MW00998174

Your Daily Dose of Happy!

Real Success Stories of the Law of Attraction

Walt Thiessen, Editor

First Edition, May 2018

Published by: LOA Today (loatoday.net)
Simsbury, CT USA

Table of Contents

Introduction

by Walt Thiessen

"Can you share your Law of Attraction manifestation story?"

That's a question most students of LOA like to get answered whenever possible.

The basic concept of LOA is simple. As Abraham-Hicks puts it, "That which is like unto itself is drawn."

But what about applying LOA in their "real world" lives? That's where students of LOA often trip up. So hearing the successful manifestation stories of others often help us all to believe, despite what "reality" insists on telling us.

I put that word "reality" into quotation marks to remind us that reality is what we make of it and that even scientists have trouble making sense out of it.

Once Albert Einstein ripped open Pandora's Box with his General and Special Theories of Relativity in the early twentieth century, human scientists stopped thinking of reality as being fixed and immutable. Now there's quantum physics, dark energy, the observer effect, and a host of other relatively new scientific terms invented to make sense out of what Einstein uncovered, stuff which often seems almost insensible.

The New Thought movement of the late nineteenth and early twentieth centuries, the precursor of modern day LOA thought, latched onto Einstein quickly, but the scientific community didn't accept New Thought explanations as anything but "nonsense" or "wishful thinking". To this day, the Law of Attraction and its other related concepts are largely ridiculed and rejected by mainstream science.

That "reality" does not stop the rest of us from exploring and embracing the Law of Attraction. To the contrary, so many people have taken an interest in LOA that it has become a worldwide phenomenon. Rhonda Byrne's movie, *The Secret,* helped LOA reach many millions of people who had not previously heard of it, and it has gained significant recognition among the population.

I discovered LOA by watching *The Secret* for the first time in November 2008. My first reaction was skepticism, but I was also in such a bad place in my own life that I was willing to consider almost anything. And so I did. I launched into a personal study of this LOA thing, determined to either harness it for myself or to prove it to be a bunch of rot.

In September 2012, with the help of my wife, Louise, I decided to start a podcast on the subject. I called it LOA Today, and it became my personal way to explore LOA concepts by interviewing other people who knew more about it than I did.

To my surprise and pleasure, I found that the podcast became one of my favorite things to do, even though I had no listeners at all at first and only an occasional listener dropping in throughout most of the first year.

In the second year after a brief sabbatical, my brother, Mark and his then-girlfriend (now wife), Uohna became my co-hosts.

By the third year, Mark and Uohna had given way to Joel Elston, one of my first interviewees in Episode 12. Joel stayed with me until April 2017, at which point he had to leave the show to attend to other things in his life.

David Scott Bartky took Joel's place, and during that summer something remarkable began to happen. Our listenership started to increase at a rapid rate. By November 2017, we had as many episodes played in a month as had been played in all the previous five years combined.

That led to me expanding the podcast to a twice daily broadcast, and I brought on board Wendy Dillard, Cindie Chavez, and Tom Wells to co-host the shows with me, with Joel Elston returning to the show as well (to my delight).

The one characteristic all of my co-hosts shared in common is that they are professional life coaches or therapists. I figured that if I was going to do a podcast, I wanted expert commentary.

In a matter of weeks, both Wendy and Cindie told me about book projects they'd been involved with. Apparently, both had contributed to multi-author anthologies where all of the authors contributed not only to the book but also to promoting the marketing of the book through their social connections online.

As soon as I heard about these projects, I wondered, *Would it be possible to use the same technique to promote our LOA Today podcast?*

Within a couple more weeks, I became obsessed with the idea of doing an anthology style book sharing personal manifestation stories with as many students of the Law of Attraction as we can find. These would be real stories told by real-life people in the LOA field from their own life experiences.

I imagined it to be an LOA version of Jack Canfield's world-famous *Chicken Soup For The Soul* series of books. No one needs positive reinforcement and confidence building more than "deliberate creators" attempting to leverage the Law of Attraction in their daily lives. What better way to get such leverage than from the real-life experiences of others who are equally devoted to studying and applying this marvelous universal law?

You hold the result in your hands.

I've organized the book into sections, to make it easy for readers to find particular kinds of stories. You can find stories about manifesting new homes and offices, relationship, careers, improved health, new cars, and even the weather.

You will find a wide range of perspectives in the enclosed stories. Perspective is a key concept in LOA, and it plays no less of an important role here. So many perspectives, 39 in all, came together to create such a great book.

So you'll find stories that range from really happy, light-hearted pieces such as Keisha Clark's "My Birthday Bath", to the dark, blunt, and even brutal experiences detailed by Misti Jackson-Derringer in her story, "Boot Camp".

You'll find stories where the main players didn't even know how LOA worked, side-by-side with stories from experienced practitioners who knew exactly what they wanted to attract and how to do it deliberately.

The stories range from being locked in a garage and using our inner voice to get out, to following one's nose all the way out to an oceanic adventure.

The emphasis on what's important varies considerably from story to story, just as the voices of the different authors also vary.

Some stories emphasize the internal self-talk and self-listening. Others emphasize physical talk and actions. Some emphasize theory, while others emphasize feeling your way.

But they all have one thing in common. They are all stories of things, experiences, and events that occurred by thinking and feeling about them **first**.

The Law of Attraction always operates in everything that comes into our lives. This book not only recognizes that fact but also plays up stories where LOA's role is clear.

The main criteria that your editor used when putting the book together was to make the book a collection of stories. Our purpose here is to entertain and inspire rather than to teach.

We hope you agree that this is really the best way to hear other peoples' stories.

On behalf of all the authors of this book, I hope you'll find this book is a bright light in your daily life. Perhaps it will take a place on your coffee table for you to read for a bit whenever you need a pick-me-up. Or perhaps it will adorn your bedside table, giving you some happy thoughts before you go to sleep at night.

Just like what we say about the LOA Today podcasts, we hope that his book becomes Your Daily Dose of Happy, one that not only provides you with inspiration and reinforces your belief in yourself and in what you want most to manifest into your life, but also gives you something you are eager to share with friends and families.

I want to thank all of the people who have played roles both in the creation of this book and in helping me to develop the LOA Today podcast over the years. Hopefully, I don't leave anyone out. If I do, please accept my apologies.

My thanks go to:

Stacey Aarssen
Linda Armstrong
Esther Bailey-Bass
Ellen Bakker
Clarissa Barraza
David Scott Bartky
Cambria Berger
Cathy Brown
Rhonda Burns

Cindie Chavez
Keisha Clark
Anik Clemens
Michael Craig
Wendy Dillard
Renate Donnovan
Joel Elston
Patricia Framo
Ruby Gangadharan
Hannah Golightly
Ana Hernando
Misti Jackson-Derringer
Anne-Marie McEwen
Mike McEwen
Susan Murray
Debra Oakland
Barbara Pinti
Geanina Roman
Galina Shadrova
Paulette Sherman
Leslie Shew
Dez Stephens
Sherry Trentini
Louise Thiessen
Mark Thiessen
Uohna-June Thiessen
Tarryn Tomlinson
Janet Warnecke
Tom Wells
Jean Yang
Susan Shearer Young

I also want to give my special thanks to program director Jesse Funk and owner Gary Null of the Progressive Radio Network (prn.fm) who began carrying my podcast on their network nearly four years ago . Without their support, I would not have reached anywhere near as many new listeners as I have. Thank you, guys!

Finally, I would be remiss if I didn't take a moment to address our primary purpose. If you haven't listened to the our podcast at www.loatoday.net, please do so. And when you like it (and we're confident you'll like it), please subscribe and share. The instructions on how to subscribe are found on that same page, and a huge number of social media links for sharing with your friends are provided there as well.

Thank you, dear reader, for picking up this book. Now, get ready for a really fun ride!

Houses and Offices

Home Sweet Home

by Wendy Dillard

After living in many rental properties, I'd had all I could stand of white-colored walls and boring color palettes that rentals provided. So, it wasn't any surprise to me that I'd been dreaming of my own house where I would have the luxury of painting the walls and decorating it in every conceivable way that my artistic heart desired. Living in a space that reflected my colorful personality felt like the kind of nurturing environment that would nourish my soul.

When we were financially ready to buy a house, I performed an analysis of home prices around our city and landed on the target area where we could get the most square footage for the lowest price.

Even though this would be my first house, I didn't want a typical 3 bedroom / 2 bath starter home because when I want something, I dream BIG! I really wanted 5 bedrooms, but realistically 4 bedrooms was more in line with our budget.

Since I had been planning for my first house for a long time, I'd developed a pretty long list of criteria, needs and wants. So, here's an abbreviated list:

- Five bedrooms (which included: a master suite, a guest room, a workroom for me to do my many artistic projects, my office, and a separate office for my husband so we wouldn't have to share an office anymore. I'm a highly organized neat-freak, and he loves his piles and piles of stuff scattered about everywhere)

- Two to three bathrooms

- An open-concept floor plan

- A nice yard for our dog

- A long and flat driveway that could park a minimum of six cars. (My husband loved to tinker with cars and always had a number of non-running vehicles that he was in the process of restoring. Our current rental house gave birth to this criteria because even though the driveway could hold four cars, the driveway was pitched at a 45 degree angle. It took me forever just to have the courage to drive up or down this steep, monster-like driveway. We ended up replacing the brakes on our cars practically every six months! So, between our personal cars and the ones that my husband was working on, we knew we wanted lots of space to park our cars, and it had to be on a flat surface.)

- We wanted it to be at a price that we could comfortably afford, so we wouldn't feel that every dollar we earned went toward the mortgage.

- And it had to be no-money down!

Needless to say, the list was long. But, my life's experience had taught me that no dream was too big for God (or the Universe) to deliver.

As the house-hunting began, we found the four-to-five bedroom houses in our price range were completely unacceptable, which left us feeling melancholy. We thought we might need to compromise or settle for less than what we wanted, causing all the air in our lofty balloon to deflate. My hope of finding my dream home took a huge blow. What do you do when you believe your dream is out there somewhere, but you don't see any evidence of it?

A number of months went by. I thought maybe the latest inventory of houses on the market could possibly provide better options. So with renewed energy and vigor, I went back to searching.

This time we still found a bunch of duds, but the last house on the list showed promise. It was a black-and-white brick, one-story, four bedroom, two bathroom house. The flat driveway wasn't particularly long, but because of where the house was situated at the end of street, it could work.

The inside of the house was darling. It checked almost all the boxes on our list. It was in super-duper, wonderful condition. There weren't any dings or dents in the walls or doors (like we saw in the other houses). The back yard was small, but it was beautifully landscaped and definitely appealed to the artist in me.

Overall, the house made my heart smile. Both of us could easily picture ourselves here. While heading home, our excitement was almost uncontainable as we chatted on and on about its attractive curb appeal, charming interior, wonderful floor plan, pristine landscaping, and spacious area for cars.

We floated on Cloud Nine with smiles fixed indelibly on our faces.

The only glitch was that we needed $2,000 for a down-payment (which we didn't have), but we thought for certain that either his parents or mine would happily loan it to us. We knew his parents had the money, so contacting them felt like a formality.

With a feeling of "this was a done-deal," my husband called them by phone while I stood close by with great anticipation and a readiness to celebrate. His smile quickly changed to a somber expression. The call was brief. They said "No." They had a reason as to why the money was not available, but the reason faded as I focused on the shock that they wouldn't lend us the money for the down-payment.

We moved on to the backup plan of asking my parents for the money. With the sale of my grandma's home after she passed on, I knew they had a large amount of cash in the bank. I knew this was a conversation that required me reaching out to my Dad (because he was the decision-maker). He hated talking on the phone, but loved email.

So, I promptly typed up an email using all the sweetness, charm, and "you love your daughter, don't you?" wording I could think up. Then we waited ...

Day One, no response ...

Day Two, no response ...

We were practically out of our minds with impatience while waiting for a response from my dad. My thoughts turned to fears as I pictured someone else snatching up the black-and-white brick house. It was not easy to keep calm. I kept reminding myself that IF this was to be our house, that it would be – and my dad's delayed response wouldn't be a problem.

Finally on Day Three, my inbox held the response from my dad. I'll never forget his words: "After much prayer, your mother and I don't feel we are to loan you the money. We wish you all the best in finding a new house."

OMG! This was not at all what we'd expected. Our hearts sank to an all-time low. I re-read his email over and over. I couldn't believe my dad's words. But, knowing their religious beliefs, if God had told them "No," there was no overturning their decision.

With no other resources available to us, our plans to live in the black-and-white brick house died. We wallowed in anger, sadness, and grief for the next several days as the realization settled in that we'd lost this house.

Fortunately, after a few days of releasing much pain and sadness, the cheerful, optimistic side of me buoyed back to the surface. I felt an unanticipated surge of knowingness permeate my entire being with this inspiring thought: If not this house, then what's in store for us must be even better!

With that, I felt jubilantly refreshed as my vision of my dream house was reinvigorated. I knew with every ounce of my being that the house actually awaiting us would be even grander than the black-and-white brick house, because what was yet to show up would truly be The House.

That thought was so powerful within me, it held me in a sense of hope for an entire year. One day, I felt the nudge to hit the Internet again in search of our house. This time I went into it knowing the exact suburb that would give us the biggest bang for our buck, so that's where I concentrated my efforts.

One day, I found a house on April Showers Way that perfectly fit my search criteria. I thought, *How cute is that street name?*

I could totally live on a street called, "April Showers Way." I decided to check it out on my own, so as not to get my husband's hopes up if it turned out not to be a good option.

I printed my MapQuest directions, and off I went. When I found the address, I thought to myself: *Something about this house doesn't seem right.* The description online was for a two story house, and this was only one story. Feeling misled by whoever wrote up the description, I drove around the neighborhood to see if there would be anything else for sale.

I meandered through the streets of this subdivision where I found a group of six model homes. I went in to check them out. Each one was beautifully staged with furniture, décor, and impeccable landscaping. As I walked through each home, my enthusiasm grew while my artistic-self resonated with the attractive décor. I was in heaven!

As I opened the front door to this two story, five bedroom house, feelings of fairy tale-like enchantment enveloped me. This enormous house was so big, I actually got lost in it (true story).

When I walked up the stairs, I couldn't help but wonder what this house might cost and if it was anywhere within our price range. I strolled from room to room. The master suite's entrance had two French doors that majestically opened up into the large master bedroom. Even with a king-size bed, there was plenty of space for this room to have a feeling of being absolutely grand.

Surprisingly, as I walked all the way to the end of the bedroom expecting to find the Bathroom area, I found yet another room that could perhaps be used as a secluded room for reading.

Tears began to stream down my cheeks as I was filled with an overwhelming flood of joy. This magnificent house was more perfect than I'd ever pictured in all of my imaginations about my dream house. I felt deep within me that I'd come home. There was something about that extra room within the master suite that filled me with feelings of royalty and grandeur like I'd never experienced. It was the icing on the top of my dream-house cake! My tour ended with an enormously sized bathroom, followed by a huge walk-in closet (the size of another bedroom).

Wiping the tears from my eyes, I pulled out my cell phone to call my husband. He worked nearby, and quitting time was coming soon. I told him I was in the area looking at homes, and asked him to meet me at the model home sales office, because I wanted him to view the model homes. I did my best not to blurt out anything that would broadcast my extreme excitement because I wanted him to have his own experience.

I walked behind him as he toured the model homes, trying to be as quiet as a mouse so as not to influence him in any way. When he came to the one I'd fallen in love with, he became enthusiastically more vocal about the things he liked. By the time he reached the master suite, he too fell in love with this model as much as I did.

How's that for synchronicity and like-mindedness?

With a particularly large bounce in our steps, we headed off to the sales office. While there, I picked up the sales sheet with the description of the "Chanticlair" Model that we loved. I laughed because it was the exact description of the house on April Showers Way that brought me to this subdivision. I love how guidance doesn't always come in the package I expect, but the path is always laid out for me.

The prices were higher than we'd hoped – big ouch! But, we still talked the salesman's ear off with our joyful enthusiasm for making a purchase, and we simply acted as though we could afford the model we loved. We left there knowing we'd have to do some creative financing, but we felt "sold" on that model.

The next weekend was New Year's Day, and we drove out to the sales office to talk more seriously about locking down one of the pieces of property upon which to build our new home. We thought for sure the sales office would be open to do business, but we were wrong. The office was closed.

Because we felt such a powerful desire to go there, we thought maybe the purpose of the trip was to drive through the development to select the property we'd build upon. Most of the properties had the driveways either poured or measured-out with stakes. Shockingly, these driveways were tiny – barely one car length long. The longest was one-and-a-half car lengths long – definitely not what we were expecting. This meant that none of the available properties would work for us.

We were back to feeling disappointed and a bit hopeless. This seemed like yet another case of getting our hopes really high, only to have them dashed.

How was this possible?

I was once again reminded of the powerful thought: "If not this house, then what's in store for us must be even better!"

This encouraged us only slightly.

While in our saddened state, we drove around the neighborhood next to this new development. I couldn't believe my eyes when I saw the Chanticlair home in an already developed neighborhood with a "for sale" sign in the front lawn. Could this be real?

As we looked for a place to park the car, we found yet another Chanticlair home with a "for sale" sign.

Were we in a Twilight Zone episode? It sure felt like it.

Before we dared to get excited, we drove through the alley where we could see the lengths of the driveways. Astonishingly, the first driveway was about four car lengths long, and the second one was five car lengths long!

We couldn't help ourselves. Our hopes sky-rocketed once again. Right before us were two Chanticlairs with long driveways already in existence, and they were for sale.

We called the listing agents on each of the "for sale" signs. The first house had just sold. The second house was still available, so we scheduled a meeting to see it. When we physically walked into the house, we knew this was truly the one.

This house was incredibly perfect. It met all the criteria on our list with a few bells and whistles thrown in. The sales price was within our budget, which was lower than the new construction home, and we could buy it with no money down!

We celebrated by dancing with joy because this house was beyond what we'd ever thought possible. It had our five bedrooms, three bathrooms, and three living rooms. It had an open concept kitchen looking into the living room, and the walls beckoned the brush of my artistic stroke as I envisioned the beautiful colors that would make my heart sing.

We went home, got all of our ducks in a row financially, and planned to put our offer on the house the next Saturday.

On Friday before my work day came to an end, I was unexpectedly called into the HR office. Without any warning, I was told that my job had been eliminated. It felt surreal like I was in a movie with a major plot twist. The HR lady continued to speak, but I could barely hear her over the sounds of my own thoughts racing about how this would impact the purchase of our house.

I didn't know what to think or what to feel. I felt certain we'd been guided to our house – and now this?

When I called my husband from the car to tell him what had just happened, he said with a sad tone of voice, "I guess we won't be able to buy the house."

To which I replied with powerful intensity: "Oh, no – this is not going to stop us! We found our house, and we're going to put on offer on it tomorrow as planned."

Saturday, we met our Realtor and took one more walk through the house drinking in the feeling of being at home. Standing at our soon-to-be kitchen counter, we quickly agreed on the amount we would offer.

As the Realtor wrapped up the discussion, he asked if we had any questions.

"Well, there's one thing. I lost my job yesterday. Will that be a problem?"

He looked up toward the ceiling and pondered as he composed his answer.

When he was ready, he looked directly at me and said, "Well, in my 25 years as a Realtor, I've dealt with worse circumstances. So your job will be to get a job before the closing."

I loved how my job circumstances didn't derail him, and it definitely gave me the encouragement to go forth and land a new job!

Our offer was accepted, and we were ecstatic. We'd finally found our dream home. We were relieved that this arduous search had finally come to an end.

For the next six weeks, I didn't allow myself to focus on anything except finding a new job. I was in the final round of interviews for a job that would pay about the same salary as my previous job, and it looked good. While driving there, a headhunter from another company called saying that he'd already shared my resume with his client, and they felt I was perfect for the job. I told him that I was really close to securing a job, as I was literally driving to the final interview, but this headhunter was persistent and begged me to call him anyway when I exited the interview.

When I walked into the final interview at the dairy company, they informed me that the company prioritized hiring from within. They had just learned of an associate desiring to transfer to this office, so they gave her the job.

As much as I was disappointed, I also felt relieved. Even though I needed a job ASAP, I didn't really want that one. It didn't feel challenging enough to hold my interest for long.

I called the headhunter from the other company. He was right. His client loved me. After one of the easiest interviews I'd ever had, they hired me on the spot. And guess what? The salary was significantly higher than the dairy company. With this salary, we'd have a financial cushion so we wouldn't just be working to pay the bills, fulfilling another criteria on our list.

I immediately called our Realtor and told him the good news. He was delighted. I told him that I would start my new job just in time for the paperwork to be drawn up for the closing to happen on time. Closing day went off without a hitch. Whew! We drove around our new city looking for a place for us to have lunch and bask in the joy of home-ownership.

While directing our movers as they carried our furniture into our new house, I could barely contain my exuberance. This house filled me with such incredible joy. Even after 11+ years of living in it, I still get giddy about its perfection.

We got everything that was important to us about a house. Thank goodness that knowing the ins-and-outs of the Law of Attraction was not necessary for it to show up in our experience, because at the time we didn't know about Law of Attraction.

Knowing what I know today, I can see in hindsight how the Law of Attraction coordinated all necessary elements to deliver to us exactly what we desired with a synchronicity I could have never orchestrated. My strong desire and never-give-up attitude played a large role in landing our dream home. And as Dorothy from the Wizard of Oz said, "There's no place like home."

Wendy Dillard is a Masterful Law of Attraction Teacher & Coach. Her expertise is in knowing how to apply the Law of Attraction to any situation. What other people call miracles and coincidences, Wendy considers normal and the way life is intended to be. Website: www.wendydillard.com

The Lot

by Barbara Pinti

In 1978 our family of six was too big for our house.

We had loved living on the last road cut into the side of a mountain. During nice weather our family had hiked through the woods up that mountain to see the white-tailed deer. With three of our kids walking and one in a pack on our backs, we loved to explore the area.

One day we had found a huge sprawling rock formation and decided to have our picnic lunch there. It became "our" rock and a favorite place to rest and eat after hiking.

But our house was too small, and our family was growing. It was time to move.

We searched for our new "family home" where we would raise our children to adulthood. We took several trips through town looking for that perfect house. Finding nothing after several months, we thought about building one ourselves so we could have all the things we wanted in our ideal house.

A builder in a nearby town put up some larger homes, and we went to look at them. He had a few different house plans, and there were some lots available. We started getting excited about it, chose a lot, and selected a plan.

The house took forever to build. We visited the site daily to check on progress.

One day, we were very upset to find that the builder had switched the floor plan to be the opposite of what we had planned. It was very disappointing, but there didn't seem to be anything possible to be done about it as the foundation was already poured.

We accepted the disappointment. About a week later we found another problem. The fireplace was done, and it was amateurish, awful, completely unacceptable. I remember at the time we said it looked like a kindergartner had built it.

A decision had to be made. I no longer wanted the house. It had become a disaster project instead of a joyous one. After consulting our lawyer, we found we were able to get out of the commitment.

So after all this time, we found ourselves right back again at step one. We began to search again for that house that would make my heart flutter.

We learned that lots were being forged out of the road further up our mountain. We took a ride up the mountain to see what was going on up there.

Nothing had been built yet, but all of the lots were marked off. We checked them out. As we perused the lots, one lot seemed very familiar. It included a large rock with some of the same parts that I had remembered from our picnics. However much dirt covered parts of the rock, so it took a while for us to realize that it was indeed "our" rock.

That was it! We wanted that lot! We started getting excited about the possibility of building on that site where our footprints had tread while our joys and laughter had rung out.

Finding the builder's number on a sign nearby, we went right home and called him up. Our disappointment was profound when he told us that all of the lots had been sold. I was crushed at first, but I remembered other times during my life when I thought all was lost.

I began imagining the house that we would build on that property and all the fun that the children would have playing in the woods. I even planned out just where I would locate my garden. I walked the land and scoped it all out as though it were mine.

I confided to several friends how much I wanted that building lot and continued to hope beyond hope that it could be ours. Every night before sleep, I would imagine all of us snug in the house that we had built on that property. I pictured us playing outside around the rock while laughing and enjoying ourselves completely. I felt as though I had claimed that property as our own, not only then, but years earlier as well.

A few weeks later, a miracle happened. I spoke to a friend who had been bowling that morning with the woman who owned "our" lot. The woman confided that her husband had just been offered a new and better job in another state. They needed to sell the lot as quickly as possible.

Events moved very fast now. We bought the lot from them in a quick, private sale. I worked feverishly designing our new home. We found a builder.

One of the first things we asked him to do was to remove the dirt from the rock so that it looked exactly like it did in the days when we picnicked on it.

Barbara A. Pinti, MA, MA, ABD, LMFT, LPC

I am a psychotherapist in private practice in West Hartford, Connecticut. I have taught the Law of Attraction in many groups, workshops and in my private practice.

Email: barbarapinti@comcast.net

Manifesting an Apartment on Central Park West

by David Scott Bartky

Many years ago before I became a professional life coach, I moved from Los Angeles to New York. While in Los Angeles, I learned about the Law of Attraction from Michael Beckwith many years before he appeared in the movie, *The Secret*.

When I moved to New York City, I became part of the masses who raced to see any new apartment listing. Since I didn't have a large budget, most of the apartments I ran to ended up being very disappointing. They were either too small or had some weird quirk about them that for me made them undesirable.

After many of these cattle call type experiences, I suddenly had an "ah ha" moment. I remembered the Law of Attraction and how powerful it is. I thought to myself, "Why am I looking at these apartments all over New York City when I always dreamed about living on Central Park West?" I thought this despite the fact that my budget didn't qualify for an apartment on one of the nicest streets in New York City. So in an instant I went from an "I'll take anything" attitude to an "I know exactly what I want, and that's all I'm interested in!" attitude. How could my dream of rollerblading from my apartment building into Central Park become a reality?

I learned from Beckwith that what I focus on is what I attract. I didn't have to know how it would happen. I just had to get into the vibration of what I wanted and expect it to happen.

After my wonderful "ah ha" moment, I called my Realtor and told him, "Don't let me know about anything unless it's on Central Park West." Silence on the other end of the phone told me he thought I was crazy. After the silence he said, "Well, that's a tall order, but I'll keep my ears open." I thanked him, and I never looked at another "for rent" ad again. I just trusted that it would happen and went about my business. Within two weeks I received a phone call from that Realtor about a studio apartment coming available in a building on Central Park West. It was $500 more than what I could afford. He asked me if I was interested. I didn't hesitate: "YES!"

Why did I agree to go look at an apartment that was $500 more than I could afford? Because I know that anything is possible, so why not look at it? I met him outside the building. The lobby was so nice it took my breath away. The elevator was the nicest one I had ever been in. It had oriental birds painted on the walls. I was ready to move in before I saw the apartment!

We walked into the apartment. I knew it was perfect for me. The tenant, who wasn't supposed to be home, was gathering some things. I asked her why she was moving. She told me her mother was ill, and she had to go back home to care for her. She also said I was the first one to see the apartment and that since she was breaking the lease, the owner didn't want it to sit empty. I got the nerve up to ask her how much she was paying per month. She told me, and it was exactly what I could afford!

I guess the owner was told she could charge $500 more, so that's why she raised the price. However, since I knew what the current tenant was paying I told the building manager that I wanted the apartment, and I offered $25 more than what the current tenant was paying. My Realtor told me that that wouldn't be enough, but it really was all I could afford, so I asked the building manager to propose my offer to the owner.

The next day I found out that the owner accepted my offer, and I got the apartment. A few weeks later I moved in. Thank you Law of Attraction. I loved living in that apartment!

David Scott Bartky
Life Coach David
Web Site: lifecoachdavid.com
Facebook: @lifecoachdavid
Twitter: @lifecoachdavidb

David is a co-host on LOA Today.

Our Dream House in Northern California

by Janet Warnecke

In 2015, My husband, Ed and I, after years of living literally in the middle of Hollywood, California, started putting into action our plan of moving to Auburn, California and away from the traffic and the crazies. We needed to sell our home and improve our credit scores and get all our financial ducks in a row. We knew we had a slightly long road ahead, but it was certainly doable, and we started doing just that.

That summer, our daughter graduated from the University of California at Santa Barbara but was still living at home and looking to find her way. What exactly does a degree in German get you? She switched from majoring in history to German because "The German Department is more fun." Sounded good to us – fun is better. Without knowing it, she clearly had her own momentum, but that's a whole different story. She is currently working on her Masters degree. So proud!

We moved to Encino as a pit stop for her to find a job and begin working. We were not exactly in a position for Ed to give up his job (we were still improving our financial situation). All that time, we constantly discussed what we wanted from the move, i.e., the feeling, the calm, the lack of rush hour traffic, the ability to work from home, neighbors we would actually get to know as opposed to the zillion people surrounding us in condos and apartments.

We rented a home from a friend in 2015 in Encino. We moved in and all was going great. Our daughter started working and boom, within a year she met and started a relationship with a very nice guy. His family was very welcoming and later that year she moved in with him and his family – all the while continuing to enjoy her job and look into her options.

Things seemed to be lining up perfectly for my husband and I to make the move to Auburn as we were only planning on staying in Encino for a year and a half.

In October 2016, my husband was diagnosed with throat cancer, and our whole world changed. Three months of heavy chemo was followed by a short break before handling 37 daily treatments of radiation. We were devastated. With Ed in a fight for his life, moving was no longer on the front burner.

The treatments were brutal. I was his sole caretaker and had no idea what I was doing. It was truly one minute at a time, one appointment at a time, one pill at a time. Without going into too much detail, I had never experienced anything so scary. My husband went from 160 lbs to 112 lbs in three months. I have no idea how he didn't fling himself off the roof, except that he was too weak to climb up a ladder.

With the help of friends and family we made it through. He had a very good result from the chemo which gave us strength to go forward with the radiation.

During this time I did not personally think about the house and the move, but my husband told me later that it was constantly on his mind to get through this treatment, so that one way or another we could make it to our dream life. During most of his treatment he could barely speak, so he did not share this vision with me, but thank God the Universe was listening and that we had been filling that vortex over a lifetime.

By July 2017. the day after my husband's radiation treatments ended, our landlords (previously our friends of 30 years) gave us a 30% rent increase. It was astronomical! Apparently, they wanted to sell the home but had not informed us. So with this giant increase we decided to move as quickly as possible. Ed was way too weak to move, but we started taking action to find storage facilities and do whatever we could to go forward. More importantly, we had gotten the news that the tumors were all gone, and Ed was given a clean bill of health, but it would still take several years to recover fully.

Our hopes were high that we would still be able to make our dream come true. Unbeknownst to me – and certainly to Ed, because we were so consumed with treatment and appointments and ER visits – we didn't pay attention as well as we should have to our financial situation. When we went to apply for a loan, we were told it would take us approximately a year or so to clean things up – again – to get a loan.

That was it for me. I cracked. After getting through the cancer and seeing the light at the end of the tunnel, I was DEVASTATED! Another year?

After I sobbed for about three hours that my life was over – not too self-obsessed or ungrateful for the good things happening, i.e., cancer free – I got a grip and pulled myself together. Well, it would take what it takes. We're not giving up. I made a list of what I wanted in a house and started thinking about it again.

By November we were ready to move, after briefly talking about our "house dreams" with the guys on the LOA Today podcast. Even with Ed's low weight and difficult physical condition, we packed and the movers came. We were out by November 30th, on our way to stay with my father-in-law up north and darn grateful that we had a nice place to stay for Ed to continue to recover and for us to house hunt.

In December, we saw several homes that first week, but we didn't have much positive vibration on the actual purchase of a house because we knew we had to improve the financial end.

But just being up here, looking at the lake, looking at the trees, the beauty – our vibrations improved whether we had our own house or not. If it took a year, fine, we were in the most beautiful place on earth for us. A lot of stress released as we accepted the situation and just enjoyed our surroundings.

We suddenly got word that Ed qualified for a VA loan, which opened up a whole new enthusiasm about purchasing a house. The day after that news, our lender said, "Hmm, your credit score is great, I don't know what happened. You can get any loan you need." We were so jazzed. Now we just had to find a house. No pressure though, we thought we'd take the next three or four months to look around.

On New Year's Day 2018, we took a walk. It was a gorgeous day. We decided to go up a street we never take, and there on the corner was a house for sale. Since it was New Year's Day we did not expect anyone to be showing the house.

I had seen this particular house on the MLS listings a month earlier, and it had just been sold and was in escrow. A week before, the previous potential buyer's offer fell through.

The agent just happened to be in the house for a private showing as we walked by. We asked if we could take a peek. She said, "Sure." And we fell in love! We made an offer, and after one day of back and forth, it was accepted.

What happened next was also crazy. It seemed at every step exactly what we needed fell into our lap. All the paperwork, people who had what we needed – everything! By February 8, 2018, the keys were in our hands!

After moving in, about every other day I'd say to Ed things like, "You know, I didn't notice this when we were looking at the house, but I remembered I always wanted a stream in the backyard – and wow, we have one!" It was that way with so many things in this house. So much of my wish list is here. The Christmas trees out front, the fireplace, the deer and bunnies running around, the lake, the sound of children playing in the neighborhood, my sliding glass doors, French doors, a guest room, a music room, etc. My neighbors brought us welcome cookies.

Here's the original wish list:

1. Fireplace In Every Room – **Got one in the living room**

2. 3 Bedrooms, Office Space, Guest Room – **Got it**

3. At Least 1800 Sq Ft – Would Have Accepted Less – **Got it**

4. Trees – Amazing Views – **Got it**

5. Close To My Father-In-Law – **Got it (three minute walk)**

6. Short Walk To The Lake – **Got it**

7. Porch/Deck – **Got it**

8. Backyard The Deer Can't Get Into For The Cats To Wander – **Got it**

9. Good Closet Space – **Got GREAT closet space**

10. Two To Three Bathrooms – **Got three**

11. Mother-In-Law Suite – Saw several in the MLS and thought it would be a great thing to have. There are not that many homes here with that situation, but i still wished for it – did not expect it in a million years. – **Got it**

12. Deer And Bunnies And Blue Birds – **Got them**

13. Super Cozy Feeling – **Got it**

14. Good Size Kitchen – **Got it, nice and bright too!**

15. White Kitchen – **Got it**

16. Decent Size Parcel Of Land – **Got it, one-half acre**

17. Double Front Door – **Got it, couldn't believe it**

18. Sliding Glass Doors/French Doors – **Got French doors in the bedroom**

19. Great Back Yard – **Got it**

20. Garage with space/shelves and could actually fit the car – **Got it**

21. Indoor laundry – Last one was outside – hated that – **Got a whole laundry room with counters and sink. Amazing!**

Plus, there were more things we didn't even think of for our wish list that showed up anyway, like a built-in sprinkler system and a golf cart.

This DOES NOT HAPPEN in the middle of Hollywood! Apparently, all the years of putting different thoughts on what we wanted our home and lives to look like were all piling up in the vortex. I like to think that while Ed was going through this time, OUR home was being prepared to be put on the market.

Janet and Ed Warnecke listen to LOA Today from their beautiful new home in Auburn, California.

Divorced, Broke and Homeless

by Mike McEwen

That's where I was in 2013, the result of 20 years of trying to make everyone else happy but myself. I guess this is what it takes to "wake up" and be responsible for your own happiness.

Looking back on it today, I am very grateful for all the failures and the lessons I learned, which helped me to write this story in the hope that I can inspire someone who's going through something similar. When one gets caught up in life's circumstances, it's like being trapped in a revolving door of lack. The Law of Attraction gave me plenty of opportunities to continue feeling all that I lacked. I eventually realized that the one thing I lacked most was happiness.

My divorce was finalized July 28, 2013. On August 1st, I arrived in Phoenix, Arizona to visit my daughter, son-in-law, and two grandkids for a healing vacation. For the first time in a long time, I felt like I was moving forward, and I was so grateful to be with my Arizona family. I arrived back in Connecticut in late August refreshed and feeling loved and appreciated ... something I hadn't felt in a long time.

I was still homeless but not broke. A good friend of mine invited me to stay at his house until I could get my own apartment. John likes big bonfires, and I arrived one Friday evening to find him building one.

It gave us a great opportunity to sit around the fire and drink some beer, so we did. Around the fourth beer, I decided to burn all of the old negative past paperwork and anything linked to my unhappiness. I made the intention to connect with new people with similar interests.

Oh what a great night that was! I had no idea what was about to happen.

Sitting at the kitchen table the next morning having coffee, I decided to go online to check out some events. I found a meditation group meeting that afternoon in the town where I grew up and decided to attend. After the meeting, I talked with the facilitator of the meditation group, telling her that I would like to find more events to attend so I could meet more positive, like-minded people, and she recommended I check out a website called Meetup.com.

Back at my friend's house that afternoon, I decided to go online to check out the Meetup.com site. I typed in "local events." The first thing that popped up was Laughter Yoga at The Buttonwood Tree. So without hesitation I signed up for it.

Not only did Laughter Yoga teach me how to laugh at things that would normally upset me, I met the director of The Buttonwood Tree, Anne-Marie, and it didn't take long before a strong connection grew between us ... something that hadn't happened in a long time. She asked me out for tea.

I replied, "It's 9:00 at night. How about a beer?"

In conversation over a few beers we found that we had a lot in common, so I invited her to sunrise Tai Chi that next morning. I was happy that she showed up. After Tai Chi we went out for breakfast. It was a wonderful start to a new relationship.

Before I knew it, we had a dinner date. The food and the conversation were great as we sat overlooking Lake Pocotopaug at Angelico's Lake House Restaurant.

What a great manifestation!

Several days after our dinner date she handed me a key to her apartment. Hesitating at first, I realized here was another manifestation: no longer homeless and no longer alone. As we say in Laughter Yoga, "Very Good Very Good Yay!"

After living with her for about a year, the landlord sold the house, and we had to move out ... in three weeks! Oh no! At that time, my contracting business was slow, and money was real tight. How could we find a place to live in three weeks?

Intend it to be and it shall be. My then fiancée just kept saying, "No worries ... the right place to move into will show up at the right time."

Okay, I thought, but where's the money going to come from? If we feel abundant when there seems like there's nothing to

51

feel abundant about, the universal Law of Attraction matches the feeling with more of the same. People, circumstances, and events line up at the right time ... and that's what happened.

Anne-Marie called a Realtor whom she worked with in the past and received a lead on a single-family house for lease that she *thought* might be available but wasn't sure. Anne-Marie investigated and found that it was the perfect little house for us.

We had five days to sign the lease, but we didn't have the $3,000 we needed up front for it.

I had sold a contracting job that would yield us enough money, but it would take 30 days to complete the job and get paid. Three days before signing the lease, I received a call from the management company for the construction project. The bank had taken over their property, creating a very unusual situation because they had to close out all the accounts for that property. He requested that I send my invoice for the job even though I hadn't started so he could pay me in full to get it off the books for the sum total of $9,600!

Problem solved. I still can't believe it.

Mike McEwen, LOA practitioner. Certified Tai Chi instructor for 25 years. Reiki healing energy practitioner. Group or private sessions are available

Email: mikegonow@gmail.com

Cell +1-203-515-0818

Wouldn't It Be Cool To Live Here?

by Stacey Aarssen

In 2003, I had spent the last fifteen years working with my parents in a retail clothing store that had grown exponentially over the years. It wasn't the easiest of tasks to work with parents who didn't always see my ideas as good ones, although with persistence they would eventually listen. It was a constant battle to be heard, and at the age of 38, I needed a change.

I did most of the buying for the store. I ran the 4,500 square foot retail space when my parents took the months of January to April off to go to Florida every winter. How would my dad run this place without me? I didn't want to hurt my dad, and I didn't know what else to do. I felt smothered, and I couldn't see a way out. Purchasing the store from my parents was not an option. I couldn't get the funding and prayed for a way out of this box.

A few months later, my husband and I took an exciting trip to Elora for a week of camping with our three beautiful daughters.

Elora Gorge is a lovely Ontario town with a historic feeling, lovely little shops, and outdoor cafes. Sitting in the outdoor café, we admired the wonderful old buildings while having an amazing conversation.

I said with a chuckle, "Wouldn't it be cool to live here?"

Elora was three hours from our home, and John and I both worked in family businesses. He worked with his dad, and I worked with mine. Wishing to live in this historical little town didn't really make practical sense.

Five months later in November, our business celebrated its anniversary. Sadly, there wasn't much to celebrate. Sales had been declining for months in a clear downward trend.

Normally November is a celebration of great sales figures. We always had a big sale to kick us off to an amazing holiday sales season.

This year was different. The sales were not coming in.

It created a lot of stress for Dad. He was in his 60's and really didn't want to see his retirement lose steam.

But after some contemplation and research, he decided to run a huge retirement closing sale.

The sale began that December. The same week we announced the closing of our family business after 28 years, John's dad's business announced they were selling his business to a foreign company. Given the uncertainty that comes with new ownership, John and I wondered about his future.

December turned out to be an extremely busy month in sales for my family's business. It was the end of an era for our store. Many of our long-time customers were sad to see us close, and at times we wondered if it was the right thing to do.

But I realized my prayers were being answered. I had prayed for a way out of the business without hurting my dad. I didn't really know what to do with the result.

A call came one day from an old friend asking if John was interested in interviewing with a firm located north of Guelph, Ontario. After some contemplation and with an open mind, John decided to go for the interview.

The first interview was four long hours, which got him a second interview. After the third interview, John got offered the job.

Decisions had to be made. Our vision of our life was changing in so many ways.

We currently lived in a small town where everyone knew each other with lots of family close by. Now, we were moving to a new area. It was exciting and scary, all in the same breath.

The following weekend, we decided to head north to check out the housing market. When we got to the Fergus area, we discovered how unexpectedly close it was located to Elora.

We called a real estate agent to view a few homes in the area, only to find that there were not many homes matching our wish list.

One of our most important wants was for the girls all to have their own rooms on the same floor. Most of the homes available had the fourth bedroom in the basement, which we didn't want.

The first house we went through was in Elora, a four-bedroom home with all the bedrooms located on the same floor. It was a little bigger than we planned, but it had potential. The view from this house sitting on a hill was spectacular.

After viewing a few other homes that were okay but didn't have the energy I was looking for, we all decided the first house we went through in Elora was the one we wanted to buy.

The amazing part: this house was empty, and it had been on the market for a while. The offer was accepted, and we were the proud new owners of a home in Elora. It was a dream come true.

Now the planning began to get our home in Wallaceburg on the market. We worked like crazy to make needed repairs to it within a few weeks.

A close friend of mine mentioned their neighbours' parents had been looking for a home for the past six months and couldn't find one.

We decided to get in contact with them to see if they wanted to see ours. It was exactly what they had been looking for.

We couldn't believe it! Our house sold in one day without needing to engage a real estate broker.

If someone would have said to me six months earlier, "Be careful what you wish for, because dreams do come true," I would never had believed them.

Stacey Aarssen
Personal Branding Specialist

Helping individuals & business owners who want to be financially better. Be Better!

Phone: +1-519-341-3691 Ext 102
Toll-Free: +1-844-474-7284
Cell: +1-519-362-6644
Website: www.path2wealth.ca

Arizona Dreaming

by Barbara Pinti

In 1995 I took a vacation right after Christmas with a friend of mine. We spent two weeks in Sedona, Arizona seeing all the sights and doing all the things that tourists do.

It was a wonderful two weeks. Each day we went to one of the popular destinations the area is known for, such as the Grand Canyon, Cathedral Rock, Oak Creek Canyon, and other places where we could feel the energies that abide there.

One of our favorite places was Red Rock Creek. We drove there each day, gazed at the beautiful rock formations of Cathedral Rock, hiked through the creek, and smelled the wonderful scent of honeysuckle from the many nearby bushes. I took a sprig of it and put it in my hair so I could smell it all day.

Red Rock Creek was one of the most photographed places in the old western movies. I remembered the movies I had seen as a girl, recalling Roy Rogers and especially The Lone Ranger.

One day, instead of continuing around the curve to go to the creek, I took a dirt road straight ahead to explore the area. I drove about a quarter of a mile and stopped at a perfect view of Cathedral Rock on the left-hand side of the road.

To the right I saw the most wonderful house for viewing Cathedral Rock. I said to my friend, "Now *that* is the house where I would love to live. It's just perfect!"

During our two week stay, I kept getting a strong feeling that I would come back to Arizona. The longer I was there, the stronger the feeling became. I even thought about starting a business there and living there. I took a four-seat airplane ride over the area, and the sights were just breathtaking! I truly wanted to spend more time here.

Before my trip to Arizona, I had a vision of a large tract of land with a barn with upstairs rooms on the top floor of the barn. I thought a lot about it as I drove all over Connecticut looking for that barn, sensing I would somehow work out of those rooms. Since I never found that barn, I decided it must have just been my imagination.

When I returned to Connecticut from Arizona, I spent a great deal of time thinking about living in the southwest. I began creating in my mind a self-made sabbatical for the summer and spending it in Sedona. I called one of the healers I visited while vacationing there and inquired whether she knew anyone who could help me with housing. She gave me a name.

I started saving money every week and putting it away for my sabbatical. I called the woman whose name I had been given and asked her about renting a place for the summer. I told her the particulars of what I could afford and the dates of my stay. She told me she would ask around and get back to me.

While I awaited her response, I kept imagining spending the summer in such a magical place with sunshine every day. I was enthralled with the red rocks, seeing them in my mind with the sunshine sparkling off them.

Not long after that, the housing helper called and told me she had a very nice place for me to rent. She had checked off all the parameters I had given her, spoke to the person who owned the apartment, and left it to us to work out the details.

I was very excited and looked forward to the beginning of May when I would take what I thought of as my healing journey. The leases on both my apartment and my office were up at the end of April, and the classes I taught at the local college ended May 9th. Perfect timing!

I put everything in storage, turned in all my students' grades, and began what I later called my "moving meditation". I drove to Sedona in my little red Honda Civic, windows down, sun roof open, hair blowing in the wind, and loving every moment.

That summer is one I will never forget. For the first time I was able to think all my thoughts to completion. I loved being by myself for the first time in many years. I listened to my favorite music and the many spiritual and holistic tapes I had collected over the years.

I spent nine days crossing the country so that I would be able to see the many sights I had read about and so often wanted to visit. During that drive I felt as though I had waited a very long time to do something this important to me. I spent each day enjoying it to the fullest. It was a dream coming true.

I arrived in Sedona early in the day and followed the directions I had been given to the house I was about to rent. I saw that I was driving on the road I had taken previously to get to Red Rock Creek.

I kept on looking at the houses, checking them against the address of the house where I would stay. Each moment of that drive became more and more exciting as I began to think that the house was surely near my favorite spot in all of Sedona.

As I kept driving and looking, I found my route taking me down the special road I had explored during my previous visit. My excitement was paramount now. Could it be? Could it be the house I had spotted and fallen in love with?

Yes!

The very same house I found during my winter vacation and designated as the "perfect" place to live was the house I rented by phone, not knowing it was the same house! The Law of Attraction had been hard at work bringing me everything I wanted.

What a wonderful summer! I awoke every morning, hiked to Red Rock Creek, absorbing the breathtaking scenery around me.

Returning to Connecticut brought some confusion. I wasn't sure what I wanted to do or where I wanted to live. I rented some temporary office space from friends and got back to work meditating on what my future held.

Within a few months, I decided to open a center for alternative and complementary therapies. I found a great location for the center, then opened and filled it with therapists doing different holistic modalities.

It wasn't what I had originally imagined, but it was very successful and one of the first of its kind. This kept me very busy with my own practice, managing the center as a whole, and teaching college.

However, there was that one niggling thought, "What about Arizona?" I just knew there was something more there for me.

About a year later I returned to Arizona and began to explore the state once more. I didn't have a clear idea of what I wanted or what I was looking for. I vaguely thought about finding a ranch where I could open a residential center like the one I founded in Connecticut, one where people would come and stay for several weeks at a time for healing. But I couldn't find the right place.

Feeling confused and discouraged, I returned to Connecticut and decided to put Arizona out of my mind for a while. However, it wasn't long before I once again felt strongly that I must return.

An old friend who lived in Arizona gave me the name of a Realtor who might be able to help me. I really liked the first ranch he took me to, but something was holding me back from signing the deal on the lease. Something wasn't quite right.

I've learned over the years to pay attention to those feelings and not ignore them.

There were several out buildings besides the main house and barn. I spent all day checking things out.

Late in the afternoon, I took my last walk around the property still undecided but trying to be realistic about the fact that everything seemed to be just what I wanted. I walked way out beyond the barn into the horse pastures.

When I turned around and looked at the back of the barn from that angle, I saw my vision! It was the barn in the vision I had seen when I was in Connecticut. It never occurred to me that I would find it here in Arizona!

Barbara A. Pinti, MA, MA, ABD, LMFT, LPC

I am a psychotherapist in private practice in West Hartford, Connecticut. I have taught the Law of Attraction in many groups, workshops, and in my private practice.

Email: barbarapinti@comcast.net

A New Healing Center

by Clarissa Barraza

In April of 2017, I felt a strong need to relocate my office space somewhere I could grow my business even more.

I easily visualized a gorgeous courtyard entrance with a glassy pool in the center surrounded by lush green palm trees, tropical plants, and plush seating for clients to relax before and after their appointments. Beyond the courtyard, I imagined rooms occupied by a variety of other healers and practitioners services.

Two nights later, I searched using keywords such as *healing centers* and *spas*. To my amazement, I found an announcement of the grand opening of a spa very close to my residence. I got excited when I saw the photograph of the storefront. It showed a beautiful Southwestern stucco building with tall, sunlit, beveled glass windows and doors, elegant Spanish tile, and archways. I *knew* I had to go view this place!

As luck would still have it, the location was only ten minutes from my home. After work the following day, I visited the address around dusk. I remembered seeing this building in passing over the years but had never been curious enough to look beyond the driveway.

I saw a "For Lease" sign at the front of the property. I parked my car and walked around, surveying the environment and even peeping through the windows.

It was difficult to see inside because the glass was tinted and slightly distorted from the beveling. A maintenance truck with lawn equipment was parked outside, but I didn't see anyone else as I wandered about.

The driveway was landscaped with manicured sage bushes with long purple blossoms, along with yellow-flowered cacti and agave succulents. It resembled a desert oasis.

There was a palpable sense of magic in the air. The area was lit with a pinkish, golden yellow and hints of purple.

A fountain stood at the center of the courtyard, accompanied by more greenery and framed with brick archways all around. Wooden beams rose overhead, and plenty of leisurely seating was spaced throughout the courtyard.

Surrounding this open area were ten individual office spaces, each with a lovely arched door and windows with etched, beveled glass. Tile entryways enhanced the already picturesque environment. I was astonished. It was just as I envisioned it!

After a bit, an older gentleman exited one of the vacant offices, so I introduced myself and told him of my interest in leasing a space. He graciously offered to show me all the spaces for lease.

As we walked, he explained that the doors, windows, and tile were imported from Mexico. He even provided a blueprint of the offices.

They all seemed so lovely, but they turned out to be too big for me to lease on my own.

Nevertheless, I called the property manager immediately and left my contact information.

Afterwards, I took photos of the exterior in the evening light. I couldn't wait to show them to my friends and family!

If I could gather enough interest, I figured we could share and create our own healing center. But while everyone loved the property, no one was interested in sharing the space.

I had met Wendy in April 2016 on an Abraham-Hicks land cruise in Cancun. We talked for about three minutes on an elevator. We were both from the Dallas area and quickly exchanged business cards.

Wendy and I did not initially maintain contact after our original meeting, but in November 2016 we reconnected at an Abraham-Hicks seminar in Dallas.

This time we kept in touch, and over the next few months, Wendy kept mentioning that I should meet her friend, Keisha, with whom she said I would have a lot in common. The following April, right around the time that I found my dream office space, Wendy organized a brunch with me and Keisha.

A few weeks later, I showed the pictures of the office to Keisha.

She replied "I know this place! I am going to be co-hosting a workshop there in a few months!"

Instantly, chills ran up and down my body.

Keisha then offered to introduce me to Christine, who occupied the dream space that would be used for the workshop. Christine and I spoke on the phone, and I liked her immediately. We set up an appointment to meet at the office later that week.

When I walked in, the office space felt like returning home to a warm hug. The energy was unmistakably healing, and the wonderful atmosphere was decorated so comfortably, complete with healers practicing their modalities and a blissful meditation room.

I was completely enamored!

Christine showed me two spaces that were available, and I nearly cried when I saw it. *My* office.

It was a spacious room twice the size of anything I had ever had with a stunning window that overlooked the courtyard.

The environment was perfect for healing work. I knew this was mine. I felt as if it had been waiting for me to show up.

Needless to say, I moved in immediately.

This is the view from my office.

Clarissa J.Barraza LMT

Email: cjbarrazalmt@gmail.com

Facebook: @ClarissaJBarraza

For 25 years in the Dallas area I have practiced LOA in my sessions, allowing Source to guide me to do what's best for my clients.

Trapped

by Esther Bailey-Bass

It was a beautiful sunny day in May, with a breeze and a slight chill in the air. I remember it was Monday, May 1, 2017, typical as any other Monday before.

I readied myself for work, and as I proceeded to leave the house, I turned down the thermostat, set the house alarm, then closed and locked the door behind me. I noticed that I was leaving on time ... in fact, a little early.

I got into the car, and using the hand remote I opened the garage door and drove the car outside onto the driveway. Again using the hand remote, I closed the garage door. Just as I was pulling away, I noticed the garage door was still open.

"Huh, that was odd," I said.

So, I tried it again, and this time I watched the door close completely, then open again.

Not wanting to leave home with the garage door open and easy access to tools, lawn mower, yard equipment, bikes and more, I got out of the car to investigate.

First, I went to the wall unit to close the door from there. The same thing happened. The garage door went up and down and then up again.

Check the sensors, I thought.

So I did, and they seemed to be aligned. How could I tell? Again, I used the hand remote, the same thing. The wall unit, the same thing – the garage door went up and down and then up again.

"What!?" I screamed.

I don't have time for this.

Then I remembered that James, my husband, had adjusted the motor. So I decided I would climb up onto a bench and check the motor. Maybe I could manipulate something there.

I did, and then again with the hand remote, I pressed the button to open and close the garage door.

It worked, the garage door was down completely. Now on the inside, I was faced with a dilemma. Do I attempt to open the garage door using the hand remote or wall unit, or would the problem persist?

I remembered James once told me I could pull the red string to detach the garage door from the motor and then lift the door open manually.

That's it! That's what I'll do.

Something inside me was a little twitchy at this idea but I went for it anyway.

I pulled the red string and heard a sound of something becoming unhinged. Now I'll be able to manually open and close the garage door then go onto work.

Not so fast.

I went to lift the garage door. I pulled and tugged as hard as could, but it was impossible to move even a little bit.

Wait, I have muscles, I'm not weak. I can do this!

So I tried again and still not even the slightest budge would the door make.

I was locked in.

It was in that moment I realized I was trapped in the garage with no way out. The onset of panic came quickly. Standing in the middle of the garage, nearly in tears, I twirled around like Cinderella.

What just happened? What did I do?

In a panic stricken voice, I said to myself, "Calm down, take a breath, think." I was going to meditatively coach my way out.

Yeah, right! That was B.S.

What could I do? Who could help me? My car, with the keys in the ignition, cell phone and purse on the seat, was on the other side of the garage door.

WTF!

What to do? Well, I did what anyone would do in a similar situation. I screamed and cried for help.

There was just a sliver of space between the garage door and wall, and through it I screamed for help, calling out, "Neighbor, neighbor help!"

It seemed utterly useless.

Looking around the garage for an answer, a way out, I heard sirens in the distance, and that triggered a memory.

"There's a phone in here," I said.

Immediately, I rushed to search for the cordless phone. I had placed it in the garage for this exact reason.

I found it, but James had unplugged it. When I plugged it into the outlet it read, "Warning check battery … warning check battery."

Surely, it won't take long to get a charge, and I could call 911 for help.

While the phone was charging, I got down on my hands and knees and began screaming through the exhaust vent to the neighbor next door.

"Help, neighbor, help!"

No one. Nothing. Crickets.

I went between the cordless phone, the exhaust vent, and garage door screaming for help.

Then I thought, *How can I trip the lock on the interior house door. I've seen this done before.*

Sure, but it doesn't work on a deadbolt lock, and I knew that before I even tried, but thought I'd go for it anyway.

The cordless phone panel kept blinking, "Warning, check battery ... warning, check battery."

I felt a sense of despair that I would be locked in the garage until someone came, perhaps the mailman or James coming home from work.

Eureka! I'll dismantle the outside lock of the garage door and use a pole with a rag attached, stick it through the hole to draw attention to passersby.

So I fashioned a kind of surrender flag and stuck it through the lock hole, waving frantically to no one. Cars would pass by with windows rolled up against the chilly day.

The UPS truck went speeding by. The next-door neighbor pulled into their driveway but was deaf to my screams.

No phone.

No response.

No keys.

No way out.

I felt a sense of exhaustion take over me, and then I heard: *RESIGN.*

From what, my job? My body felt exhausted and I surrendered. I had been planning to leave my employment over the past 5 years.

Pausing to listen, the word settled in me, and I obliged myself to sit down. I pulled up a bench and sat in front of the garage door, looking back and forth asking myself, *How does it work?* I don't know how a garage door works. *How does it work?*

It was like asking a genie in a bottle for a wish.

Before I could say or hear the word "hands" I sensed them, and there they were, right in front of me. Then I heard, "You can do it," in a warm, confident, encouraging tone.

It was a familiar voice. Somehow I knew this voice. It was an aspect of myself from long before college, marriage, and the mundane.

She was my encourager, a voice of wisdom, clarity, and certainty. I knew her because we had played together before, and I was inclined to follow her lead. So, I reverse engineered my steps.

Hands.

What did I do?

You did this.

When I did that, what happened?

This happened.

If I do this, what will happen?

76

So, I climbed up onto the bench looking for what had detached. Using my hands, I latched two metal arms together. Something in me said, "That's it, now try." With the hand remote still in my hand, I stood suspended and pushed the button. Just like magic, the garage door opened.

Now free, I was dumbfounded. I remember looking at the clear blue sky, uncertain what to do next. I was baffled. So I got in the car and sat for a while before calling work to explain why I would be late. Then I called my mother to tell her what had just happened. After being trapped in the garage for nearly two hours, I ended up being my own rescue.

Seven months later, I did in fact resign from my employer after nearly 18 years of service. Life on the other side is already proving sweeter.

Esther Bailey-Bass is a Certified Professional Coach helping women in mid-career who are ready to embrace the role of leader and champion.

Esther can be reached by email at engage@ebbnflowcoaching.com or found on major social media platforms @ebbnflowcoach.

Our Dream Home

by Linda Armstrong

The funny thing about how we manifested our dream home is that I was really FINALLY happy in the home we were living in. I did not plan to move. We lived in a very small Cape Cod style home on a very small lot, about one-eighth of an acre.

When we purchased that house, we actually had to settle for it. It was the only house we could afford in the town where we really wanted to live. We wanted to live there because the town had a very good school system.

The house was filthy because of the hoarders who occupied it. So there was a lot to confront. I actually had a knot in my stomach when we made the offer. I was horrified at the thought of living there.

Luckily both my husband and I were very good at visualizing what the house could be, and we knew that we could do the work needed ourselves while hiring out work that we could not do. Knowing that we could make the house into a home that we could enjoy, we purchased it.

I am very interested in Feng Shui, so I had a Feng Shui Master come to the house and do a floor plan for us to make the energy in this house work best for us. Well, after she did a walk through and took some notes, she told us that she saw red ... blood ... and that it would be best if we were to move. Since we could not move, we had her create a Feng Shui plan designed just for us to make the energy work better.

We rearranged furniture and placed crystals in specific places throughout the house. She told us that we would have to move our front entrance. She said it had to be moved to another side of the house.

Cape Cod homes generally have a staircase that leads straight out the front door. In this house the entrance had literally three feet between the door and the staircase, just enough space for the door to open. The staircase led straight upstairs into the bathroom ... more bad energy. The more she looked around the house, the more bad energy flow she saw.

We did move the entrance, adding a new foyer. We purchased a really cool carved wood door that had a large sun and moons carved into it. It was such a happy door. I actually miss that door. It set the mood for the whole house.

I created a custom mosaic floor in the foyer, making it very inviting and improving the house's energy. We removed walls and opened up the stairway so that it had a wall on only one side. We added a nice iron bed foot board as a see-through railing for the basement. It was quite unique. It really did turn out to be a great little house full of character.

Always in the back of my mind, I thought that once we renovated the kitchen, we would be able to sell the house and move to a home that we really wanted. We added all new cabinets, granite counter tops, a tiled floor, and a really interesting stone mosaic back splash that pulled out an amethyst color that ran subtly through the granite counter top, which was mostly black with shades of grey. We added all new stainless steel appliances, making the kitchen a wonderful space.

After seven years of work, we were very happy with the house. We loved this little house that was as different as night from day compared to when we moved into it. I landscaped the whole property myself. I enjoyed doing that as well.

There was no garage. When we created the new front entrance, we added a large pergola that acted as a carport. We really put a lot of ourselves into that house, adding so much LOVE to it.

While sitting in my living room with my sister-in-law, she asked me if, now that the house was totally renovated, would we consider moving? She knew I hadn't been happy when buying it, but she admired the work we had done. Would we want to sell it and move on or stay and love it since it was a really cute and unique home?

My answer to her was, "The only way we would move is if we found a ranch style home that was contemporary in design. And it would have to be on a large piece of property."

And that was that. I didn't give it another thought. I merely stated what our ultimate dream home would be.

Then my son, Steele, who always hated school since preschool, asked if he could drop out of school and get his GED. He was miserable in school. We had done Child Study Team each year, but not one of the so-called professionals could ever figure him out. You see, he is very smart. He never fell into any category that would place him with any sort of learning disability. He is a very respectful kid, never got into trouble. But he just hated being in school all day, every day.

He had a way of outsmarting his teachers, in a respectful way. He would only do the bare minimum of any requirement he was asked to do. The teachers wanted more.

I had to tell his teachers to be specific when giving him an assignment. If they asked him to summarize a book he read, he would turn in one paragraph that told in a nutshell what the book was about. He had an algebra tutor. Before the tutor could write out the math, he would already have the answer.

Kids actually do know what is in their best interest. Steele had long used Law of Attraction. He made things go his way without any resistance.

At first my husband and I were not too thrilled about him wanting to leave school, but Steele was so sure of himself that we decided he knew best.

Since Steele was leaving school, there was no reason to stay in the town we lived in any longer. Now that there wasn't anything keeping us there, we decided to look around for another house to live in. Our current house was very nice now, and it would be easy to sell.

We started looking around and found a nice house on an acre of land. It met most of our requirements except that it was a split level. We put our house on the market. It sold for full asking price, and we then put a bid on this new house, which was accepted.

Everything was good … until our buyer backed out. Now we had to try to find a new buyer. The house was on the market again, and although everyone seemed to like the house and made nice comments about it, we weren't getting another offer. And then the seller of the house who had accepted our offer lost patience with us and decided to accept another offer. We lost that house.

We did then get another offer on our house from a new buyer. This offer was $20,000 less than our asking price, but they were very serious about purchasing it. My husband was in the hospital having hip resurfacing/replacement surgery. As I sat with him in the hospital room, I thought that I might as well start looking for homes in our slightly reduced price range.

I found a very contemporary-looking ranch on nearly two acres of land. I remembered the conversation with my sister-in-law about my dream home. It seemed perfect.

We couldn't wait to go and see it.

I went to see the house first. A few days later, Gavin could hop around using crutches, so we both went to see the house. We loved it.

This was the house that we wanted. We made an offer and it was accepted.

Next came the legal details of purchasing a home. Gavin's brother and his girlfriend came to visit us from California. They stayed with us for a week. During their stay, they started talking about the Law of Attraction. We had never heard of it before. We were very intrigued. They spoke to us about Abraham-Hicks, and once they were back in California, Gavin's brother sent us a video clip of the Abraham material. Soon, we were hooked!

We always thought that everything happens for a reason … that was for sure with us. And always in both of our lives, things always did work out. But, now for the first time we fully realized that we do create our own reality and that the Universe will guide us to our desires as long as we are in alignment with the energy of the desire.

While we were in attorney review, someone else put in a higher offer on the house that we were in the process of purchasing. While the sellers considered that offer, the buyers of our old house were having some difficulties with their Realtor and their mortgage commitment. It was turning into a real struggle, and at times it didn't look good, but thankfully we had learned about the power of our thoughts.

So I started showing appreciation for my current home (I actually miss it even now). I also thought about why I wanted this new house and why I thought I would receive it. I created stories in my mind of living in the new house. I really did A LOT of visualization.

I looked at the listing photos, decorating each room in my mind and creating experiences of living in the new house. I saw us hanging out in the backyard entertaining guests. I sat with these images in the listing and imagined living in the house before we even had the keys. I did this every day.

I took on the feeling of what it would be like already living there. I did NOT let myself think about it not happening for us, I only thought about how great it will be when we moved in. I really felt into it. That's the power of imagination: anything is possible.

I swam in the energy of living in that home so much that the owners decided to sell it to us and our buyers were able to complete their purchase of our old home. WOW!

Linda Armstrong is a Master Certified Law of Attraction Energy Coach, and Energy Healer. She works with The GATE Healing Method and Theta Healing® Technique. She is also a Reiki Master Teacher, and Light Body Meditation Practitioner.

Website: www.lovemylife.coach

Treasures From Tikashi

by Renate Donnovan

I lived in a shared accommodation. It was a cute, rented duplex with plush off-white rugs and rustic wood trim on the doors and ceilings. I shared this space with two roommates.

All three of us were going through divorces or some version of massive "life-restructuring." These restructurings took the forms of career changes, recovery from financial losses, and ending relationships.

One of my roommates was a drug addict who created chaos in the house through both a remarkable lack of hygiene (personal and home) and through the unpredictable, Dr. Jekyll/ Mr. Hyde behavior he displayed depending on his level of drug-induced high or withdrawal.

We had a controlling, prying, noisy landlord who attempted regularly to bypass the landlord-tenant laws in every way from unannounced, surprise visits, to using the garage we were renting for his own purposes, to spying on us by looking in our windows, to holding yard sales on our property without asking or notifying us.

One day, my already frayed nerves encountered more than I could manage.

My stoned roommate blared heavy metal music while dancing around the house in his underwear screaming lyrics at the top of his lungs.

Our landlord worked in "our" detached-garage while peering into our house windows through a pair of binoculars.

I attempted to deal with legal needs created by my "life-restructuring," failing miserably. I felt frantic. I needed peace. I needed an escape.

Despite the drizzling, cold late-March rain, I bundled up in rubber boots, a rain-slicker, and gloves. Pulling the hood of the slicker over my head, I bolted out the front door like a house cat making a desperate play for freedom and went for a walk.

Walking usually has a therapeutic quality for me, but on the day in question I was stirred up ... not just because of my roommate and landlord, but from the personal archaeological unearthing that deep inner work and personal growth create.

I was enrolled in a personal growth program that would last several years. I was trying to reconcile concepts of the Law of Attraction with my current reality.

I was also reading Maximum Achievement: Strategies and Skills that Will Unlock Your Hidden Powers to Succeed, by Brian Tracy.

My heart was heavy, and my thoughts were disjointed. One minute my mind replayed the antics of roommate and landlord, the next minute it practiced Brian's technique, then it swung between thinking about what I didn't want and what I did want, then back to my roommate, and so on.

Somewhere in that swirling shamble, an inner voice said, "I would really like to own my own home. Is that possible? What would have to happen to make it possible?"

The thought had barely registered when I spotted an odd purple square on the sodden ground, partially tucked into the winter grass. Enough of it was visible to display the words, "Treasures from Tikashi."

I recognized the purple square as one of those inspirational/spiritual cards that the reader can use as a personal motivator, provoking insights for daily guidance.

The card was soaked through, wrinkled, puckered, and darkly stained in one corner. It had obviously been there for some time.

The strangeness of it stopped me. There were no other cards or objects anywhere around. Knowing how valuable these types of cards are to those of us who have them, it seemed wrong to leave it lying there, abandoned. I took my right glove off and carefully (to ensure I didn't rip it) lifted the card and turned it over. The face of the card read:

ABUNDANCE

Love, security, freedom, happiness, support and finance are yours in abundance. The universe provides, it is up to you to say 'Yes!'

All life flows with love, and you are an energy being of love, you are not separate from what you desire. Let go of limited expectations and acknowledge that you are worthy of all things.

Participate in life's joy and you shall receive the rewards of your efforts.

The rain changed from drizzle to downpour as I stood there blinking, awe struck, for a full five minutes as the synchronicity of the situation sunk in. Then, with a squeal, I jumped for joy.

Rarely, before or since, have I received such a clear answer. With a combination of irrational joy and expectation, my feet carried me back to my shared accommodations.

Later that night, my mother called me. She worried about my living situation and wondered what the current housing prices were in Calgary. How much would I need for a down payment? She only had "this amount" that she could spare – would that be enough? Could I manage the mortgage payments? We talked for several hours about my options.

The first night I slept in my new condo was June 21st – the Summer Solstice, the longest day of the year, exactly three months to the day after I found the Abundance Card on the day of the Spring Equinox.

I sent an email to the contact address on Brain Tracy's website. I'm not sure why; I just wanted to share with him the impact his work had made on my life.

I wrote that when I started reading his book, like so many of the people he wrote about, I thought to myself, "I'm not special. Can I really do this?"

And, like the people in the stories he shared, I put aside my fears and used his Law of Attraction technique.

I assumed one of the staff who monitored the email would read it. I simply hoped the person who read it would pass along my appreciation to Brian.

The response to my note was simple. The email contained one line, "Congratulations on discovering you are one of the special people. --Brian Tracy".

Renate Donnovan MAL, CEC, Cht, MNLPP, PhD Candidate

Website: emergencehypnotherapy.com

Beginning Again

by Sherry Trentini

Grief sucks. I know this to be true. I became a widow at age 40. My daughters, ages 8 and 10, lost their daddy. Then five months later my own father died.

It was an exceptional year for us, to say the least.

Grief has the unique ability to make everything feel like it's going too fast, while simultaneously feeling as if you are standing still. It is plump with conflicting emotions, disconnected and scattered feelings, and there can be more questions than answers.

And those questions are endless when the cause of death is suicide. I didn't have answers to those questions for my daughters or anyone else.

Why did this happen? Why did he do this? How can this be happening? To us or to anyone?

In the months that followed, I did my best to field my girls' questions. They were valid. They wanted answers. In their way and at their age they needed something, anything, to try to make sense of it all.

I believe that grief is a part of life, but it didn't have to be our life.

I made the decision to move overseas 14 months after my husband passed away. I put our acreage on the market, boxed up the contents, let go of a large amount of stuff by either selling it or gifting it, and we set off for our international adventure.

The home we left was over 3,400 square feet of living area. In contrast we moved into a quaint furnished cottage of about 700 square feet.

Talk about downsizing!

We lived simply, and I measure "simply" not only in actual size but in features. The comfort I found in making that change was that we lived within what we needed. There was zero unused space.

I hosted a Canadian-style Thanksgiving for twelve people, feeding them all the traditional fare, and did so without having things like...

- a double oven

- a double sink

- a dishwasher

- a formal dining room table

- an 8' x 4' counter for the buffet

- various kitchen gadgets and accouterments, etc...

Everyone ate, drank and enjoyed the celebration.

Would I have attempted to make such a drastic change in houses if we'd stayed in Canada? I doubt it.

Did I miss certain creature comforts? No question.

Am I blessed that my girls adjusted to sharing a bedroom smaller than either of their previous rooms was? Absolutely.

Before you would have to look for where a person was in the house.

Now you were acutely aware of everyone's breathing patterns.

Not to mention one bathroom for three girls ...

In order to move forward, I believe it is necessary to lighten your load, literally and figuratively. I asked myself If I didn't have the physical space to keep these items, what would I do with them? Would I pay to store them elsewhere? How much would I invest to do so?

I didn't question the contents that my amazing team of friends came and lovingly packed up with me. Not only did I have a tight time constraint to get this done and on the airplane, everything that I did not let go of retained a high level of value, especially emotional value.

I attracted the most perfect people to help me move forward with these tasks, and I also attracted the most perfect people to be caregivers of our property in our absence. Both our bags and my heart were tremendously lighter because of that.

Selling property can be a true test of patience. When that property doesn't sell, it can be a pop quiz on one's self worth. The house I was selling burst with emotions. It wasn't just a property. It was:

- the house my husband and I built,

- on the land that he and I loved,

- in the community that we helped to create,

- in association with the business he had dreamed of starting and owning for years,

- for friends, family, Thanksgivings, Christmases, birthdays, and celebrations of all things,

- in our family home that our girls were to grow up in, move out of, and come back to.

I am keenly aware of and attuned to listening to my "gut" as my intuitive guide. Three main things came up for me:

1. Whenever I thought of the house, I felt a clenching in my chest ... not good.

2. I felt that as much as I wanted to sell it I was clutching it to my chest ... not conducive to manifesting a buyer.

3. Whenever the girls and I talked about the house, it sounded like we were talking about their dad, not the building ... tricky.

So I asked myself two questions:

1. If we weren't in Europe right now would I be selling the house?

    Answer: Yes

2. If we were to repatriate to Canada tomorrow, next month, or next year, would we move back into the house?

    Answer: No

So I created some affirmations, "I am so grateful for receiving the most perfect offer on my house now. I willingly let it go to the new owners with love."

Every time I thought of the house I immediately started to affirm letting it go with love.

Every time we spoke of a family memory, I would thank the house and affirm letting it go with love.

Every opportunity I could change the language in association with the house, I did. And it began to feel better and easier.

The next thing I did was write a letter and asked my girls to do the same. The letter was dual purpose: first it was to express our gratitude to and for the house and land; and secondly it was a welcome letter to the "Most Perfect New Owners."

I started by expressing gratitude to the house for keeping us safe, warm in winter, cool in summer, for being the most perfect place to live, for being such a gracious host to our celebrations with family and friends and for daily living.

I thanked it for being "the most perfect place" for the girls to have grown up. I thanked it for all the attributes that sprung to mind.

I then thanked my husband for choosing the location, for creating such an amazing yard, for tending to the land and respecting it. For all the things he did to make the house our home.

I thanked everyone who ever came through my door and for adding such positive energy to our space.

Next, I welcomed the new family. I told them how they had made the "Most Perfect" choice to live there. I excitedly told them about all the wonderful reasons they will love living there. How the yard and valley craved for kids to run, play and explore. How breathtaking the valley was in every season and to watch for the ample wildlife. I shared how strong and secure the house was and that it would love being freshened up to reflect their style. And I affirmed all of their reasons for choosing to make this their home.

After completing the letters, we read them out loud, which led us to share stories and memories. When we spoke about those things, it felt good. It didn't feel like loss. It helped us shift from "clutching onto it" to "releasing it peacefully".

To finish what now had become ceremonial, we burned our letters and released them ... with love.

I then asked my agent for a blank copy of the offer to purchase, which I then filled in with every detail as if it were the real deal.

For the names of the Purchasers I put: The Most Perfect Family or Better

For the price, I put in my walk away price: $XXX,XXX.XX or Better

For the date of possession I wrote the date and added: or Better

I signed it as the Seller and signed it for the Purchaser as The Most Perfect Family or Better.

Then put the document away and let the energy flow!

I'd love this next sentence to read, "And after I put my pen down my agent called ..."

Alas, the phone did not ring right away, although how cool would that have been!

Months later there was a family celebration planned in Canada that we wanted to attend. The timing of the event coincided with a school holiday. However, to justify traveling that distance, I wanted to extend our stay, which exceeded the girls' school break. I had to apply for the girls' absence well in advance.

The application form asked, "Why do you require the children to be out of school outside of normal holidays?"

My answer, "We sold our house in Canada and needed to go back to move out."

Which technically was not exactly true, but my intention was for it to BE TRUE.

This really amped up my energy by way of believing it! Every time the school break came up in conversation, I told people we were going to Canada to move out of the house! Yes I was affirming it!

Three weeks before we left for Canada, I received an offer to purchase that ticked all of our boxes, and I eagerly accepted.

And, yes I did a little jig!

Sherry Trentini

Life Coach &
Grief Recovery Specialist

www.SherryTrentini.com

Signs from the Universe

by Susan Shearer Young

I lived in Washington, D.C. in a beautiful neighborhood near the National Cathedral. I loved everything about it. Our house was a 100-year-old Victorian with a large front porch. I had installed a porch swing with pillows and comfortable wicker chairs. I loved to sit on the porch and wave hello to neighbors and people passing by.

People constantly yelled up to me, "I love your house. You look so comfortable."

And I was. The huge draw of this particular neighborhood was several excellent schools, all within walking distance. My three children attended three of the schools, and it felt magical to have them walk to school after years of commuting in heavy traffic into the city.

Our house was a haven for their friends as well, and there were constantly kids in our house, plopping down and talking about what was going on at school, who said what, who did this. It was so nice to be connected and tuned into the lives of my kids and their friends.

It was very hard to get a house in this neighborhood, precisely because of all of the good aspects this highly desirable neighborhood featured. Houses rarely came on the market, and when they did they were snatched up, sometimes in just one day. It took us nearly two years to get our perfect home, and there were multiple bids.

My very close friend also had kids who attended those schools, and she still drove the very stressful commute into Washington daily, back and forth for school events and sports practices. It was exhausting. It meant getting up earlier, getting home later, and it was much harder for her kids to socialize with their friends, which required navigating D.C. traffic during rush hour. My friend really, really wanted to move into D.C. Her top choice was our neighborhood.

I sat in my home office one day, working on a book about the Law of Attraction, which I ultimately published. I was in the zone, focusing upon great ideas, writing, thinking, and just absolutely enjoying what I was doing.

Strangely, I felt the impulse to go to our basement and straighten out a bookcase. We had moved into the house nearly a year earlier, and it popped into my head that I had never really organized any of the things in that bookcase. It felt a bit strange, as it wasn't a top priority. It was in the basement after all!

The basement was mostly a kid hangout, and I had plenty of other things to do. Yet, when I reflect back, it was like I was being moved, nudged to go to that bookcase and put things in order.

As I began to stack up the books and some files, I noticed on top the closing file from the purchase of our home. I have no idea how it ended up in that bookcase, because I had a filing cabinet. For some reason I felt the nudge to look in the file. On the top of the papers was a check in the amount of $2,500, made out to my husband and I. It was a refund of excess funds from our escrow account. It had never been cashed, and I was happily shocked to find it.

It occurred to me that because the check was rather dated, I should call the real estate agent who wrote the check and let her know that I would be depositing it. She was a very successful and connected agent who had helped us to get our home in that desirable neighborhood. She could sometimes get people houses when there was stiff competition, and she had done exactly that for us.

So I phoned her about the un-cashed check. As we chatted briefly, she mentioned that there was a home near ours that was likely to come on the market that weekend. She was going to make a presentation to try to get the listing. I was thrilled when I heard the news, as I knew of the house, and it was beautiful and only ONE BLOCK FROM MY HOUSE! My friend would love it; it was perfect for her family.

Despite being excited, I knew that having that information was no guarantee that my friend could get that house. It would be competitive. There were lots of moving parts. I told the agent about my friend and arranged for them to talk. As I'm sure you're imagining now, our agent represented my friend and her husband in the stiff competition, and they got the house.

Not only did I appreciate the manifestation and my ability to sit on my front porch and drink a glass of wine with my dear friend with no need for prescheduling, but I really appreciated learning how sometimes our best manifestations come with just a series of gentle nudges that light up the path of least resistance. Very ordinary nudges can lead to extraordinary results.

Susan Shearer Young is an award-winning Law of Attraction coach who helps her clients live the abundant lives they desire. She is also the author of *How to Allow*, chosen as Best of Books on Law of Attraction in 2012 and nominated in 2015.

Website: www.howtoallow.net

The Seller Who Was The Buyer's Ally

by David Scott Bartky

Several years ago, I decided I wanted to move after visiting a home with gorgeous views on a very quiet street.

Although my house was very nice inside, I didn't realize until after purchasing it that you could hear all the noise from the busy street corner on which it sat. I could hear every car, bus, or truck that drove by. There was no view except of the street or the neighbor's house. So between no nice view, and lots of street noise, it was time to move!

Besides a nice view and a very quiet street, I wanted a single story home, one with an attached garage. The idea of not having to deal with stairs sounded really good to me – not that I can't walk up and down stairs, but my parents were getting older, and I had a dog who can't climb stairs, so a single story home would be much easier.

After meeting with a Realtor, I was not surprised to be told that single story homes are very hard to find. Her negativity didn't concern me in the least. I know that the Universe knows what I want and will make it happen.

She did have one good idea: to sell my current home before finding my next home. That way there would be no chance of paying two mortgage payments at once, and I'd have the down payment for the new home.

As anyone who knows about selling homes can tell you, the best time to put a house on the market is in the Spring. However, it was December, and we wanted to be in a new home by the Summer. So we didn't want to wait until Springtime to list the house.

Two weeks after we met with the Realtor, a *For Sale* sign appeared in front of our house, and the open house occurred two days later on Sunday. We were unsure what price to put our home because home prices in the area were all over the place. Our Realtor suggested we price low to start a potential bidding war, which is what we did. There's no guarantee of a bidding war, but it's a risk we were willing to take.

The day after the open house, the Realtor called and told us we had two offers. She said that one offer was good, but the other offer would have us "dancing on the tables!" Of course I was most interested in the dancing on the tables offer, since the more we got for this house meant the more we would have for the purchase of the next house.

We met with the Realtor, who told us we had a full price offer. Then she told us the other offer was WAY higher than the first one. It turns out the couple who made that offer had tried to buy a few other homes but were outbid. So this time around they came in with their best and final offer.

Our Realtor cautioned us not to get too excited about such a high offer because the house had to appraise at that amount in order for the deal to go through. I honestly had no doubt that the house would appraise at the full amount, even though others involved did have doubts. The Universe knew that we needed that extra money, and I knew it would all work out.

Needless to say, the home did appraise at that amount, and the buyer also wanted a quick closing, which is another thing we really wanted. A month later, we sat at the closing table, where they handed us a very large check! Thank you Law of Attraction!

Now we needed to find a new house to buy that met our requirements. We must have looked at 50-60 homes. Some our Realtor found for us, and some she didn't.

One day I drove by a home in our preferred area and saw a *For Sale By Owner* sign on the lawn. I quickly went home to my computer and plugged in the address. The home was very nice and had 90% of what we were looking for. It was on a very quiet street, was basically a single story home – only had two steps up to the 2nd floor – and had a great back yard.

The only issue was that it was way above our price range. Even our Realtor, who didn't find the home for us, told us not to look at it because of the price. However, knowing how the Law of Attraction works, I decided not to let that get in our way.

The day before we found it, the owner decided to list it with a Realtor because he wasn't getting any action trying to sell it himself. We went to look at the house, and once inside we knew it was the one. The owner liked us and told us to come back again to look at it if we wanted to. So we took him up on his offer and went back a few more times.

Soon the seller's Realtor called me and asked if we were going to make an offer on the home. We said we wanted to but it was out of our price range. He then told us a long story about how the owner listed the house at a price that was way too high. That's the reason he didn't get a lot of people coming to look at it. The Realtor also told us that the owner had to move by a certain date because of plans he had made, so that we should basically make an offer because he had to sell.

We decided on an offer two days later. When I called, the Realtor told me that the day before someone else made an all-cash offer, and the owner accepted! How could this be? I just knew this was my house! I decided to stay positive about it and didn't get upset because I trusted it would work out.

My parents saw the house with us a few times, and they clicked with the owner. After my mom heard that he accepted another offer, she called him and demanded, "How could you do that?" He told her that we were his first choice, but he didn't know we were going to make an offer when he accepted the other offer. He also told her that he would try to get out of selling the home to the buyer. My mom told me what he said, but I didn't believe it. Why would he let an all-cash offer go?

A few weeks went by, and I started looking at other homes on the Internet. One day, I received a text message from the seller's Realtor asking, "Are you still interested in that house?"

I replied, "Yes! Why?"

The deal fell through with the other buyer. The owner refused to fix anything on their list! The buyer pulled out because they didn't want to spend the money to fix everything.

The Seller kept his promise to my mother and got out of the deal! How crazy is that! He accepted our offer, telling us to wait before we ordered the home inspection so he could fix everything that had to be fixed. How often does that happen?

When he finished (including installing a brand new heating system), we got the house inspected. It passed with flying colors.

A few months later we moved in, and it has been a wonderful, quiet home with great views out of every window and with only two stair steps. Thank you Law of Attraction!

David Scott Bartky
Life Coach David
Web Site: lifecoachdavid.com
Facebook: @lifecoachdavid
Twitter: @lifecoachdavidb

David is also a co-host on LOA Today.

Careers and Finances

A Financial Surprise

by Barbara Pinti

About a year ago, I began working with a woman who for many years had a poverty mentality. Money was always short, and there was never enough to get to the things that weren't absolute necessities.

She inherited a life script from her parents concerning money and honed that script to perfection for 40 years. She often talked about not having enough money for this or that. She resented not being able to travel, her greatest desire. She blamed everyone for her living a life of lack rather than abundance. Her words put forth a low vibration, and that low vibration returned to her daily.

I helped her write some affirmations about money while teaching her how it could come to her easily by simply changing her beliefs. We worked on raising her vibration by carefully keeping her thoughts and words very positive. She became more consciously aware of her thoughts and her words whenever they became negative or discouraging. I explained to her that everything she desired was right there in the unseen world and only needed to be claimed by her.

I introduced her to visualizations. I asked her to imagine herself and her family having a wonderful time traveling to all the places she so wanted to experience. She began to see herself enjoying life with more than enough money to take those long desired adventures.

This education about the Law of Attraction went on for about a month, and I did the exercises with her.

We examined the words of several famous people from Einstein who wrote, "Imagination is everything," to Buddha who wrote, "All that we are is the result of what we have thought."

Henry Ford informed us, "Whether you think you can or can't ... either way you are right."

Wayne Dyer added, "I will see it when I believe it."

We also studied the work of Masaru Emoto, who conducted many experiments with water showing that the vibration of the words and thoughts connected to vials of water affected their molecular structure in dramatic ways. Knowing that both our planet and our bodies contain approximately 70% water shows us how important it is to keep our vibrations high.

After a few weeks of our working together to change her poverty script to raise her income, she told me about a new job offered to her son that would take him to many interesting places in Europe. Her husband, who previously struggled with a low-paying, commission-only job, also received a wonderful job offer from the same firm as her son and began making much more money than before. My client herself got back a former job that she loved, this time with the hours and at the wage she asked for. She later reported receiving a bonus of over $2,000.

That didn't surprise me. What surprised me is that even though I wasn't purposely intending her exercises for myself, I began making more money than I ever had before! My business phone rang all the time, and my case load filled to capacity.

This universal law knows not who you are or what it is you desire. It just WORKS!

Barbara A. Pinti, MA, MA, ABD, LMFT, LPC

I am a psychotherapist in private practice in West Hartford, Connecticut. I have taught the Law of Attraction in many groups, workshops and in my private practice.

Email: barbarapinti@comcast.net

Sailing

by Cambria Berger

Follow your happiness. That phrase is something that I used to say often as a carefree college student with her whole life ahead of her and a history of loving family and solid friends.

Little did I realize just how much that sentiment would shape the rest of my life and, more specifically, the year following my college graduation.

Since my teenage years, I had always been a bit of a dreamer with a love of the outdoors and adventure. In college I became fast friends with a fellow with sailing in his blood. His grandparents were sailors, and his cool demeanor and quick mind convinced me that that was the sailor's way.

Since we lived in the rugged part of Northern California – practically in Oregon – his fanciful warm water sailing stories seemed more like fantasy. His images of sunshine and sea spray were a welcome distraction from the cold and musty reality of the weather we endured 70% of the year.

The more he shared, the more I desired to be that brave and resourceful soul who would cast off the lines and sail into a world of adventure and exploration. I could taste that this was going to be a part of my future.

Enter Robert ... the man who would make my dreams come true! I was instantly attracted to him. As I got to know him, I learned that he was building a massive 60-foot-long sailboat a couple of towns over.

Robert was a fascinating guy. He was welding the hull together himself and had grown up in a Caribbean Island. He had sailing in his blood, as his grandfather was a Captain in the Coast Guard. His father built sailboats, and being an island boy, he had a deep love for the sea.

We dated, schemed, dreamed, and worked to turn his hunk of steel into a glorious sailing machine. But as time went on, and my days as a college student began to dwindle, it became clear that Robert and I were not on the same timetable for setting sail. I was willing to work with that, but then our relationship began to implode of its own accord.

We partied more than worked, played more than schemed, and burned out as fast as we had sparked in the beginning. I was crestfallen. I felt incredibly sad that the relationship ended and mourned the death of my dream of sailing around the world … especially with someone I cared deeply about.

In the end, I had to leave. I lived in that small town for so long that my wings were damp with the Northern Pacific rains and slow ways of a mountain town.

I planned a trip to New Zealand with an old friend as a graduation gift to myself. At least I had that to look forward to. It patched up my heart and stoked the dwindling embers of a capricious life at sea.

Footloose and fancy free in New Zealand with one of my best friends was a feeling of expansion like I'd never known before. All of this "growing up" and becoming an "adult" was supposed to be hard work, nose to the grindstone, sacrifice according to many.

Granted, I was on vacation, and although a career and work life was imminent, I couldn't help but keep "follow your happiness" at the forefront of all of my decisions.

I was responsible. I worked my way through college holding down 30 hours/week jobs and 15-18 units of science courses simultaneously. I worked since I was 15 years old. I understood responsibility at a visceral level. Surely I had earned this vacation, and deep inside I knew that this journey would open up my perspective on life and how to live it to the fullest.

The trip was nothing short of magical. My travel partner Rose and I ran track and cross country together in high school. Part of a close-knit friend group from those days and throughout college, we stayed close and visited one another regularly, even when seven hours of driving time separated us.

She was bubbly and had this constant sense of curiosity that I adored. As your friend, she made you know that she was truly interested in you and everything that you were up to. That curiosity also drove her to incredible academic heights.

At the time that we traveled, she was between a rigorous undergraduate degree and an imminent graduate program, taking a break. She was all about squeezing every last delicious drop from our trip.

As we explored New Zealand, we saved money where we could, opting for hikes and treks into nature while going along with new friends on group adventures.

We even found our way onto a sailboat for a few days! My taste for sailing around the world bobbed back up to the surface. It turns out that it had been bubbling and gurgling deep inside looking for a fissure, an opportunity to erupt into the ultimate adventure.

We sailed for three days, though it was cold and wet, and the captain seemed to have more interest in my friend than actually teaching us to sail. I had to let the immediate fantasy go, hoping that the sailing life was growing closer.

Our travels continued, but after some time my friend had to leave me. She scheduled one month for the trip, but I scheduled two. I was sad to see her go, but our trip had been incredible. We had marvelous synergy, got into epic adventures, and our friendship was now closer than ever.

Being on my own was a new kind of thrill, though admittedly not as carefree without a second set of eyes and opinions. My money was running low, and I wondered how I could pay for the last two weeks of my trip, since I barely had enough money to cover accommodations.

I put my "follow your happiness" theory in front of me, as I had in the past. I comfortably moved from town to town safely.

I even managed to find work in a restaurant for a couple of nights to pay for a diving trip in the Milford Sound, which is an incredible glacier-formed fjord in the southern part of the country.

Slowly I made my way back up the eastern side of the South Island. Catching rides where I could, I kept calculating how far my money would go, hoping to squeeze in one last touristy excursion, though the thought occasionally occurred that I ought to turn tail and head home a few days early.

I landed in a little town called Nelson up at the top of the South Island. It was a sleepy, sweet, and artsy town, and I figured it would be a great place to hang around until I was ready to hop back up North to Auckland to conclude the trip.

I caught a Sunday farmer's market festival with folk music and sunshine. I rode a bike through the streets imagining living in such a quiet little town. And then honestly, a bit of boredom crept in. It was time to go.

On departure day, I hemmed and hawed and dilly-dallied until it was almost too late to go. I finally committed, and as I walked to the outskirts of town to catch my ride, I walked past Cambria Street.

Awesome! I had never seen a street sign with my name on it. Delighted by this detail, my step lightened, and I figured that I must be on the right path.

I got several blocks away before I realized that I really wished I had taken a photo. I kept walking and then heard clearly in my head, "You may never walk this path again." I promptly turned around to take the photo.

As I juggled my camera, a familiar voice called my name. I looked up to see an Israeli fellow my travel partner and I had met at the beginning of our trip. He was gregarious and kind, with a goofy grin, bushy dark hair, and an overgrown beard. He was also on his bike.

He and his friend (I could never remember their names!), who was equally as friendly and likable with bushy blond hair and a struggling beard, were biking around the whole of New Zealand. When my friend and I met them, they were just starting out. We talked about routes and sights and listening to people tell them they were slightly crazy for attempting such an endeavor. We adored them.

We saw them all over the country, however only one at a time! We'd roll into town and there would be one of them asking if we had seen the other after they had gotten separated. A few towns or days later we would see the other one, asking about the first. And so it went, all over the country, six weeks of leapfrogging and near misses.

So when he rode up to me, he excitedly told me they had finally reunited and were staying just down the road in an amazing hostel where you could sleep in an actual bus, and didn't you know there was a party tonight, and I just *had* to be there!

I laughed at his boyish ways and exuberant ramblings while instantly agreeing to join them for the night at the hostel.

I followed him to the hostel, got settled in, and made plans to meet for drinks and the party later. With a bit of down time, I decided to take a quick jaunt down to the Internet café and report to my mother that my plans had changed. She was keeping tabs on me, and I was diligent about notifying her of my movements.

When I walked into the café, there was a flier posted on the wall that changed my life forever. It was a black-and-white photo of a pirate ship (well it *looked* like a pirate ship), that said "Crew Wanted, S/V Alvei; French Polynesia Contact Evan". Hand written below that was a local phone number and an email address.

My heart stopped. Could I dare to dream about being a crew member on this incredible ship? Immediately the chatter in my head began … you know the advisory board that lays in wait to chime in on any major decision, or anytime you put yourself really out there? Yes, them … they all woke up and started deliberating. Through it all, I had this silly girlie giddy feeling inside like maybe this was it. Maybe I could go. My dream could begin right here!

It was not lost on me that the series of "coincidences" that put me in this place at this time were nothing short of miraculous. Cautiously, I tempered my enthusiasm and typed out an email to Evan, followed by one to my mom.

Needless to say, that night I felt restless, yet cautious. I couldn't see how this was going to work, but what I knew down to the core of me was that I was going to do whatever it took to make it work!

The next morning, I rushed over to the Internet café to see if Evan had responded. Dashed by finding no response, I brightened to learn that my mom, who though she expressed concern like a mother can do, said she was also excited to learn what it was all about.

Now what? I was too excited to sit around, so I made my way down to the docks in search of the ship.

Nelson is known as the maritime gateway of New Zealand. It is perfectly situated for many commercial and private boats to have a protected place to tie up, because it is located directly top and center between the two islands. As I strolled along a marina filled with sailboats, my heart began to sink. I didn't see the masts that would surely tower over all of these others.

I asked a fella walking down the docks, and he told me that he thought that the ship had departed. My heart kept sinking. The 'opposed' members of my advisory board smirked. But that fire deep inside of me still burned, and that little girlie dreamer demanded that I not give up that easily.

I wandered a bit more. Another fellow came down the dock, and I asked him as well. He told me that he thought the ship was on the other side of the buildings at the commercial dock. Quickly I walked up and around, and there she was! Her masts stood tall and proud among the metal smoke stacks and tall bridges of the cargo ships docked there. As I neared, I saw several confident young people working on and off of the S/V Alvei. They smiled, and when I asked, they found Captain Evan for me.

Evan was lanky and tanned with a knowing look in his eye. He told me that he hadn't checked his email recently as they had planned to leave yesterday, However they were waiting on a delivery of engine spares that was due to come in that day or the next. The next day was Friday though, and sailors (suspicious lot that they are) never set sail on a Friday.

He did still have room for one more crew member. If I signed on as crew, he asked for a 10 month commitment, to return the ship to this port after sailing through the South Pacific Islands. He took on passengers as his ship was sort of a combination floating hostel/ learn to sail/ life of a traditional sailor training program.

The ship was a 'gaff rigged top sail schooner'. She was 126 feet overall length and 82 feet on the water. There was no running hot water, no refrigeration, all 15 sails, and the anchor had to be raised and lowered by hand (well several sets of hands).

Everyone was expected to do their share. I wouldn't be paid. It was all volunteer work, but he would waive the $25 per day fee everyone else was paying. I just had to post a bond in Tahiti of $700 as a part of their immigration process, and the money would be returned when we departed the country.

Holy smokes! I was SO up for that! Living in Northern California when I was at college, my campus was literally in a Redwood forest. I loved camping and roughing it. I loved the physical challenges of hiking and crossing rivers, much as I had loved surfing and playing in the beaches of my home in San Diego.

Having exchanged pleasantries with some of the other crew members and passengers, I knew that I could quite easily live and work with them. I just had to see about the money and handle the details of my life back at home.

Rushing back to the Internet café, I'm not sure if my feet even touched the ground! I nervously dialed my mom. My parents were going to have to help me with the money. I had $200 left to my name, and I needed $25 of that to change my plane ticket to get back to the US.

As luck would have it, and at the end of a very intense conversation, my mom told me that she had just received her tax return and would be happy to lend it to me, even though I knew it was a stretch for her. She agreed to care for my little dog, and my dad agreed to take on payments for my student loan and my storage unit.

Exhilaration was redefined for me that day. Two days later we sailed. The trajectory of my life changed forever.

In the ten months that followed that I lived on the S/V Alvei, I fell in love with the sea. It enraptured me. I became enchanted with slowly watching land rise up from the sea and take form as the next paradise to be explored.

Fruit never tasted so sweet as when pulled fresh off the trees. The smiles and generosity of locals, expats, and fellow sailors settled into my soul as a knowing of "this is how people are meant to be with one another." Any ideas about sitting at a desk for the rest of my life disappeared.

I became a sailor that year. The stories and experiences of those island hopping days are a novel all their own.

In the 13 years since, my itchy feet have touched 15 countries, and I spent close to three years of my life with the rolling deck of a ship beneath my feet as a research technician for a prominent oceanographic institution. I successfully combined my love for the sea and being aboard a ship with my oceanography degree.

Follow your happiness. I am so glad that I did.

Cambria is a long time student of personal development. She retired from oceanography in 2012 to raise her two wonderful boys with her husband in San Diego, California and is now a certified Law of Attraction Coach.

Web: www.CambriaBerger.com
Phone: +1-619-880-0714

It's No Accident

by Cathy Brown

I learned about negative manifesting the hard way.

A few years back I was driving home from a visit with my Mom, who was 96 at the time and living in an assisted living facility after my Dad transitioned (passed away) a year earlier at age 94. (I've got good genes ... thank you Universe). The visit didn't go too well. She was not in the greatest mood. At 96, Mom's demeanor was often unpredictable.

I was not in the greatest mood either as I drove home. I felt a little sorry for myself, focusing on why can't Mom be happy to see me, since I was so busy yet I had taken time to spend with her when I could be doing so many other (in my mind) more productive activities. I was far from accepting of her feelings, aches and pains. I now realize it would have taken so little to be more understanding.

What energy or thoughts do you think I was sending out?

About halfway home, a large SUV in the middle lane suddenly decided to make a right turn. Too bad I was in the right lane! I slammed on my brakes just as I saw her cut in front of me, but I couldn't stop quickly enough to avoid her smashing into by left side. At least by hitting my brakes, I avoided a much worse collision.

I went ballistic.

We pulled over and the negative energy swirled as she spoke only in broken English. She couldn't find her license and was driving her brother's car. I could feel the anger flaring up inside of me. This was my first accident in over 20 years.

I didn't think to call the police, just my insurance company. My agent tried unsuccessfully to understand the other driver. Getting nowhere, my agent suggested I just stop the confrontation and take my car in for an estimate. She booked an immediate appointment.

I was still furious as I drove to the dealer for a damage estimate.

Why did this happen to me?

I didn't take responsibility for creating the events in my life at all. Cooling my heels in the dealer's waiting room helped a little, but you could still cut through my negativity with a knife.

The mechanic kept coming in to say, "Relax, it will be fine", but I wasn't buying it. The estimate came to about $1200, of which $500 was my deductible. This just increased my anger and negativity. I didn't stop to think that if I was not at fault, I would be totally covered, nothing out of pocket.

I begrudgingly thanked the mechanic, got back into my car and backed out of the service bay – right into a brand-new car. That's right, I ran into another car – my second accident that day! This time there was no question who was to blame: me.

Sometimes if I don't get it the first time, the Universe has to whomp me up the side of my head.

Now whenever I start to go negative, I take a step back, take a few deep breaths, and focus on something positive. It takes a mere 17 seconds to start to reverse a vibration and 68 seconds to start to manifest that new vibration. Much better than having two accidents. Lesson learned!

In 2014, I enrolled in Christy Whitman's Quantum Success Coaching Academy's (QSCA) program totally focused on becoming a great Law of Attraction life coach. I was about halfway through the program when I heard about the annual QSCA business meeting in California.

Invitations were sent to all graduates and students to gather for the weekend to network and learn from noted metaphysical speakers while meeting the instructors and Christy herself. This sounded like something right up my alley. I hadn't had a proper vacation in a few years, and the opportunity to meet Christy was just too much to resist. I signed up on the spot.

On the flight from Ohio to California, I read *The Prosperous Coach,* by Steve Chandler and Rich Litvin. The authors said you can only take a client as far as you are willing to go yourself.

131

How can you expect a client to buy into the concept of coaching if you don't buy into it enough to have a coach yourself and continue to grow in your business and personal life? That was an "a ha" moment for me.

At 30,000 feet, I set my intention. *I am going to get a coach this weekend.* I had no idea who, or how, but I would get my coach this weekend. I closed my eyes and asked the Universe to assist in bringing my coach to me. Then I let to go of my intention. Every time I thought about the upcoming meeting, I totally focused on finding my new coach.

The flight was great, the hotel in San Diego was fabulous, and the meeting was really inspiring. I met so many spiritually minded people and developed many lasting friendships. I sat in the front row for all the sessions, as my 5'2' stature made it difficult to see over people sitting in front of me.

I had almost forgotten about my intention of finding my coach with all the activities and excitement of the speakers and seeing Christy Whitman live.

Then on Saturday, just before lunch, it happened. Christy began to explain a new mentoring program she was starting. It was not for everybody, only a select group of five to six coaches who wanted to excel in their business.

I nearly fell off my chair. THIS IS IT! Christy is going to be my coach. I just have to do this.

It never crossed my mind that I was only six months into the training and there were over 100 people in the audience, most more qualified than me. I just knew Christy was going to be my coach. I can't explain it, I just felt it in my bones.

I came back to reality to hear Christy say she would give all the details after lunch.

As she finished and released us all for our lunch break, I jumped up and ran to the stage where Christy was collecting her notes. On pure adrenaline, I stammered quite loudly, "Christy ... I'm a ... I'm Cathy Brown, and I want to do this ... I really want this." I must have sounded like a crazy person, a bit off balance. I felt the Universe was setting this up for me.

Christy turned around, smiled and sort of giggled I think, and said "OK Cathy, I'll get the application to you after lunch." I was on Cloud Nine. I wanted a coach, but I never thought it would be Christy Whitman. Christy was the *New York Times* bestselling author, CEO and founder of the QSCA and top spiritual leader. WOW!

Once again, I didn't give any energy to the fact that I was probably one of many applying for the mentorship and one of the least qualified.

That afternoon, along with many others, I filled out the application and just let it go. I allowed the Universe to take control, trusting that the result would be in my best interest.

Little did I know, Christy was intrigued with me. She was genuinely impressed that I was willing to commit and trust the Universe to bring this to me without having any of the details, investment or anything. I appeared to have total trust in her and in the Universe.

Unknown to me at the time, Christy started to "check me out" by talking to my instructor and others who knew me from the program. The Universe was setting things in motion.

During the final session on Sunday, Christy thanked all of us who applied saying she would email those selected early next week.

My homeward bound flight was scheduled on Monday morning. While waiting in the lobby for the airport taxi, Christy and her husband walked by the front desk, and I heard somebody call my name. I turned around to see Christy Whitman walking over to me smiling. She gave me a big hug while whispering "Congratulations, you are in the Mentor program. I'm going to be your coach."

This is one of the few times in my life that I was speechless. When I finally regained my composure, all I could say was, "It works, this stuff really works", then of course, "Thank you so much".

Christy looked a bit puzzled and replied, "Great, yes it does work."

Cathy Brown holds an MBA and is a Certified Law of Attraction Life Coach, Hypnotherapist, Reiki Master, Creating Money Coach, a best-selling author and highly sought after speaker and teacher.

Email: cathy@lifecoachingbycathy.com

Website: lifecoachingbycathy.com

Making Changes

by Galina Shadrova

A man in his late sixties made an appointment in my Tarzana, California office. When the man walked into my room, he nervously stated, "I don't think you will be able to hypnotize me, but you were highly recommended from my friend, and I would like to give it a chance."

This is a really promising beginning, I thought.

All his life he was the provider for the family, and everybody constantly acknowledged him for it. This made him very happy.

Time passed. He got older and lost his job with little savings for his retirement, resulting in him lashing out at his wife and kids. He feared that they would leave him.

After the first session he awoke happy and relaxed and immediately made another appointment for nine days later. He returned for the second session in an angry mood. He screamed that the hypnosis did not work and that this would be his last session.

"Okay. That is absolutely fine, but as long as you are here tell me about this past week," I said.

"After the first session I was calm and happy and everything at home began to feel good. However, the past two days I began yelling again, and everything became bad again," he replied.

I never promised to fix his entire problem in one session. I am a clinical hypnotherapist, not a magician!

Usually hypnotherapy works for about seven days. Then you must do it again to reinforce it. I hypnotized him again, and he fell into a very deep hypnotic state (so much for not being hypnotizable). Afterward, he decided to make another appointment for seven days later.

After several sessions his wife called me and asked, "What did you do to my husband? He is a totally different person. I don't think I've ever seen him so happy. After 20 years together, we are planning a second honeymoon. Life is great. Thank you!"

Two months later, he called me again for an appointment, asking for my help to get a job and make more money. He entered my office with a smile on a much younger looking face and with confidence stated, "Everything is good in my life, and I am very happy, but because of my age no one wants to give me a job. My wife is still working, and I would like to make some extra money. Is that possible?"

Time for Law of Attraction! After two sessions he got job with a 10 minute drive from his home twice a week. After a couple more sessions, another employee left, and the owner offered him two more days of work per week.

He recently e-mailed me about how he was now working six day a week and had won $500.00 from the lottery.

I got another call from a woman who said she wanted to make an appointment to help cure her of depression.

I asked her if she knew that this was a hypnotherapist's office and that she would need a doctor's referral for me to help her with her depression.

"I didn't know that this is a hypnotherapist's office. I just called because somebody told me that you would be able to help. I am glad you are hypnotherapist! I believe that hypnosis is my last hope. I saw a psychiatrist for three years and even asked shamans for help. I do not want to live, but I can't leave my children. On weekends I do not feel like getting out of bed."

When she entered my office, I saw a woman without make up and a tired face in her 50s.

She got divorced after 27 years of marriage. Her husband left her for a much younger woman. Her oldest son lived alone, but her two teenage kids still lived with her.

I advised her to have hypnotherapy sessions twice a week until they were not needed anymore.

For the second session, she came in with a nice hair cut and pretty make up, and she was beautifully dressed.

I knew hypnosis helped, but *that* fast?

Two more sessions later, she declared, "I want to make repairs in my bedroom. I already bought wallpaper and began to apply it myself."

I switched her to one session per week.

She decided to take a few private drawing lessons. Her life became more and more enjoyable.

A few months later, I got a call from her. She said that she was ready to start dating again but did not know how to find the right person.

It was time for her to learn about the Law of Attraction. We had a total of five sessions in which I taught her what she should do for herself.

Six months later she called me and said that she had met a man with whom she is now very happy!

Galina Shadrova is a hypnotherapist and a life coach who believes we are never too old to make positive changes in life. She helps her clients to become magnets to reach their goals in life while enjoying every step on the way. Web page: hypnosis.edu /hypnotherapists /galina-shadrova

London Calling

by Geanina Roman

The first time I visited London was during a three day trip. That was all I needed to fall in love with the city. It wasn't just the beauty of the place that drew me in but also the feeling that I'd been there before. I remember sitting in line at the airport. As I boarded the flight that would take me back home to Romania, wanted to return so badly.

Back home I had recently started a very promising full-time job. I was hired as a translator by a prestigious company. This was the sort of job that sounded really good on paper, particularly for a fresh graduate. I thought that I would be happy as long as I was using my language skills. My previous experience as a volunteer translator for cultural events during University made me feel confident about that.

I didn't take me long to realise that my new job, where I had to deal with soulless technical details and monotonous press releases on a daily basis, was nothing like my volunteering experience. I felt disconnected from my work. It felt hard, and I began to doubt myself.

I also missed the small town where I went to university and the friends I made there. The lack of job opportunities there led me to move to a big city that felt cold and unfriendly by contrast. I couldn't find anything exciting at work or outside it. I began to feel lost and too hopeless to even think about finding something better.

Only my daily meditation practice prevented me from wallowing in anxiety and helped me regain some of my balance.

The thought of going back to London was always at the back of my mind. So a few months later, the news that I was being made redundant came as a relief. It also came as a permission slip to finally do something about my dream to go to the U.K.

Exactly one year to the day from when I stood in line at the airport to leave Britain, I found myself at the Arrivals at Heathrow ready to start my new life.

That new life revolved around my job as an au pair. This meant that I lived with a British family taking their children to school and helping out with household chores, all in exchange for some pocket money, my own room, food, and no bills to pay.

My schedule gave me plenty of time to do some soul searching and to explore London. There was so much to see and do! I went to as many parks, galleries, cinemas, and other sites that would allow me to visit. There was so much beauty around me and in the people I met. Everywhere I went I experienced an underlying feeling that anything was possible, that I was supported no matter what. It was so easy to be myself in London, and I had a familiar feeling of belonging there.

During this time, a deep knowing came to me. I discovered that my thoughts and the things I give my attention to create the events in my life. For example, my strong thoughts about Britain brought me there, and I realised that landing there on the exact same day one year after I made the wish couldn't have been just a coincidence.

Also my love of the English language that I'd acquired from a young age when I watched Scooby-Doo on TV must have influenced me to end up in Britain. The deep feeling of peace that I experienced in Britain matched perfectly the feeling I'd practised during my meditations before I arrived.

I came across a book on the Law of Attraction by Abraham-Hicks, and although a bit doubtful about some of its claims, I decided to buy it. Idea after idea presented in the book resonated with me in a way that nothing did before then. The Law of Attraction became my life philosophy as I learned how to shift my thoughts to create happy experiences as my self-confidence grew with every day.

Living in London was the most joyful thing I could imagine. I wanted to stay there for as long as possible. But in order to do that, I needed a different job, one that would give me a proper salary and thus more freedom to be more than just a guest in another family's house, no matter how kind and friendly they were to me.

My interests were scattered, and my work experience was limited. I had no idea how I could use them to get a good job.

The most interesting experience I had was volunteering for cultural events while I was still a student. I acted as a guide for tourists and for other volunteers, translated movie scripts, and offered information to festival goers, among other things.

I loved working behind the scenes in events related to the cinema and the theatre because of their ability to transport the audience to new places. It felt good to contribute to that purpose in my own way. As for my other skills, my previous work as a translator wasn't particularly helpful because Romanian isn't exactly a sought after language in Britain (or anywhere else!)

As an au pair I learned that I loved children, and I would have liked my dream job to involve them somehow. But my au pair job was too informal, and it didn't qualify me to work with children in an institution.

Nor did I have the finances to study and eventually obtain such a qualification. All I knew for sure was that I had good administrative skills so, that's what I applied for: any job that would make use of them. The more I thought about it, getting a job I liked seemed hard.

Could I find something I enjoyed doing despite my lack of experience? Where could I find this job? Would it mean starting from the bottom and thus having to put up with some shortage?

Those questions went through my mind as I started my search. Thinking about them brought a lot of the old anxiety back, and there were many times when I had to remind myself that the Law of Attraction expands anything I focus on.

Lack wasn't what I wanted, so I did my best to snap myself out of negative patterns. Instead, I remembered how the Universe orchestrated my arrival in London, how it brought me to my wonderful au pair family, how easily it helped me meet people who encouraged me, including a boyfriend. The Universe had already brought to me so many things that made me happy. Surely, my dream of staying in London must have been heard too.

The first time I realised that something was beginning to manifest was when I got a call from what sounded like a potential employer. Except that I was in a place with poor reception and I could hardly hear what the caller was saying. I hung up disappointed, unable to reach them back.

That seemed like an awful start to my search. I felt sad, but I tried to remember Abraham's words about there being more than one opportunity lined up for each desire. So that if you miss one, there's always another one around the corner. This helped me keep my hopes high.

Once, more or less randomly, I applied at a big entertainment company only to get a rejection email, politely saying that they don't need anyone with my skills at the moment. Again, I tried to see it as just another opportunity to keep focused on what I wanted and to ignore any evidence of the opposite.

So I kept visualising the expansive and exhilarating feeling of embracing London more and more, having fun there, meeting more interesting people, going to a job I loved where I felt at ease and happy. My daydreams were as real as I could make them.

About two months later, I found myself sitting in the office of an employment agency whose furniture was exactly like what I'd visualised. I couldn't help but smile. At the same time, I was also blown away by how I got there to begin with: I was headhunted!

The lady sitting in front of me had been looking for someone with my language skills for a while, and she was wondering if I'd like to interview with a big broadcasting company.

Soon afterward, as I walked through the building of the company for my interview, I was in awe and a bit star struck because this is where my favourite cartoons as a child were broadcast from. The walls were covered in posters of Scooby, Tom & Jerry, Dexter's Lab, and many others. I thought to myself: *How cool is that?! Even if I don't get the job, I'm just happy to be here!*

It was the only interview I went to during my job search and the only one that I needed. Shortly afterwards, they offered me the job, and I accepted it. Despite the fact that I didn't have any experience in broadcasting, they were happy to train me because I was a Romanian speaker and because as a student I used to volunteer for a film studio.

My main responsibility was scheduling the children's TV channel that went out to Romania, the same one I learned

English from as a child! This meant so much to me because I could contribute to making other children happy too. It made use of my organising skills as I had to put together programs, trailers, and commercials into a schedule according to broadcasting rules before I delivered them to Transmission. It was also fun to use my language skills as I had to check and edit scripts for trailers and also watch programs and graphics to make sure they were in the right language.

Everything else lined up in a way that met all my needs at the time too. It was an office job in central London, in a building filled with toys that reminded me of childhood and fun. The pay was even higher than what I asked. The work environment was positive, and my manager taught me so many things, appreciated my work, gave me a raise a year later.

I've been living in London for a few years now, and I still can't get over how perfectly the Universe brought together so many aspects of what I wanted and needed then. It felt like a nod to carry on following my joy because I was on the right track.

Geanina Roman is a certified career and Law of Attraction coach with a background in media and translation.

When she isn't helping people, she photographs and explores the British countryside.

Website: geaninaroman.com

Getting Published

by Paulette Sherman

While I was in graduate school getting my doctorate, we were told that our dissertation could be a literature review instead of lab research, and we could choose our topic. Since my grandparents and mother were Holocaust survivors from Romania, I became interested in how holocaust survivors used creativity and play to survive psychologically during extreme trauma. My mom told me a story about how she made a slide out of an old storm door when there was no food in the ghetto, and I wondered what similar stories others had.

I started reading survivor's accounts and heard that a new Holocaust museum had opened in Washington, D.C., so I made plans to visit for the day. They had video testimonials with survivor's stories, and I spent the day watching them.

During a break, I went up to the librarian, Mishlee, and mentioned that my grandfather was originally from Chotin in Bessarabia and had been killed during the Holocaust. I asked whether she had any photographs of him or the town. She came back with one Hebrew book, and at first I did not understand the names, nor did I know what he looked like. She helped me look for the name Avraham Wolkove, and by some miracle, there he was.

In those days, people took few photographs, but my grandfather had been a known speaker in the town and was sitting at a meeting with several other people in the photograph. She gave me a photocopy of that black and white photo in the book.

This was the first time that my sister and I saw our grandfather. My mom also did not know what he looked like because she had been two years old at the time of his death. In my heart I had wanted to find that picture, but I had not planned it, and this missing piece of our family puzzle seemed to fall magically into place.

After graduate school, I knew that I'd like to write a book and maybe a column. One day I picked up a free magazine, called *The Improper Magazine,* from a kiosk on the street in Manhattan. I looked at the masthead and had the thought to email the editor Keith Girard to ask to write a column. I had not written a column before and did not have much writing experience, but this limitation did not occur to me at that time, so I just did it. He wrote back and said he'd be glad for me to write a monthly column on relationships, which I then did for two years until the print magazine went digital.

At the time I was dating, hoping to meet find a husband while working as a therapist and wishing I would publish my first book before I married. I took notes on what I learned in my own dating process and subsequently developed a manual for a dating class I facilitated for single clients.

I went into a Barnes and Noble to look through a *Writers Market* book and jotted down the contact information of four publishers on an envelope. Then I sent in my dating manual via snail mail with my resume. I got calls back from two editors, both of whom told me it was something they'd been looking for.

One editor submitted it to the editorial board review, but they passed on it. The other editor was Cynthia Black, who was also the publisher of *Beyond Words,* which formed an imprint called Atria Books with Simon and Schuster.

I did not know that at the time, nor did I know that she was in the process of publishing the book, *The Secret,* and was looking for other books on the Law of Attraction. My dating book was about the Law of Attraction, but that term was not in the subtitle until she added it, and it was not mentioned in the book. She suggested that we go back and forth with rewrites, and if she was satisfied with the final book then she'd offer me a contract.

I signed the publishing contract right before I got married. What were the chances of getting my first deal with Simon and Schuster without an agent and with little writing experience (except for a column), and then sending it to the person working on that topic? It was not something I could have planned consciously.

After the book got published, I married, and we later had two kids. I had little time for writing then and had to focus on more practical things.

At age 41, I was diagnosed with breast cancer. I walked on the beach and prayed and asked whether I was going to die. I heard that I would not and that I had a legacy of at least 22 books left to write. I went through chemotherapy and radiation for a year and lost all my hair. I continued working as a therapist and wrote on the subway and in the hospital. The idea of 22 books seemed crazy to my conscious mind, but my spirit accepted it as a clear command, so I just went to work, learning self-publishing.

I was on a mission to write these books, but didn't want to go into any debt in the process, since our kids were our practical priority. My desire was to have those self-published books paid for even if I did not make a profit. I did not have many book sales and had no energy or budget for marketing at the time and had not yet worked on much of a social media platform. My goal was to get my messages of love out there and to put my books in hope chests for my kids as a legacy, which I did. I trusted it would all work out, even if I didn't know how.

I happened upon a blog by Gordon Burgett who writes about self-publishing where he said that he made more money by getting a foreign agent and translating his self-published books into a few languages than he did with a traditional American publishing deal. I didn't know anything about this, so I searched the term foreign literary agent in Linked In, and a woman named Marleen Seegers came up.

She looked beautiful and smart, and her agency looked new. This was the first and only foreign agent that I wrote at that time. She liked my book, *When Mars Women Date: How Career Women Can Love Themselves into the Relationship of their Dreams,* and it subsequently got published into Chinese, Korean and Czech. The sales more than covered my basic publishing expenses for my ongoing book legacy.

Later, another foreign agent from Linkedin helped me to publish two other books I wrote into Chinese. I later read a publishing book by an expert who said that one of the main reasons to get a traditional publisher is they have a much better chance to sell your translation rights, but I hadn't known that or adopted that limiting belief.

As I wrote and worked on my self-care, I started to take sacred baths where I would have silence in the morning to align my thoughts and feelings with my intention and goals. I'd relax, pray, meditate, and receive guidance. In this way I got many creative ideas for my books, and they flowed out of me. I published them one after another (literally) on Amazon and soon had 20 published books just five years after my diagnosis.

I was doing well emotionally, physically, and spiritually and felt that this morning bathing ritual could be helpful to others. So I wrote a small book about it. I had given my Reiki teacher, Raven Keyes, several of my books as gifts. She had never said anything about them, but for some reason when I handed her book number 21 (which was about using different sacred bath rituals to improve your love life), Raven said that she loved the idea and encouraged me to create bath rituals in many other life areas as well. She said she'd never done this, but she thought her editor at Llewellyn might consider the book a good fit .

So, I submitted a proposal and several chapters. Llewellyn came back with a publishing contract. This felt like a miracle to me because of the ease with which it happened. My latest book, *The Book of Sacred Baths,* came out last year, and now I am writing book number 22 in my legacy project.

Dr. Sherman is a psychologist, certified life coach, author, teacher and speaker. She offers international phone coaching and specializes in relationships.

Twitter: @kpaulet
FB: @pauletteshermangroup
Instagram: @paulette_sherman
Web: DrPauletteSherman.com

The Poker Tournament

by Walt Thiessen

Here's a very simple manifestation story that happened on March 10, 2018. I play poker online ... play chips, although I used to win money before the U.S. Government shut that down. I'm pretty good at it. I've accumulated over 90 million play chips in my account over the years while playing sporadically and casually.

This particular Saturday I played in a tournament, my favorite way to play. It was a pretty big tournament, over 700 players. I decided to use it as a sandbox, so to speak, for practicing LOA.

In the past, when I tried deliberately creating while playing poker, I usually tried manifesting particular hands at particular times. However, like everyone else, I have my own levels of resistance, and I usually ended up failing to manifest the right hand at the right time.

This time, I did it differently. I decided to stop trying to micromanage the hands and just leave it to the Universe to provide the ideal results in its own way and time.

So instead of trying to attract winning hands, I visualized doubling my chips and/or reaching new and higher chip levels.

Before I started doing this, I'd already lost half my chip pile. I was way behind and in danger of losing all my chips and being eliminated from the tournament. So I figured, "This is a good time to really put my new LOA approach to the test."

I had about 700 chips at that point. (All contestants started the tournament with 1,500 chips). So I decided I wanted the Universe to double my chip count and got really excited about it. A few hands later, it happened.

So I decided to do it again. This time I wanted 3,000 chips. Once again, I just kept thinking about having 3,000 chips, building my emotional excitement about it while playing the hands. A few hands later, I reached that goal as well.

As the tournament went on, I kept asking for a higher chip count than what I had already achieved. I got myself into a really great feeling place each time.

I didn't worry about my fortunes from one hand to the next. Sometimes I won, and sometimes I lost.

Overall, out of 125 hands played, I won about one out of every five hands I played, while managing to avoid having any big losses. It didn't matter to me what the results were. As long

154

as I was still in the tournament and successfully focusing on my goal, without getting attached to any particular hand, I was happy.

Nor did I worry about how it would happen. I only focused on the goal. I didn't care which particular hand got me there, regardless of what cards I had, good or bad.

At one point, my goal was to get 20,000 chips. I had about 9,000 at the time. I got a really big hand, but only won about 3,000 chips with it.

I thought, *Oh well.*

But I'd forgotten that I was also in a tournament where you get bonuses for eliminating another player. I did just that with this particular hand, and my reward was – you guessed it – 20,000 chips!

This kept going and going. Over time I got to 30,000 – then 50,000 – then 80,000 – then 100,000 - then 150,000 - then 200,000 chips.

Each step of the way, I visualized my goal, got really excited about it, and held it in my mind as I played each hand, not allowing myself to become attached to the result of any particular hand. Without exception, I kept reaching my goals!

When I reached 500,000 chips, I was the leader in the tournament. I also got greedy. I tried to micromanage, scaring players into folding with big bets and "captaining" the table as it's called.

The result? I lost more than half my chips!

Okay, I thought. *I get the message. No more micromanaging! No more trying to make it happen.*

Normally, losing that many chips would have put me into a downward spiral of expecting more bad hands to happen, but because I let go of micromanaging the hands ... well, see for yourself what happened next.

I went right back to focusing on my next chip goal and getting really excited about how I would feel when I got there.

Much faster than I expected, I got back to 500,000 chips after about 10 more hands.

When I got to 600,000, there were just two players left, me and the guy I'd been butting heads with for some time.

I got a King – Nine pocket, off-suit.

I didn't know it, but he had a Queen – Seven pocket, off-suit.

A "pocket" is the two cards each player gets dealt face down in the No Limit Texas Holdem style of poker.

"Off-suit" means that the two cards are from different suits.

Neither hand was a strong hand, but both were worth betting.

I raised, he called, and then the first three cards flopped: King – King – Seven. I had three of a kind ... three Kings! That's a very rare kind of flop, and I got it at the best time.

My opponent had two Sevens, and since the odds are about 4:1 against matching anything in your hand on any given play, and since he saw two Kings on the board (which made it even less likely in his mind that I would have a King), he figured the odds favored him.

So he went *all in* with his remaining chips. I called, and I won the pot, all his chips, and thereby won the tournament!

 Walt Thiessen is the founder of LOA Today, where he does daily podcasts on the Law of Attraction with co-hosts: David Scott Bartky, Cindie Chavez, Joel Elston, Wendy Dillard, and Tom Wells. He lives with his wife, Louise in Simsbury, Connecticut.

Website: www.loatoday.net

Health

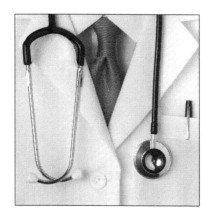

Healing Myself

By Jean Yang

Since I became a young woman, I dealt with severe menstrual cramps and heavy bleeding during my periods. I dreaded that time of the month. Things got so bad for me that I finally went to the doctors. They found a large growth the size of an orange on my left ovary that needed to be removed. I had my surgery, and the doctor had to remove my left ovary as well as the growth, which turned out to be benign endometrioma. The diagnosis was endometriosis.

After recovery from surgery, I remember still having to deal with very painful cramps every month, as well as heavy bleeding that sapped my energy and stamina. It was so bad that one day on my 70 minute morning walk, I could not make it back home.

I had to lie down on a concrete bench because I did not have enough strength to move my body. I rested for a good bit of time before I could gather enough strength to slowly get back home.

I became desperate and sought help on the web. I found a lady named Carolyn Levett and got her book, *Reclaim Your Life – Your Guide to Aid Healing of Endometriosis*. Along with dietary and lifestyle changes, Ms. Levett suggested Reiki as helpful for those suffering from endometriosis. Reiki piqued my interest, even though I had never heard of it before.

I found a Reiki instructor named Karen Harrison from Kansas City, who came into the Dallas area a few times a year to teach. I quickly signed up for her class, which started not long afterward.

Meanwhile, the changes in diet Ms. Levett suggested in her book and on her website, www.endo-resolved.com, helped me quite a bit with pain management. A Reiki news magazine mentioned Louise Hay, whom I had not heard of before. I bought her book, *You Can Heal Your Life*, and watched her movie of the same title. I enjoyed the movie, but none of the authors and teachers interviewed stood out to me.

About a month later, I watched the movie again with my friend, Elizabeth. She pointed out to me her favorite speaker interviewed at the end of the movie, which turned out to be Abraham, a collective consciousness received by Esther Hicks.

I went back to watch that particular interview again after my friend left and took note of the book mentioned in the interview, *Ask and It Is Given.* After I purchased and read the book, I cannot tell you all the changes that it made in my life! I have read many of their other books, watched their DVDs, attended workshops, and traveled the world on several Abraham cruises. Coincidentally, those Abraham cruises helped me realize one of my fondest dreams, which is to travel and see this beautiful world of ours. As an artist, I must say those experiences in themselves are priceless!

A beautiful young man I met on an Abraham cruise in the Mediterranean showed me a book he'd been reading that fascinated him. It was *Seth Speaks: The Eternal Validity of the Soul,* by Jane Roberts. I later overheard an older gentleman mention the same book. Then on my plane ride home from the cruise, a lady sitting to my left next to the window was reading a novel, and I was inspired to look over at what she was reading. Lo and behold the name Seth popped out from the left page of the book she was reading, as if a spot light was shining on it! Obviously, the Universe was trying to get my attention. Of course I took the hint and purchased and read the book. It absolutely blew my mind.

Everything was delicious on my journey of discovery: the people I met, the clarity I received, ever improving health, all of the synchronicity that guided me to even more fun and stuff that I have asked for through the living of life. Needless to say, I am so much happier than I have ever been, so much so that others who have known me have remarked upon my transformation.

One transformation that is clearly visible to those around me is that my skin that use to give me trouble has cleared up, and friends and family often tell me how much happier and better I look these days. Louise Hay's book, *You Can Heal Your Life*, gave the probable cause of acne as, "Not accepting the self. Dislike of the self." It made sense to me.

As for the endometriosis, I prayed for and received an early menopause at the age of 48. I had some trepidation about menopausal symptoms, but they were really mild and easy to deal with compared with the pain I had to deal with on a monthly basis. And since then, I just keep feeling better and better.

I so appreciate the joy and clarity I have discovered and am passionate about sharing it with others who are ready for this information. This is such an exciting time to be alive on Earth. It really is the time of awakening as more and more of us are ready to remember who we really are and the power we hold in our own hands.

Jean Yang is an intuitive adviser, a licensed massage therapist, a Reiki master, and an artist.

Jean can assist you in pinpointing those thought patterns or beliefs that are hindering you from success, health, and happiness.

Website: jeanyangwellbeing.com

Boot Camp

by Misti Jackson-Derringer

Nearly one year had passed since my mom's last drink. She seemed okay, having made the transition into living a normal life, but the shadows crept and crawled around, as shadows do. Something **big** needed to happen. We needed help seeing through these shadows to a better life, a better connection, and certainly a better understanding.

The Shadow Process is a catalyst for our healing as we embrace our darkest side, the pdf read. I checked the dates for the next event: Miami, end of June. My mothers birthday is June 24, Miami is warm, and there's a beach. She loves the beach, as do I.

I booked the flights and bought the tickets as a birthday present. A vacation in June seemed a perfect way to celebrate her one-year mark of sobriety.

My childhood was spent in limbo between two parents stuck in their own shadows. I survived the harsh realities of divorce, drug, and alcohol addiction. Years of unworthiness and fear of neglect kept me stuck in a place of complacency. From the exterior I appeared exceptionally grounded, while the inside was a different story.

We landed in Miami and checked into the hotel, feeling relieved of our daily responsibilities and hopeful to create a newly meaningful relationship between mother and daughter. The Shadow event started the next day, so we sat by the pool sipping cool (non-alcoholic) fruity drinks.

I felt very good about providing my mom this opportunity to get away, to dig deeper.

This will be good for her, I told myself.

I forgave her long ago. Had to. The grief I felt from mourning my motherless childhood was too much to bear, and forgiveness was freedom from my pain, even when the sadness became a security blanket as I hid behind a confident smile and warm laughter. Her growth would mean my growth. More growth, more forgiveness.

The next morning, my mother and I showed up excited and ready to take on the program. Armed with our venti lattes and chatting like school girls, we had NO CLUE what we were getting ourselves into.

Within minutes, the facilitator began giving us her "expectations'" for the next 72 hours. She was attractive and well dressed. She knew things, and you could tell. Her story had scars, and she shared them fearlessly.

She laid out the rules.

Rule number one: Noble silence except for group exercises.

She went on: No meat, no sugar, and ... *no caffeine!* She set aside her notes and looked silently at the group. The coaches in the back row sat tall, also knowing something we didn't. Each of them looked like wounded soldiers who hadn't lost the spirit of the fight. From the first moment, I trusted them.

We each took a long delicious gulp from our over-priced mochas and stared at each other, in shock and awe.

This was not a vacation, we both realized. *This was a battlefield, and we had just been informed we would be on the front lines to fight for our healing.*

At the first break, forbidden to discuss what had just happened, we tossed out our precious $7 drinks and got some bottled water. The simple fact that we didn't run screaming out of there indicated progress for us.

In the first session, we listened to story after story of fearlessly facing the shadows from our coaches. I trusted them even more. Stories of loss, pain, grief, and shame poured out from their hearts. We cried, we laughed, but we didn't talk. We listened.

Over the next three days, we both experienced something deeply profound. We slowly began to understand the *nobility* piece of the silence. After the first awkward meal with the other noble souls, we started to see the benefits of not blabbing our guts out to everyone and each other.

We kept our vow for the retreat (minus the initial mouthing and failed attempts to make hand motions to signal what we desperately wanted to say out loud) as we learned then and there that words have power.

And no words? Even more power internally.

In my own personal silence, it became a wave of relief not having to explain or excuse myself or listen to others' explanations or excuses. It was peaceful to not feel the heavy obligation to make meaningless small talk about ignorant things with people we barely knew.

Most of all, it quickly brought a depth to this experience that nothing else would because when you can't speak, you **must listen**. You must be open to receive.

As a southern girl from Tennessee, I had always heard the saying, "The good Lord gave you two ears and one mouth for a reason," but I just thought that was some redneck saying for "shut the hell up." And I suppose it was, but not in the way I had once considered.

Our coaches led us through a shadow-laden process to reveal deeply held judgments and beliefs about ourselves and others. When we weren't listening to our program leaders, we had to listen to our own thoughts. Scary stuff there.

But without this experience, I would not have the awareness I *even had* scary thoughts, much less listened to their meaning or intention.

On the last day of the retreat, we participated in several group exercises in which we journaled things about ourselves we did not want to hear or believe. Some were things we'd tell ourselves and some were things said to us with hurtful intention.

In short sentences we were expected to speak what we had written, and the group repeated back our words to us. The instructions were simple. Execution was brutal.

My mom's list included: "I was a horrible mother."

She choked out the words over and over. As I wanted to run and silence her, it became clear that I didn't want her to admit this because then it WAS true. With each time she repeated it, I was reminded how terrible it had been and how deeply wounded I was.

Our group drove in the knives as we repeated, "You were a horrible mother." The knife of her words hit me over and over. Repeating the words in confirmation of this fact stung like a thousand needles.

Then in an instant, I realized – where I felt a knife, she felt a sword. Where I felt needles, she felt razors. My compassion arose as hot tears fell down both our faces.

Working our way through our breakout tribe of shadow warriors, we continued. When my turn came, tears began to flow. Where to begin? Which shadow that had been hidden in my wounds could I choose.

I took a long breath and tried to gather myself. My mother's eyes welled as her own shadow wounds lay open, bleeding for all to see, and she knew the pain I felt in my heart. Yet she looked at me with a fierce love that gave me the courage to speak. I had her support, and in that moment I had never needed it more.

"I am unlovable," I whispered, voice shaking.

My group spoke it back to me, and their words pierced my soul. I continued saying it over and over until something loosened inside. I wept as I looked at my mother and said what I had always felt. We connected and again her fierce look of love gave me the push to go on until I heard these words as only sounds.

The power of my words had not been in the sounds but in the meaning and truth I granted them.

We were strictly limited to the script we had written, and no one got out of the hot seat until they were crying their damn eyes out and shaking all over.

Believe me, noble silence came easily that day as no one wanted to say a word during the break. We were all so shaken up, it was as though there had been some sort of mass spoken exorcism of words.

The final program exercise was to set up in the same groups. This time, we had the chance to say what we wanted to say. What we really needed to say to ourselves, out loud, to set a new intention for our lives where the raw hole had been hallowed out before.

After a weekend of cultivation and awareness of words (or lack there of) we were more than ready to express our truest selves aloud. Statements filled with love and compassion. Words of hope and intention.

Again my brave mother took her seat opposite us. She took a breath and stated timidly, "I am a wonderful grandmother."

We confirmed her words with ours, "You ARE a wonderful grandmother." Loudly enunciating each word for her as we were given the chance to repeat her bold statement. "YOU are a wonderful grandmother." Again, "You are a wonderful GRANDMOTHER."

She began to smile as we saw a visceral acceptance of pride grow in her eyes, melting my heart with her truth. She is a wonderful grandmother. My children have had the very best of her, which meant I had also received that precious gift.

She went on to admit another truth. "I am safe," she proclaimed. I realized I had never considered my mother to be fearful of ANYTHING. Yet here she was telling us she desperately wanted to feel safe.

We confirmed her statement. "You ARE safe." Our embrace when she completed her turn was all we had both wanted and needed.

Once again, it was my turn to speak truth. I sat with an excitement for the next words I would speak.

"I am a good mother." I said firmly. I locked eyes with her first as she repeated the fact back to me the way only a mother can do.

Each time I said it, her heart healed more and mine leaped for joy. Our eyes locked deeper and we both knew in that moment the reason we had come here.

The healing that took place in these brutal and honest statements sealed off the wounds we had carried for one another.

I looked down at my next statement, but as I opened my mouth those words didn't come out. Instead, as though a voice from my soul spoke into my heart I blurted out instead, "I am a spiritual guide."

Electricity shot through every cell in my body, as I looked shocked at my mother who leaned forward and confirmed it loudly with her fellow team of repeaters, "YOU ARE A SPIRITUAL GUIDE." I said it again and again until the words were very much my own: "I am a spiritual guide."

I had found purpose for the pain that feeling unlovable for so long had gifted me.

After the program ended, my mom and I went for another venti coffee and then for a huge steak dinner that night. We spent the entire evening recapping the incredible gift we had received, a powerful tool that separated fact from fiction in our awareness. We now understood the power of our words, spoken or not, and how they created the life we called our own.

Our words attract our outcomes, and we were both amazed at how something as simple as "noble silence" could be the catalyst to speaking with intention.

My words, "I am a spiritual guide," connected me to the universal power of attraction. Today, I am a spiritual guide, a certified yoga instructor, and a certified holistic leadership coach. I now do the work to guide others spiritually back to their own truth. I travel, speak, and train others to be guides.

Almost five years later, my mom continues to feel safe in her sobriety, and she supports my family by being a WONDERFUL grandmother.

Quite literally, our life is the words we speak both inside our head and out to the rest of the world. We are living proof that your words most definitely have the power to create your reality and to redeem your past.

Misti Jackson-Derringer is a poet, speaker, author, Certified Holistic Coach, Intuitive Energy Worker and Yoga Teacher.

She is a teacher and leader in her local community and worldwide who helps others design a life they legitimately love.

Website: meetmisti.com

Nizhoni

by Ellen Bakker

Help came when I was almost 24 years old.

When I was 7, I was diagnosed with Type 1 Diabetes. By the time I was 21, I started having problems with my eyesight. It didn't come as a surprise. At age 12 the doctors had already told me and my parents that I had symptoms that would lead to future eye problems.

I was diagnosed with retinopathy, a diabetes-related eye disease. In the years that followed, I was treated with laser therapy many times. The results were not successful.

One day, when I was at the hospital again, I asked the doctor a simple and very direct question: "Am I going blind?" His answer was: "Well, I cannot say that you won't go blind. I am sorry..."

Now I wasn't brought up religiously at all, and I don't remember having ever prayed before, but that night I prayed very hard and intensely for help! I remember vividly while I cried that I prayed with the words, "I don't care what I have to do, if you want me to hang upside down here on this lamp, I will do it! Please, please, please help me!"

Help came a couple of months later. My aunt knew a homeopath whom she thought could help me. So I went. My parents went with me the first time, very reluctantly though. They had always been non-believers when it came to alternative practitioners. Spirituality was not in their book and definitely shouldn't be in mine either!

My parents were very dominant, especially my father whom I had always been afraid of. Even though I was 24 years old and not living at home anymore, they still believed they could forbid me things. After that first visit to see the homeopath, I decided to go again alone and didn't tell them about it.

On one of my visits, I told one of the employees working for the homeopath that the doctors had said that the problems with my sight were irreversible. I could tell she wanted to tell me something but felt hesitant. I encouraged her to tell me.

She said she knew someone who could probably help me but that the woman was very unconventional. I said that I didn't care about "unconventional" and convinced her to tell me more. Today I am so grateful that she did!

The first time I went to see Marian, I remember walking in feeling as if my back was pushed to the wall. When I saw her, I knew immediately that I had come to the right place and person. I simply thought, "Okay, this is good."

As I learned about her methods, I became really interested in spiritual matters. I also started to attend the courses she gave.

The courses took place at her house, which is how I got to know her family as well. With her husband Peet, she had two children a little younger than myself, Yosi and Richard.

The first time Marian told me about her son Richard, whom she was clearly very proud of, I immediately felt a connection to him. I didn't know why or how this was possible. I had never met him and probably never would because he was studying in the U.S. at the time. And obviously I had much bigger issues!

One evening, just before the start of one of the evening classes, I had the following conversation with Yosi.

"I have been going to the library many times, looking for books on spiritual subjects. As usual I really didn't know what book to pick, so this time I decided to choose a book in a different way. I made sure no one watched me.

"I closed my eyes and touched the spines of the books with my fingertips. There were approximately a hundred books to choose from, so it took some time, but at one point my fingers started to tingle. So I chose that book, took it home, and started to read."

"And, was it good?" Yosi asked.

"I couldn't even finish the first page, simply because I just couldn't stop crying. It was a story of a young girl having spiritual experiences. For her, they were as normal as breathing. Somehow it felt like it was my story. And my God! ... the description of the landscape she grew up in!

"That touched me even deeper. Apart from that I am intrigued by the way the regression therapy is done at that institution the author talks about. So I read and cried and read and cried and now I have decided I want to go there!"

Yosi looked at me, amused, and asked me who the author was.

"Chris Griscom," I answered.

The look on her face changed from amused to totally shocked and even a bit nervous.

"What's wrong," I asked.

"Are you sure?" she replied.

"Well, yes, of course I am sure," I said, not understanding her reaction.

"Chris Griscom is the director and teacher at the school my brother is studying at, in the United States."

Now it was my turn to be completely blown away. Yosi didn't know that I so much wanted to meet him. I couldn't wrap my head around this so-called coincidence!

Of all the dozens of books I could pick, I unknowingly chose the one that made me decide to go to that awesome place in the

U.S. not knowing that the one person I so much wanted to meet was living and studying there.

Yosi got up, and told her mom about it. Marian didn't seem surprised and simply said: "Well, I think some things are awaiting you there."

So here I was in September 1993, 26 years old, still studying, no job, no money, determined to go to the Nizhoni School for Global Consciousness. Studying there was not an option, but I learned they organized summer camps as well.

The regression sessions described in the book and that I so much wanted to experience were part of the program. I was not and am not a very patient person, so I decided that next summer would be the right moment to go!

Of course I knew I needed a lot of money that I didn't have. The regression sessions were pretty expensive, and I knew I had to save at least $6,000. I had no clue how to do that. I just knew I wanted to.

The next week a professor from Leiden University where I was studying Child Education and Development asked me if I was interested in working for him for 16 hours per week. He was looking for someone who could help him with the book he was writing.

The book was about a French pedagogue, and since I already had a master's degree in French he figured I would be the right choice. I started in October and thus made some money ... not enough to be able to go to the U.S., but it definitely was a start.

What happened during the following months is still a mystery to me. For some reason and in ways that I honestly cannot recall, I was able to save money. I "found" money everywhere, and I saw opportunities everywhere to cut down on my regular expenses. It became sort of an exciting game to me that I turned out to be very good at!

I ran into Richard four times that same year. The first time wasn't a coincidence. I heard from Marian that her son would come home for two weeks. I knew that I wouldn't have a chance of meeting him unless I visited on an evening with no classes. Marian had a lot of spiritual books. I asked her if it was okay for me to come over one evening to take a look at her books to see if she had some that I might want to read. Luckily, she agreed!

It was typical Dutch winter weather, cold and rainy, so I put on something nice, warm, and comfortable . I always wore glasses, but for this occasion I put in my contacts. I felt prepared and ready to go. Still, I had no idea if he would actually be at his parents' home.

As I came in, Marian immediately noticed I wasn't wearing my glasses. I had a perfect excuse: "Well, it's dark and raining, and I suffer from night-blindness (which she knew was true). I don't see well with raindrops on my glasses." She bought it.

My preexisting feeling of connection was confirmed. I fell in love with him. Actually, that wasn't accurate. A better word would be soulmate, someone I once knew.

That same year, Chris Griscom came to the Netherlands to speak at a Congress organized in Amsterdam. Of course I went with Yosi's family. Richard was there too.

That was the last time I saw him in the Netherlands. The next time would be at the Nizhoni summer camp in 1997.

I somehow had been able to save up $8,000 in nine months time! I still remember the look on the face of the bank employee. I booked the camp and flight.

She said, "Well, now you will have to pay $6,000."

Since I had saved the money all in cash, I simply took the $6,000 out of my pocket and gave it to her. I remember wearing a red pair of trousers with huge pockets and a long white sweater covering them. I figured no one would be able to see or least of all expect me to have so much money on me.

I didn't know her thoughts, but I could tell she was surprised to say the least! Now that I am older, I understand, but at the time I thought there was nothing unusual or odd about it.

So that is how I overcame the money hurdle, but there was yet another hurdle to clear as well: my family. I had to tell them I was going to the U.S. alone to a spiritually-oriented camp.

They reacted the way I expected: upset, angry, scared, and dead set against my plans. My father simply forbade me to go, even though I was 27 years old. He told me that if anything went wrong I couldn't count on the help of my family.

My sister refused to talk to me all together.

My brother didn't understand why I had to go and what the hell I was going to do there.

My mom agreed with my dad.

I felt terrible. A week before my scheduled flight I took a long look in the mirror and seriously imagined for about 30 seconds not going.

I felt my energy drop drastically. The things around me and in the mirror lost their colour. At that moment, I knew I wouldn't be able to live with myself if I didn't go.

So I told my family my decision was final, and I went.

I only have a few regrets in my life. One of the biggest, or probably THE biggest, is that I didn't get up when Richard showed up with a friend at the tent I stayed in at Nizhoni Camp close to Santa Fe in New Mexico.

I was lying on my stomach on the floor. I was still so ashamed of my body that I didn't dare to get up and walk over to him. I felt awful! I didn't know what to do, so I did nothing.

Maybe that didn't matter to him, but I felt and still feel deeply ashamed of not getting up. I just said, "Hey, hi." ☹

Even though he wasn't the reason I went to the US, I really wanted to see him there. He showed up, unannounced, and what did I do....?

"I told you there would be a Dutch girl here."

Those were the last words I ever heard him say and the last time I saw him.

The Nizhoni camp was fantastic, and I never regretted going there for a second. The environment was magical and "home" to me. I had great fun with the people I met and learned a lot!

In the regression sessions I discovered a lot about about myself and the role of certain people in my life. I also understood why I had the absolute urge to come to this part of the U.S. And yes, I also found out the reason I felt such a deep connection to Richard.

When I got back home after almost four weeks, I had trouble sleeping in a bed in a house. In the U.S. I was part of a group that slept outside instead of in the tent. I had slept outside on the ground for weeks, and I missed that. Once back home, I tried sleeping on the balcony. It obviously wasn't the same. No clear sky filled with stars, no coyote sounds, just the city sounds. After a couple days of this, I went to bed, my head and heart full of amazing experiences and blissful memories. Today I am so grateful I had the opportunity to go and darn proud of myself that I actually went.

PS: My eyesight improved from 5 percent to 90 percent in one eye, and from 50 percent to a 100 percent in the other.

Ellen Bakker is a certified Law of Attraction Life Coach, master in Child Psychology, and a former member and coach of the Dutch national table tennis team.

Web: ellenbakkercoaching.nl

Email: info@ellenbakkercoaching.nl

Coping with Arthritis

by Tarryn Tomlinson

The pain was unbearable, sometimes stabbing and hot, other times dull and throbbing. The doctors said there was no cure for the arthritis that ravaged my joints. I took the medication, but it did nothing much for the pain and discomfort. Not being one to take the opinions of others as law, I decided to research this affliction and how I could go about getting some relief.

I had always believed that the mind was powerful and that life was far more magical than what I had been experiencing. I took the practical approach to attempt to heal the illness; I changed my diet, took homeopathic meds, tried acupuncture, went for body alignment and yoga. I tried just about anything and everything, and it helped to a marginal degree. Over the years the disease slowed down, and the pain lessened, but it was the mental work that got me through the worst of it.

I intensely studied the mind-body connection, my emotions, the power of positive thinking, the perils of negative thinking, and the Universe at large. I believed that our bodies and lives are the result of our thoughts and set about understanding my route to constant physical pain.

In 2007, things clicked for me in a big way. I had heard of the Law of Attraction and had studied books on creative visualization, but only after I watched *The Secret* did the simplicity of it all became apparent. The documentary in itself was a confirmation of all that I have learned up until that point. Cutting away the philosophy and mysticism introduced me to the simple three step process: Ask, Believe, Receive.

There is a point in the documentary when one of the teachers speaks of how he decided to set a big goal for himself, one so big that if he achieved it, he would know it was only because of what he had learned. I decided to do the same.

However, I never concentrated on walking. What set my heart on fire was the idea of going to live in Italy. For a long time I felt guilty about not concentrating on my health but later came to understand that if a topic is too emotionally charged and brings up too many fears it is best to get off the subject. The thought of living in Italy felt free of the past, the pain, and the limitations. It brought me joy to think about visiting Italy and excited me. I needed something to feel excited about.

I decided that I wanted to visit Italy, but not just to go on a holiday. I wanted to stay there for longer than a year, and I wanted to live in absolute luxury. I wanted to experience the best Italy had to offer, because if what I was learning was the truth, if the natural state of the Universe is one of abundance, and if any experienced limitation was just a product of my own thoughts, then there was no reason why I should not experience abundance on my trip.

Dreams are beautiful things. They give you hope and make you live out in fantasy what seems so far from reality. The reality of my situation at that time was that I was wheelchair-bound with no source of income, no job, and no trust fund. There was absolutely nothing in my reality that even resembled my dream, but I did not let that stop me.

I re-watched *The Secret* and did my journaling work on a daily basis. Each time I watched the documentary, I carried myself away during that hour in complete belief. The journaling helped me to process emotion and understand what I was thinking. I used it each day to write down my affirmations.

Months passed, months of watching, writing, believing, and standing guard over my thoughts. I would be lying to you if I said I had perfect faith. I just gave it the best attempt I could.

I started watching *The Secret* in August, and by the time December came around I had reached the height of my frustration. You could hear a pin drop in the silence of the nothingness the Universe presented to me. I remember sitting on my chair in my mother's room, crying because all I wanted to do was to go to Italy, and all my mental work was producing nothing.

My mom hugged me and wiped my tears as she tried to alleviate my heartbreak. She then decided that we would go to Italy together. She had leave coming to her the following year in June, and we could go for 18 days then. Though this immediately eased my hurt, I still had to figure out how to get my airfare, and 18 days was not what I asked for.

Being desperate to get to Italy, this small move in the right direction to me was a great relief. The money for the airfare quickly manifested when my aunt, who had promised to purchase me a plane ticket years prior, made good on her promise.

It was not until sometime towards the end of January of the following year that something spooky started to take place.

It was late in the afternoon, and I was going to have a bath. I decided to take my phone with me into the bathroom, and I turned it on to listen to my messages. The first voice I heard was that of a man: "Hi Tarryn. You don't know me. My name is Mike, and I am a friend of Nadia's. She is not sure if you remember her, but she asked me to contact you and pass on her details. She has some information about your health."

Nadia was an acquaintance I had met four years prior. She contacted me from Paris, saying that she had some news about my health. There was some type of natural medication that was said would help decrease inflammation and abate the disease. She had access to this medication because she worked at UNESCO for a well known virologist, the very man who discovered HIV back in the 1980s. The problem was that they could not send the medication to me because it was still in its trial phase. I needed to go to Paris in order to have it administered.

Though the offer was one worth trying, I simply didn't have the funds to go to Paris and financially look after myself for a month. I communicated this to her and said that I planned to come to Italy in June/July. It just so happened that they would be in Italy around the same time and could meet up with me to give me the medication.

Something was brewing in the Universe. I just didn't know what or how all the pieces would fit together.

My first trip to Italy with my mom and friends was amazing. I remember the Trevi fountain like it was yesterday. Rome on any given day is packed with tourists, and that day around the Trevi fountain a horde of tourists stood to take in the magic of the place, and of course to take pictures. A friend suggested that I throw a coin into the fountain. Apparently, if you throw a coin in, you will come back to Rome. I simple shrugged it off telling him that I do not have money to waste. I knew I was coming back.

The fateful day arrived when Nadia and her boss came to meet me at my hotel room. What an honour to meet face to face with such a great mind! Professor Montagnier and Nadia sat down with my mother and I to explain the medication, reminding us that it might or might not help, suggesting that it would be worth a try.

It was the second-to-last day of my stay in Italy. At one point in our conversations, Nadia turned to me, and with her excitable French accent said, "But Tarryn, you know that you cannot go? You have to stay here in Italy." She looked at her boss and said, "Professor! Tell her!"

After asking Nadia to calm down began, Professor Montagnier said the words I had been praying to hear.

"There is a possibility for you to stay in Italy. I know of a man who is a very famous song writer who also has a type of arthritis like yours. He healed himself with diet and a number of treatments and is now doing a trial on his estate. Maybe we can talk to him about you being one of the candidates for the trial."

As cliché as it may sound, time stood still. I do not remember breathing very much as each and every hair stood up on my arms. Listening with such intensity to what he said, all my senses became heightened as competing thoughts were drowned out. It felt like I was in the eye of a storm in my mind.

This is it! I thought. *This is it.*

After the moment passed and my mind reactivated with expressions of joy, I told them that I simply could not stay as I had a Visa that was about to expire and roughly 10 Euros left to my name.

Both Nadia and the Professor suggested I return to South Africa, while they would see what they could do from their end regarding the trial. A part of me disbelieved it would work out. That censor voice said, "Don't get your hopes up. You know how people say stuff and do not follow through."

I did not allow that type of thinking to sink in. During the days that followed, I argued against it, telling myself that I will not entertain negative thinking.

My arrival back in South Africa was filled with wonder, gratitude, and excitement. Instead of visualizing and affirming, I trusted that everything would work out perfectly. I had put sufficient energy into the creation of what I wanted, and now it was running of its own accord. I simply needed to trust.

Four weeks after my arrival in South Africa, I ended up back on a plane to Rome. I planned to stay in Umbria at the home of one of the most famous Italian lyricists of all time, a man who goes by the name of Mogol. The estate is a sight to behold, and I had everything I could possibly want and more.

Close to midday, we finally drove the private road leading to the estate. The tall trees hanging overhead provided shade as we drove down the winding road that led deeper into the forest. I rolled down the window to feel the cool breeze caress my face, a welcome reprieve from the stuffy, hot air of Rome.

As a passenger, I had the luxury of taking it all in: the breeze, the shade, the forest, and the other passengers in the car, one of them being the man who discovered HIV. The chauffeur took the bend, and just like most things unexpected in Italy, a huge clearing appeared ahead where I saw for the first time the magnificent estate I would call home for what I thought would be a month. It took my breath away, and as time slowed while the hairs rose on my arms, it dawned upon me that my manifestation far exceeded my dream.

My first week there I made headline news in a national newspaper and was treated like a celebrity. Professor Montagnier and my friend stayed with me the first week, when he learned he had won the Nobel Prize for Medicine for his discovery of HIV.

The treatment was best suited for people at the onset of arthritis, and too many of my joints had been destroyed according to the doctors. They told me there was nothing to be done. I was less than a month into my stay!

I kept calm. A little while later, Mogol came to me with a proposal. He knew of a good surgeon who could operate on me. I could stay on the estate, and he would support me.

The occurrences that followed are too numerous to mention. I traveled around Italy, had amazing experiences, met fascinating people, and underwent two operations.

When I returned to South Africa after close to two years living abroad, I did the tally. The trip would have cost me about $150,000. I did not pay a cent out of my own pocket. I am still wheelchair bound, but what is life without something to work towards – something else to manifest?

Since I have had this experience and manifested many other things, I have become a coach. I also started a foundation for underprivileged kids by teaching them the Law of Attraction.

Tarryn Tomlinson is a life coach and public speaker living in Cape Town, South Africa.

She helps people learn to take responsibility for their own thoughts without blame.

Website: tarryntomlinson.com

All is Well

by Susan Murray

With my husband's death grip on the steering wheel, our minivan careened down I-540 keeping pace with the ambulance ahead of us. What began as concern that one of our children was dehydrated after a night of vomiting became one of the most harrowing experiences of our lives.

Barely 15 hours earlier, our sweet family of five: mama, papa, daughter Laura, just shy of 15, and our two sons, Eamon, aged 13, and Liam, almost 10, had just completed our final Saturday night community theater performance of *Oliver!* We looked forward to the final Sunday matinee performance the following day, and the next chapter in our lives promised an overseas adventure for which we had been preparing for eight long months.

Laura, a member of an elite all-girl's choir, had labored over knit goods she sold in the community. She developed a loyal following of people who appreciated her artistry and talent and were happy to pay for it. Together, the kids and I began a small house-cleaning service to help further secure the funds necessary for Laura to travel with her choir to Salzburg to perform in the Mozart Festival that summer.

Ours was a single-income, unschooling family. Funds may have been scarce, but love and generosity were abundant. Even in our more cash-strapped times, through the love and generosity of others, we managed to get what we needed and even much of what we desired. Dennis, Laura, and I intended that Laura would travel to Salzburg with her choir, and we were open and willing to do whatever was in our power to get her there.

Just when we'd nearly secured Laura's travel fare, my mother decided to give Eamon and me the gift of joining Laura on this once-in-a-lifetime adventure. We spent several months studying German, planning and preparing for our European excursion. With Saturday's performance "in the can," we had just one more matinee until we could begin the countdown and fully devote our energy to our upcoming trip to Austria!

Following that Saturday night performance, after changing out of her costume, Laura complained of nausea and headache. A viral infection had been plaguing much of the cast over the past couple weeks. We were grateful our family managed to avoid it up to that point but assumed Laura was an unhappy recipient of the nasty bug. What we wouldn't know until days later is that she collapsed backstage during the curtain call, requiring her scrambling cast mates to help her to her feet. Like a consummate theater professional, she mustered the strength to walk out on stage and take her bow.

Once home from the theater, I did a web search of her symptoms: she was severely nauseated without fever, and had headache radiating down the sides of her neck. My little visit to "fearmongers dot com" did little to assuage our concerns, but Dennis and I put her to bed, giving her some Boswellia extract to relieve her pain, and then tag-teamed staying with her throughout the night. By morning, we were finally convinced there was something seriously wrong with our beautiful daughter.

On Sunday morning, Dennis gingerly placed Laura into the van, and we drove to our local emergency room where a CT scan revealed she suffered a potentially fatal brain hemorrhage.

In an instant, a life full of hope, joy, and promise was turned on its head.

We had no idea what lay ahead of us, but we knew that, though our lives were about to be altered irrevocably, allowing ourselves to be beaten down by unforeseen circumstances was not an option.

Dennis and I had weathered many storms over the course of our 25-year relationship. Whether it was due to the power of prayer, gratitude, affirmations, or the deep, abiding belief that "all is well," every time we pulled through and overcame whatever hardship threatened to destroy the life we'd built together.

We were determined this time would be no different.

Matching the ambulance mile for mile, Dennis and I endured a fairly silent 30 minute drive from our local emergency room in Raleigh, NC, to the Duke University Medical Center E.R. in Durham. We may not have spoken many words, but our hearts and minds hummed in harmony: *All is well. All is well. All is well...*

Scans revealed that a mass in the fourth ventricle of Laura's brain was the cause of the hemorrhage; she would require emergency surgery to remove the mass and repair the bleeding.

Facing such a terrifying and unexpected event, I immediately began looking for what was going **right** that day and found many things worthy of gratitude.

Despite this emergency occurring on the Sunday of Memorial Day weekend, an internationally respected pediatric neurosurgeon was on call, and Laura was in a world-class medical facility near our home rather than on an airplane 30,000 feet over the Atlantic, which could have easily been her fate had the brain bleed occurred three weeks later.

Despite living a 10-hour car ride away, my mother found a direct flight from Cleveland to Raleigh, allowing her to arrive at the hospital before Laura was wheeled into surgery, thanks to dear friends who conveyed her from the airport to the medical center and then hosted her in their Durham home overnight.

Thanks to the coordinated efforts of dear friends in our home town, not only were our sons able to participate in the final matinee performance with the community theater, but they were cared for in our absence.

Home-prepared, nutritious food was brought to us at the hospital.

We were surrounded by the people who loved us most and supported by the rapidly expanding circle of prayer and affirmation warriors who blanketed us with the energy of healing, protection, and God's Highest and Best outcome for this untenable situation.

Our daughter sailed through the surgery, which took less time than anticipated. The surgeon was confident he removed 100% of the mass.

My husband and I brought great comfort and support to each other, and our different perspectives helped balance and strengthen our decision-making process.

More friends and acquaintances, some traveling great distances, came to the hospital to comfort us and support Laura.

We had a lot to be grateful for.

Laura enjoyed a robust recovery following the trauma of surgery. But though we held out hope the mass was a benign tumor, the results were not in our favor. Diagnosis: medulloblastoma, an aggressive childhood brain cancer.

It's easy for hope, faith, and the enduring trust that, "the Universe has your back" to quaver in the face of immense challenges. Holding on to the trust that *all is well* when all physical evidence points to the contrary is itself a major feat of manifesting.

My husband has always been the more optimistic person between the two of us. It comes naturally to him to see his glass as perpetually overflowing. I, on the other hand, have my work cut out for me whenever it comes to trusting that all that is happening in and around my life is "well with my soul."

Not surprisingly, our plans for the summer took a dramatic turn. Europe would have to wait while Laura endured additional tests and procedures, including painful and risky spinal taps and the collection of stem cells through pheresis. Treatment included six weeks of head and spine irradiation, and four consecutive rounds of inpatient, high-dose chemotherapy and stem cell transplants.

We agreed that this challenge would be met head on, frequently irreverently, often with humor, and always with unrelenting optimism.

We treated every milestone of Laura's protocol as a cause for celebration, whether it was throwing a party at the salon, complete with guests, to mark the occasion of Laura having her hip-length hair bobbed into a pixie cut prior to radiation treatments, or celebrating the end of radiation with fireworks in our cul-de-sac, or popping open a bottle of something sparkling to mark the end of a round of treatment.

Our family found things to celebrate and mark with gratitude throughout the entire year.

We also chose to incorporate holistic, natural healing strategies with the mandatory cut, burn, and poison allopathy. Careful research and investigation, followed by meticulous implementation helped all of us feel empowered and actively part of the process.

The gifts from that year have been abundant and are still revealing themselves to us. Laura continues to be 100% cancer-free since her surgery on May 30, 2006.

The integrative practices we utilized during and after her oncology treatment protected her from the aggressively toxic protocol; with the exception of some mild cognitive challenges and very, very thin hair (thanks to the radiation treatments) she emerged from the experience relatively unscathed and even has her fertility intact. She graduated from college and is employed in her chosen field.

Our "cancer year" inspired me to author a book, *Walking on the Ceiling: Reflections on Life Turned Upside Down by Pediatric Cancer* and to become a certified holistic coach. I now help others experiencing cancer develop and implement their own anticancer lifestyle.

And Europe? It was still there a year later, but this time, thanks to the generosity of the Make A Wish Foundation, our entire family enjoyed an enchanting, life-affirming visit to Italy. All is well!

Susan Murray

Certified Holistic Coach, Radiant Health Institute

Reiki Master, Certified through Lisa Powers, CRMT

Website: CoachSusanMurray.com

Facebook: @CoachSusanMurray

Relationships and People

The Boyfriend

by Ana Hernando

I was sitting in my office working. My 16-year-old daughter came in crying.

"I don't understand! Why is it that when Johnathan was my boyfriend he never took me out, and now that Sarah is dating him, he is treating her like a queen? She isn't prettier than me. She isn't smarter than me. She plays like she's a ditz. What is it about me? I don't get it! What's wrong with me?"

I desperately wanted to ease my daughter's pain, but I also knew that this was a chance for me to empower her and show her just how amazing and potent she is.

I wiped her tears and softly spoke. "Who do these tears belong to? Are you not a child of the most high God? Do you think you are unequipped to create the life you desire? Do you honestly believe that you are not enough? Are you an infinite being?"

"Mom!"

"Well, are you?"

"Yes, Mom", sounding congested while wiping her eyes.

"And as such, you know that whatever you ask for with gratitude in your heart and knowing, you will receive?"

"Yes, but, it doesn't feel that way. I ask, and I ask, and I ask even more. And NOTHING!"

"Sweet One, when our words ask one thing and our mind and beliefs ask another, there is confusion and we get a mixed-up version of what we asked for. We must get extremely clear in our asking. It's kind of like the movie *Weird Science*. Remember? The two boys created this woman, every specific detail of her. And ****POOF**** she appeared.

"Go get a piece of paper and a pen."

She looked at me perplexed, then went up to her room. I could hear her moving stuff around; her room was typically disorganized but not dirty.

"Got it, Mom, but I don't see how goal-setting is going to *poof* my perfect boyfriend to appear."

She knew that writing goals is what I coach my clients to do. She stood at the top of the stairs, pen and paper in hand.

"With each step down the stairs, clear your mind. Stop thinking. Each time you take a step down towards me, get into your body and become aware of the feelings you will have when you are in the relationship of your dreams."

Rolling her eyes, embarrassed, she took a step down.

"I know this seems weird, but trust me."

Once she reached the bottom step, we sat at the table. I picked up the remote to turn on some music and asked her, "What kind of music does your ideal boyfriend like?"

She played the music from her Spotify account.

"On your paper, you are going to write a list of the desired features for your boyfriend. Be very specific.

"Do not write 'tall'. Write how tall: 'minimum height of 5'9".

"Do not write 'smart'. Write 'scores in the top percent of his class. Is witty and can think on his feet.'

"Do not write 'is rich'. Write 'has a positive relationship with money'.

"These are examples. Ask yourself what color are his eyes? What color is his hair? How long/short? What about his nose? Hands? Feet? Build? Teeth? What does he like to do? Hobbies? How often? What are his characteristics? Humorous? Honors his family? Self-confidence? Self-Worth? How does he make you feel? Where do you go on dates? What are his ambitions?

"Once you have his picture in your mind and you can feel the energy of him, write your list. Read over your list in the morning when you get ready for school. Read over your list right before you go to bed. When you read the list, picture all of it and feel the vibration of the relationship and the person."

She wrote out her list. She put it up on her vanity mirror and reviewed it just as I said.

"Mom, I met this guy named Jake, but he's a little short."

"Go back to your list. Does Jake fit everything on your list? Does he make you feel like the person on your list? You put your order in. If what you asked for comes out wrong, don't settle. Send it back with a grateful heart, and be patient."

A month went by. My daughter came to me again.

"Mom! I met this boy named Grant. Guess what? He is the boy on my list!!"

She has been dating Grant for over a year. Now she understands how the Law of Attraction works. Getting very specific, visualizing, writing it down, reviewing it daily ... all of these work together to create neuro-synapses in the brain, electrical impulses, vibrating molecules, radiating through the universe attracting similar vibrations.

Ana Hernado is a National Board Certified and Licensed Occupational Therapist with more that 20 years experience who works extensively with people who become victims of negative mindsets and beliefs. Phone: +1-214-762-6989 Email: ana@holisticsolutionsforlife.com

Fire Alarms to Wedding Bells

By Anik Clemens

The paper I held in my hand started to crumble in one corner as the flame took hold. I blew out the match and tossed it in the kitchen sink. As the flame grew larger, the words began to disappear from the page, slowly at first and then more quickly. The written attributes of my ideal mate were turning to ash and floating up toward the ceiling. One day, at the right time and place, my ideal partner would arrive, and we would be a family.

That was my wish, anyway. To release this three page document I had written of all of the characteristics of my ideal partner into the atmosphere, so that the Universe would conspire to one day bring me the man of my dreams.

But then....

Eeeeernt! Eeeeeernt! Eeeeernt!

An alarm ... a fire alarm!

I was pulled out of my reverie and into reality.

Perfect. Just perfect. I had set off the fire alarm.

My daughter ... she will surely wake up.

I ran into my daughter's room, and there was my one-and-a-half-year-old wide awake and sitting up in bed.

"Mommy!" she started to cry.

"Don't worry sweetie. Mommy set off the fire alarm by accident. It's not a real fire. Come with me."

I swung her out of her crib and onto my hip, and we walked out of the apartment and into the hallway to see if the fire alarm was in the whole building.

Luckily it was just in our apartment. Phew. I was sure I had woken up a number of neighbors. My brilliant idea to burn my list came at 11 PM when everyone was already sleeping.

I was a single mother of one daughter, and we lived in an apartment while I looked to purchase a townhouse. We had just moved out of our single-family ranch house where we had lived with her father, my then fiancé, which had not been a good situation. We were just so wrong for each other.

I was sick and tired of being with the wrong guy, and now I had a daughter to take care of and wanted only the best for us. I knew I deserved the man of my dreams. But how could I meet him?

I had heard about writing a wish list of attributes that you want in your ideal partner. Now looking back on this fire alarm incident, I have to laugh! It must have been the Universe telling me that my list was all wrong!

The men that came into my life after writing this first list were not my ideal partner. They had some of the attributes on the list but not all of them. And there were some things that were clearly wrong. One had opposite political views. One was sweet but not very attractive. One was chauvinistic. I dated all kinds of men, but none of them were the right one for me.

Two years later I wrote another list. This time I narrowed down the attributes to one page. I included only those attributes that I wanted in a partner. I skipped the things I didn't want.

The next person that came into my life romantically was an old friend who had had a crush on me for the past 10 years.

A salty seaman he was, with dark wispy hair, sun-kissed skin, strong legs, and a musical talent that sent me to tears. He could play any instrument including the guitar, banjo, ukulele, didgeridoo, bongos, fiddle and flute. He'd woo me with beautiful melodies and put my daughter to sleep at night with lullabies. After six months of Facetime flirting, he decided to come for a visit.

He bought an old pickup truck, packed up all of his belongings, and drove from Arizona to Florida. Two weeks later, he unloaded all of his things into my garage and moved in. The three of us cooked together, went to the beach, played at the park, paddled out into the ocean, laughed, took long walks, and sang songs. It was a beautiful time together.

But something was missing. We had the here and the now, but there was no future. We didn't have the same goals or the same aspirations. It was time to say goodbye. And just as quickly as he came, he was gone.

Why was I not attracting the right person into my life?

What was I doing wrong?

Two years later I wrote my third list. And this time I simplified it down to four things. This is how I wanted to FEEL in a partnership. These were not attributes I wanted in my mate, but how I wanted to feel when I was with my mate. I wanted these feelings to last a lifetime. So, I wrote them down. I said them out loud. I embodied them.

I am LOVED.
I am SUPPORTED.
I am CHERISHED.
I am ADORED.

That's it. It was super simple. It became my mantra. I would say it over and over every day. Day and night, I said my mantra, I felt my mantra, I embodied my mantra. Soon enough I was living and breathing my mantra.

I changed the way I treated myself. I supported, loved, cherished and adored myself. And this is how I wanted my ideal partner to treat me.

I met my perfect match, the man of my dreams, my partner and my best friend after six months of repeating my mantra out loud over and over again every day.

At this time, my daughter was five years old. One of the things we loved to do together was to go stand-up paddle boarding. It's something we could do together, while being in nature, getting some sun, exercising, and seeing all the amazing creatures that live in and near the water.

Also at this time, I was looking for a new business partner with whom to lead retreats. Being a life coach, one of the things I find very rewarding for people is getting back to nature and having a reset time where they can connect more with themselves in a peaceful location. I started leading outdoor retreats in 2014. In 2016, I was looking for a new partner. A mutual friend introduced me to a lovely yoga teacher named Heather.

"Of course, I'd love to partner with you. I have a whole fleet of paddle boards, and I know just the location we could hold our retreat ... Rainbow River. It's a beautiful spring fed river in northern Florida. It will be perfect for an outdoor adventure. And my twin brother helps out with all the paddle board stuff. We'll make a great team."

I had no idea what to expect when I met her twin, but if he was anything like his sister, I was sure going to like him.

The first time I met him was at a unique paddle board spot on the Gulf of Mexico called the Stilt Houses. It's where nine stilt houses were built a mile offshore in the early 1900s as a fishing village. We took a group of paddlers to check them out and explore the island nearby.

He and I were the first to arrive.

When I saw him walk towards me, I knew it was "him".

The first thing I noticed about him was how tan he was. Glistening from his suntan oil and the sun hitting his chest, he looked very Italian! He wore a gold chain with a crucifix pendant around his neck. He smiled and his crooked tooth in the front stood out to me. He was absolutely gorgeous.

"Hey there. You must be Heather's brother," I said nervously as we approached each other.

"Yes. I'm Fred."

Fred. I would have never guessed his name would be Fred. He didn't look like a Fred. It didn't seem to match his looks or personality ... an Ian maybe, or an Eric, but not a Fred.

"Well then, Fred, it's nice to meet you. I'm Anik. I'm partnering with you and Heather. Shall we go check out a good launch site?"

"Yes we shall."

The rest of the day we were glued to each other. It was like we were on a date but with six other people there.

We chatted about our lives and got to know each other as we paddled out into the Gulf of Mexico. So many of our interests lined up. Both of our families were tight knit. We came to find out we had similar values. We both have kids and neither of us wanted any more children. We seemed to want the same things in life.

Conversation flowed easily. We managed to keep an eye on the other paddlers and help them out when needed, but then we would find each other again and continue the conversation. We were enraptured.

The first time he met my daughter was on another paddle. This time we paddled Weeki Wachee Springs, a six-mile river that is home to many manatees in the winter. My daughter absolutely loves this paddle. She sits on my paddle board right in front of me and points out the wildlife.

"Mommy! Look over there. It's a manatee!!"

"Mom did you see that turtle on the log? Look, it's right there. No, there's actually two of them. Mom. Loooooooook!"

"I see them sweetie. That's soooo cool!"

After our paddle, we had dinner at a great restaurant at the end of the river. Kyra sat next to Fred. I could tell Kyra was sizing him up deciding if she liked him or not. She was teasing him and asking him a lot of questions.

"Kyra, you keep that up and I just might have to bring out the tickle bug."

That did it. Kyra loved being tickled. It wasn't too long before he had won her over.

Early on in our relationship, I let Fred know about my mantra. I told him that the most important thing for me in a relationship was to be loved, supported, cherished, and adored. That's what I was looking for and that's what I needed in a relationship. Above all else, that's how I wanted to feel. Could he give that to me? Was that something we could have together?

Over the course of the next year and half, Fred has shown me how much he loves, supports, cherishes and adores me. He fulfills my list. And I am so grateful.

In 2017, Fred and I got engaged. We are planning our wedding in St. Augustine, Florida in June 2018.

He is the man of my dreams.

I am LOVED.
I am SUPPORTED.
I am CHERISHED.
I am ADORED.

I am getting married at 40!!!

Pinch me!!!!

Anik Clemens is a Certified Law of Attraction Life Coach, doTERRA Essential Oils Mama and owner of Anik Perspectives, LLC. Anik specializes in working with women in transition. She has worked through many transitions in her own life and feels blessed to empower others.
Website: anikperspectives.com

Welcoming a New Child

By Dez Stephens

My current (and second) husband, Chuck, proposed to me on my 40th birthday. It was a total surprise, and one of the mental flashes I had in that moment was, "Because of my age, we need to get pregnant right away if we want a child!"

My OB/GYN doctor agreed. She said, "Let's get you on folic acid and prenatal vitamins ASAP because you're not getting any younger." Then she described to me all the reasons to be urgent in this matter, facts about the higher chances of Down Syndrome, Spina Bifida, etc.

When I was younger (in my 20s), I got pregnant quickly and easily. My first husband and I had a daughter when I was 23, and I never had a thought like, "Is it going to be hard to get pregnant?"

But now, every month counted. Every month mattered because the statistics showed the increased chances of pregnancy challenges due to "old eggs." (Boy did I get tired of hearing that term from my doctor, friends, and family members – not the mention the Internet with all of its scary data.)

My husband and I luckily got pregnant within two months when I was 40. We went through the typical testing including an amniocentesis, a super long scary needle in my belly to extract tissue to determine whether my child had any birth defects. The whole pregnancy process was nerve-wracking because there was always a sense of "tick tock, tick tock" based on my age.

The initial test results came back "normal," but our ultrasound at 22 weeks was a very different matter. We were scheduled on a Monday for the appointment, and I remember feeling a bit strange the weekend prior, like I had a stomach ache that I'd never had before. When the technician put her equipment wand on my stomach and started searching for the baby, her face went white.

None of us heard a heartbeat. She said, "I'm going to get the doctor," and that was simply terrifying. My husband and I waited in frozen silence – even holding our breath it seemed. Then the doctor came in to exam me and unfortunately had to deliver bad news. Our baby had died. In a rare occurrence, the umbilical cord got wrapped around his neck and suffocated him. Yes, our genetic testing just six weeks prior showed it was a boy.

We spent the next couple of days in the hospital with a procedure to remove our baby boy from my very-pregnant looking body. When he was "born," he had all his fingers and toes and looked like a beautiful porcelain doll.

We named him. We held him. We cremated him. Then we left the hospital without him.

It was such a painfully intense week for us that led to an excruciating month or so of, "What now?"... "Do we try again? Do we adopt instead? Do we let the dream go?" At 41, these questions were not easy to answer.

After two more years of trying, we realized that we were still grieving and not emotionally ready at a subconscious level to get pregnant again. Then I had one of those life-defining days.

It was my 43rd birthday, and it was also Mother's Day. My mother-in-law gifted me with a white wrist flower corsage to represent the baby that we had lost. Then she gifted me with another wrist corsage (for my other wrist) – with one blue and one pink flower. (Yes like the kind that prom dates wear!)

It was one of those very surreal moments we have in life. To my mother-in-law, the pink and blue flowers represented the twins she wanted to help us "have" in vitro. I was stunned.

I walked into our pseudo-nursery and realized that we hadn't officially welcomed our baby because the nursery wasn't finished yet. Then I noticed that everything in the room was "dead." There was a Purple Heart framed on the wall – my husband's Great Uncle's from World War II. There was also his military outfit hanging in the closet. In the corner was an ivory elephant tusk – a family heirloom.

I immediately removed all the "dead stuff" and emptied out the entire room. Then I placed a sweet little painting on the wall, painted by a friend specifically for our nursery. We called it "Pinkie" because it was a cute little pink elephant.

In writing down this story, I JUST NOW REALIZED that this "new" elephant item was, in a way, the opposite of the "old" elephant tusk which, frankly, represented death and animal abuse and negativity to me.

It was May 11th, and I took yet another step toward something positive – anything positive – to welcome a child into our lives. I emailed all my friends and family to ask them for a favor. I knew that so many of them were feeling "bad" for us about our miscarriage two years prior. I asked them something very simple – to see me as a healthy happy pregnant mom-to-be. I basically asked them to change their sadness into hope.

Later that month, we got pregnant again! At the 12-week mark of our pregnancy, we had a genetic test called a CVS (Chorionic Villus Sampling) so that we could test for early signs of birth defects. It's basically a DNA map of your child. The nurse said to call the office "by Friday" if they didn't call us with the results.

Friday came and we hadn't heard anything, so at 4 PM I called the doctor. The nurse said, "Oh, let me get the doctor," so I started to panic. Minutes went by and I tried to stay calm. FINALLY, she got back on the line and says, "I can't find the doctor so let me just tell you the results. It's a 26Y."

I had no idea what that meant. I tentatively asked, "What is a 26Y?" and she replied, "Oh, sorry. That means that your baby is a boy and he has all of his necessary chromosomes. In other words, he's perfect!"

PERFECT. Our baby boy was PERFECT.

And he is. His name is Merritt, and he'll be nine years old next month.

We are so grateful. We are always thinking, "Thank You, Thank You, Thank You!" We are constantly in a state of gratitude about our son and our beautiful lives together.

Dez Stephens is the Founder & CEO of Radiant Coaches Academy, a coaches training school for holistic life coaches, wellness coaches, and business coaches. She is a certified life coach, master trainer and marketing strategist.

Website: dezstephens.com

Man of My Dreams

by Hannah Golightly

For the past five years I have been pretty much desperate for a boyfriend. It's a bit embarrassing to admit, but it's true! I wasn't just desperate for any old boyfriend though. It had to be the right one. I was obsessed with finding him and bored my friends by constantly talking about dating all the time.

I signed up for all kinds of dating apps and sites. I had the occasional fling with completely unsuitable men. I briefly dated an abusive partner who cheated on me, was violent, spread malicious lies, and carried out a narcissistic smear campaign about me in my home town, while I tried not to give up hope.

Being in my mid-thirties with most of my childhood friends flaunting their marriages, babies, and children on Facebook day in and day out, it was hard at times. I felt left behind, rejected, left on the shelf. I didn't feel like it was going to happen for me.

I tried to lower my expectations after years and years of refining what I was looking for in a man down to specific details. I began just wishing for a man who didn't abuse me or hit me. I guess I thought that was more achievable considering that I believed that all the good men were married or taken by the time they were my age.

Dating sites were full of men with very obvious issues. I spent hours and hours trawling them looking for someone special, someone unique, a good match for me.

I am pretty unconventional in style, approach to life, music taste, and clothes. I started feeling like I would be better able to attract a man if I looked more normal or more mainstream. I mean, I thought I was cool … but I wasn't surrounded by any men who appreciated me the way I was.

My recent short-lived abusive relationship was with a man who wanted me to completely change the way I dressed! I didn't give in, but it did make me wonder if I was missing out on love because I was "different" in my dress sense. But I have a fashion degree, and I firmly believed that my dress sense was part and parcel of "the point" of a guy getting together with me. I'd suit someone a bit less conventional and that was what would make me special to the right man. But my faith got tested over and over again with loneliness and failed attempts to get with men from dating sites.

I started to see that when things manifest in our lives, they often ease their way into our experience gradually. All the men I dated in the last year leading up to finding the love of my life prepared the way in some respect. They each got me used to the idea of a man who shared qualities that my partner now has. In meeting each one, I sort of leveled up my expectations about what I could expect in a partner.

I mostly dated wealthy men for the first time in my life. Meeting them online, I had no clue to their wealth. Previously, I had dated men who sponged off me, and I paid rent for four of my ex boyfriends! I started to expand my idea about getting comfortable with a man who had money and would have a lot to offer me in terms of being a provider. I didn't actually get together with any of these men, but they had this impact on my mindset.

I had previously in my twenties written lists of qualities I was looking for in a partner and had boyfriends with those exact qualities manifested in my life. As the year wore on, I grew more and more disappointed with my dating experiences and lack of success. I would meet men, we would get on, and then after two dates or a couple of weeks, they would disappear or show their true (unpleasant) colours while I ran for the hills.

I wrote another list of qualities for my ideal partner at the end of 2016. I deleted it some time in 2017 from my phone. I realised that whenever I manifested a man to order like that, there was always some catch, something I had overlooked. They didn't make me happy, and it didn't last.

I persevered through terrible dating experience after terrible dating experience. Being often housebound due to a health condition, I saw online dating as my most likely way to meet a partner, but in all honesty, I didn't truly want a love story that started with meeting on a dating site. I think that's why in spite of being addicted to trawling them, I didn't meet anyone on there worth dating.

I even had some very scary experiences including a stalker and someone who spat in my mouth! The final straw came when a guy put his hands around my neck repeatedly on the first date, in the street, just a couple of hours after I had met him! I told him I didn't like it, but he kept doing it. That's the point where I just took the hint and deleted my dating accounts! The Universe was clearly steering me away from them!

After that, I completely gave up on men. I asked myself: do I even wanted a boyfriend after all? I mean, most of my exes in my twenties had been abusive, and dating had become scary and dangerous. What was the point?

As many people know, depression can be triggered by giving up on a dream. I gave up on love and men. I got very very down in the dumps and barely left my house for about two months. I started to feel like I was literally going to die from loneliness.

My parents have a happy marriage and are still best friends forty years later. Growing up, I didn't really perceive them as being in love, because it wasn't like love in Hollywood films or on TV. My mother always told me she "married her best friend," which didn't sound very romantic to me at the time. It took me many years to see what they shared together clearly and to understand that what they had was true love, what people should aim for in their life partnerships.

I used to love the story my dad told about how they got together. They met in Greece in the seventies while traveling, before this became a commonplace thing to do. They discovered after getting together that my dad had actually visited my mother's hometown before they met, meeting her dad in the shop her family owned. I always found that magical to hear! I started to want that sort of thing for myself, an epic love story rather than a convenient online dating boyfriend experience.

I came to terms with the fact that actually, no, I didn't know what I wanted in a partner because whenever I had manifested from a list of desired qualities, these men had arrived in my life and not made me happy. I usually ask the Universe for the things I want to manifest. But on this occasion it resonated with me more to ask God. So one day, I just asked God to "send me the perfect partner for a soulmate relationship and send me signs so I know it's him."

As I said that, I pictured my dad walking into my mum's shop and meeting her dad long before they met in another country. To me, that was how I pictured a sign.

Suddenly one day out of the blue, I was scrolling on Facebook and saw the friend request icon appear. *Who is the Universe sending me now?* I have no idea why I asked this. I often get random friend requests from strangers or people I just met and don't even think anything of it. But I felt at that moment connected to the Universe and open to its messages for some unknown reason.

It turned out to be David, my ex-boyfriend from when I was a teenager. I wasn't too excited to speak to him as he had asked me out in 2011 and then stood me up. But I didn't mind adding him again, so I did. I just wasn't that bothered either way.

By this time I was really low. I usually think positively and upbeat and don't often suffer low feelings or moods. But I wasn't myself, so I chatted to David but wasn't as friendly as I would usually have been.

I'm pretty blunt and open. So when David asked me how I was, I told him, "Right now I feel suicidal." I wasn't in any danger of acting on these feelings, but I just answered honestly about how I felt. He told me that he was feeling the same way. This worried me, and I encouraged him to talk. I listened to him and did what I could to support him and help him feel better.

I somehow persuaded him to come over to my house a few days later. Both of us were in a bad way. I hadn't showered for days, and my hair was a mess. I had no makeup on, and I wasn't dressed. His eyes were dark, and he was very guarded. He had a dark aura about him. He sat on the end of my bed and poured his heart out to me, telling me things he had never told anyone before. I listened and listened.

Eventually, he was about to leave, and I asked him for a cuddle. He gave me a really awkward cuddle at first. I was quite concerned for him as he was so low in himself. Then we lay down together, and we held each other tightly for the first time. I felt like I had never been so emotionally close to anyone in my whole life! It was by far the most intense hug I have ever experienced. It was genuinely life changing.

As we held each other tightly, both feeling the same thing, my heart spoke up. It said directly, telepathically to David's heart the words, "I love you." My ego mind kicked right in to protest! Thoughts like *Don't be ridiculous! Of course you don't!* occurred, but my heart was sure.

It was really weird, because I didn't feel that chemical high that I had previously associated with love. It was a calm knowing feeling from my heart to his. It had nothing to do with my mind or opinions.

David later told me that I saved his life.

As the weeks went on, we spent more and more time on the phone and at my house together, reconnecting and getting to know each other again. Over time it became more and more clear that there was something very special between us. There were all these signs and synchronicities!

We discovered that we had a matching scar on our chins.

We finally saw significance in the fact that he had spent so much time in my village as a teenager (before meeting me in a nearby town and dating me for about a month), even though he lived about 30 miles away. He had visited my mother's home town in a foreign country, just like my dad had done!

Even though he lived about 30 miles away, he had visited my mother's home town in a foreign country.

He had a son born on my birthday. It blew my mind!

We fell deeply in love, in a way that neither of us had come close to experiencing before. As time goes on we continue to discover more layers to our compatibility and see more signs and synchronicities that tell us we are meant to be together. We have the same dream lifestyle that we are working towards living together.

It dawned on me that he is the man two psychics predicted that I would end up with. Laul Richardson gave me a reading recently and told me I would get with "a man who I had already met," telling me he was a chef. After we got together, David decided to change careers and become a chef, with no prompting from me!

She also told me that we would "live an alternative lifestyle," and we are doing just that, planning our eco house that we both dreamed of living in and building before we got together.

Last summer for my birthday, so many people who came for my night out were called Dave or David that we actually nicknamed everyone Dave for the evening, even the girls!

I also spent a lot of time with two of my best male friends, both called Dave, in 2017. Now I know this was the Universe preparing me for David to come into my life. I love how it does that!

He is everything I could ever wish for in a partner and so much more. I am so glad I asked God to pick me my partner because he picked me someone far better than I would have dared to dream of.

David loves the same things as I do, prefers an alternative lifestyle, likes a lot of the same music and fashion, and enjoys a lot of the same food. We have so much fun and laughter together. We seem to be compatible in every way possible.

His family loves me, and I love them as well. He's more than a dream come true, and vice-versa. He treats me like a queen, and I treat him like a king.

He is my ultimate partner, and even though we had to wait 20 years to be together, it was worth it for what we have together now. He taught me to dream bigger and to believe in love.

Neither of us have ever been happier!

Follow your heart and you will find yourself happy.

Hannah Golightly is a Law of Attraction Life Coach based in the United Kingdom. She discovered conscious manifesting naturally as a child before rediscovering it when she read *The Secret* in her mid-twenties.

Web: www.hannahgolightly.com

Markus

by Joel Elston

A few years ago, I received a call from a foster care caseworker. She explained that she had been given my phone number by a colleague who thought I could help one of the kids on her caseload.

Since Medicaid doesn't pay for life coaching (foster care kids have Medicaid), her request began with the explanation that my services would need to be *pro bono*.

I agreed to hear the details and then decide what course of action to suggest.

She said that Markus was 12 years old. He was placed in foster care when he was 8 due to his mother being sent to prison for drug distribution. She died a few months into her four year sentence. Markus had no relatives that were able to take custody or even provide minimum emotional support.

Markus had been in multiple placements during his time in foster care: group homes, therapeutic foster care homes, and regular foster care homes. At that time he lived with a single foster parent with two other boys in the home. The foster mom had asked for Markus to be moved to another home, mainly due to his defiance.

His grades were all F's when he would bother to take tests. He would not read the question and often drew inappropriate drawings in the answer section. He was frequently suspended, both in-school suspensions and out. He was on nine different psychotropic medications to treat several mental health diagnoses. He has seen multiple counselors and therapists, but none could get him to participate.

The case worker said there was something about this particular kid that got to her. He really had been dealt a bad hand. After hearing the details of Markus' case, I agreed to meet with him to see if I could help.

For our first meeting, I met Markus at my office. I put my hand out to shake his and said, "Markus, I'm Joel. It's good to meet you."

He put his tiny hand out and lightly shook my hand. He said, "Good to meet you."

His voice seemed to be closer to that of a five-year-old than a 12-year-old. After he sat down, he was not able to look me in the eye for long. He moved his legs back and forth, his feet not touching the ground.

"Markus, tell me about yourself," is how I began our session.

"I am oppositionally defiant. I am depressed and have ADHD," was his response.

I smiled and said, "No, tell me about you, what do you like to do?"

"I don't know," he replied.

When I asked which medications he was on, he seemed pleased since he knew the answer. "Prozac, Ritalin, Tegretol, and Remeron are the ones I know. There are some others, but I forget what they are," he answered.

"Do you know why you are on those?" I questioned.

"The Prozac is for depression," he responded.

Before he could go on to the next drug, I asked him if he was depressed.

He said, "Yes, I think."

"Do you know what depression is?" I asked.

"It means you are sad," he said, looking at the floor.

"Being sad can be a part of depression, but being sad doesn't always mean you are depressed. Do you have a reason, or reasons, to be sad?" I asked.

"Well, I am in foster care, and my mom died. Nobody cares about me. I'm stupid and will always be a fuck-up. Are those reasons to be sad?" he answered in a cross between a mocking and angry tone.

"Yep, I would be sad, too. There is one thing you said that I know for sure is not true. You are not stupid. In fact, you are very smart," I said with confidence.

"That's not what my teachers say," he quipped.

"*FUCK THEM*," I said with a deep bass in my voice.

"Can you say that?" he asked with a shocked look in his eyes.

"I can say what I want, especially when it is the truth," I answered.

He smiled at the fact that I had used such strong language. I could tell he was starting to invest in our session emotionally.

I began explaining to Markus the concept of negative inner dialogue and the role it plays in our reality. Markus had many people telling him what was wrong with him, and as any kid would do he believed them. Doctors, counselors, and parental figures had all told Markus how bad or disordered he was.

I explained to him that he was behaving defiantly and that some one had labeled him as having, "Oppositional Defiant Disorder," a condition listed in the *Diagnostic and Statistical Manual of Mental Disorders, 4th Edition* (DSM-IV).

He had created his inner dialogue based on what he heard and observed. He basically had become what they had told him he was. After I explained my theory to him, I could tell he was buying it with a little skepticism.

"What if everything I told you was true, and you created this obnoxious version of yourself because you were given false information about yourself?" I asked.

"What about all the damn medication I'm taking? That's for real stuff," he argued.

"Let's look at your medication. The first one you said you were on was Prozac. It is for depression, right? You said you thought depression is about being sad. Does it help you to not be sad?" I asked.

"No," he quickly answered.

"You said your Mom died, and you are in foster care. I think anyone would be sad if those things happened, right?" I asked him.

"Yes," he conceded.

"Does Prozac in any way help your Mom not be dead or get you out of foster care?" I asked.

"No, it doesn't," he said, with a bass and power in his voice that wasn't there before.

I spent the rest of our session explaining to Markus how he is in charge of his own happiness, how his thoughts create his reality, and more details about the Law of Attraction.

I gave him a copy of the book, *The Secret*, by Rhonda Byrne and asked him to call me when he wanted to meet again, but only after he read the book. He told me he would read it. We stood up, and I was caught off guard seeing tears in is eyes as we shook hands.

The next day I had a message on my voicemail from Markus' caseworker asking me to call her back. When I returned the call, she was excited. Markus went home after our session and told his foster mom that he was misdiagnosed with Oppositional

Defiant Disorder and he would no longer be giving her a hard time. He apologized to her for his past behavior and thanked her for taking care of him. The foster mom said he was a different kid the rest of the day.

He got up the next morning without prompting and got dressed for school with no arguing. On the way out the door, he asked his foster mom to get him an appointment with his psychiatrist, saying he needed to discuss his medications.

The case worker was shocked.

"He has never listened to any counselor before. What did you tell him that reached him?" she asked.

"The truth," I replied.

A few days later I got a call from Markus' foster mom. She reinforced what the case worker had reported and said his remarkable change continued.

She also reported that Markus' teacher called her to let her know Markus apologized for his past behavior. He committed to work hard in her class. He even asked to be moved to the front of the class to avoid distractions.

She also asked if I would go to Markus' psychiatric appointment with him the following week. She was worried that the psychiatrist would not listen to what he had to say. I agreed to go.

I met Markus and his foster mom outside of the psychiatrist's office. I asked him, "Are you nervous?"

"Not a bit," he responded with confidence.

After a 30-minute wait to see the psychiatrist, Markus and I stepped into his consulting room. The psychiatrist asked who I was several times and asked Markus if he wanted me in the appointment.

Markus looked him in the eye and said, "I asked him to be here." He had a resolve I didn't know he possessed.

The psychiatrist began to speak, and Markus interrupted, "How does Prozac help with my mom dying? How did you determine I needed 80 mgs of Ritalin? Where is the evaluation that shows I have ADHD?"

Markus was relentless but remained in control. He clearly had researched each medication. The psychiatrist tried to answer along the way, but Markus kept asking medication questions. It was clear the psychiatrist was frustrated and no match for this amazing kid.

"I want to get off all this crap as quickly as possible," Markus demanded.

The psychiatrist was clearly angry but agreed. When he handed Markus his new prescriptions, Markus asked me, "Will you help me find a new doctor?" I nodded in agreement.

In the parking lot I told Markus that I was impressed with what I saw. I reminded him of his power over his perspective, saying his new perspective should include seeing himself as powerful, resilient, and brilliant. He gave me a hug.

His foster mom hugged me and then hugged Markus. She told him, "I have never been more proud of anyone than I am of you. I have never seen anyone make such a positive change so quickly. You make me want to be a better person."

Markus told her, "Let's help each other."

I had several more sessions with Markus, and his change was amazing. His new attitude caused others to change their attitudes toward him.

His teacher became his biggest advocate and worked with him to catch him up. He went from all F's to the A/B Honor Roll. Markus started to love school, and he continues to thrive in the educational environment. His only medication is a small dose of Ritalin to help him focus. He only takes it on school days.

A few months ago, I had a call from Markus. He was joyful as he yelled, "I'm getting adopted!" A family had been identified as an adoptive placement.

Markus is now 14-years-old and living with his new family. His adoption hearing will occur sometime in March 2018. I will be there!

A young man changed his entire world for the better by simply changing his perspective. The Law of Attraction is always at work. Knowing how to use it to your advantage is the key. Younger people actually respond better than older people to this message because they have less negative baggage to release.

The Law of Attraction cannot change the past, but understanding it can change your perspective of the past. Markus decided he was no longer going to be a victim of his past. He chose to be strengthened by his experience instead of defeated by it. He realized that he, and he alone, was in charge of how he viewed the past. We each have this amazing power.

Markus recently told me he wants to be a psychiatrist who uses Law of Attraction concepts in his practice. Trust me: if this kid wants it to happen, it will happen.

Markus' story is based on a real case. However, Markus is not his real name, and other details have been altered to protect his confidentiality. One day this outstanding young man will let the world know who he is and share even more details of his amazing story.

Joel Elston, CCP, CHC, Certified Life, Health, Success, Addictions & Recovery Coach specializing in gambling and alcohol addiction, substance abuse, and other related issues. He is also a featured co-host on the LOA Today podcasts.

Website: joelelston.com

Being Found

by Walt Thiessen

During the first 40 years of my life, I was less than successful when it came to the opposite sex.

That's putting it mildly!

In truth, I had not had a single successful relationship in all my years that lasted more than one month. One month! On numerous occasions I asked friends and family to please explain women to me using small words, short sentences, and illustrative diagrams. I was that confused.

After 22 years as a legal adult, I was so depressed and so discouraged that I was ready to just give up. I could not see any way around this seemingly insurmountable problem.

It's not like I hadn't taken any steps to try to improve my situation over the years. I had signed up for dating services and even started a dating newsletter, a singles dance with a friend that produced exactly one dance before we decided it was uneconomical, and a singles magazine that produced just one issue.

I had met more women than most men meet in a lifetime, leading to one crushing disappointment after another.

During the most recent 10 years, I had crawled out of my shell as an extreme introvert by becoming a swing dancer, which introduced me to dozens, even hundreds of women. I was good at it too, so for the first time in my life I was popular – as a dance partner in demand, but that was about it.

I felt that my biggest hurdle was the fact that I stand 6'8" tall, and the limited feedback I received from women I met for romantic purposes was that I was just too tall. I even joined a club for tall people and was told by one of the members that I was STILL too tall for her!

With no idea what I should do about that, all I managed to accomplish was to become more depressed.

So by the Spring of 1998, after a particularly bad series of dating experiences with a "friend," I had enough. I threw in the towel. In my gloomy perspective, I tried to come to grips with the fact that I would likely remain an unhappy bachelor the rest of my life.

I knew nothing about the Law of Attraction at the time. I later realized that my real problem with women was that I had rapidly become more and more negative in my outlook toward women over time, so I expected relationships with them to not work out. And so of course, they didn't. How could they?

Heck, I practically forgot how to smile, let alone laugh!

Meanwhile, about six months earlier, my future wife's cat died. She and Shadow had been together for 16 years, and losing him was understandably difficult. But as she emerged from her grief, she made a conscious decision to switch tracks.

One day a friend asked her if she planned to get another cat.

"No, I am going to get a husband!" she replied without skipping a beat.

Her luck with relationships had not been much better than mine. She had one serious relationship that lasted a few years, but in the end it just did not work out. They were not a good match.

But unlike me, she was determined not to be alone for the rest of her life. So she began a concerted campaign to ask as many people as she could about whether they knew of any emotionally healthy single guys who were available.

Many years earlier, as a graduate student seeking a degree in Marriage and Family Therapy, she filled out a written "wish list" identifying the characteristics and traits of her ideal mate, an exercise required by one of her professors. Now, after updating it in her mind, she put it out to everyone she knew that she wanted to find that man.

Not surprisingly, as a professional therapist she had many friends and business associates in the field. Because of what she learned from her own therapy, as well as what she learned through the therapeutic services she supplied to her clients, it had become critically important to her to find someone who was emotionally stable and healthy. That became the basis of the question that she asked everyone with whom she came in contact during her daily life.

One of the people Louise asked was a fellow therapist whom she did not know really well and perhaps might not have picked as her first choice for making such a request. Dee was a consulting therapist in the family services outfit Louise worked for. She was a little new-agey in her interests, and Louise was not entirely sure that she would know a man that would fit Louise's requirements.

But she did not let that deter her. She asked anyway. Dee's immediate response was, "Yes, I do know one. Shall I ask him to call you?"

Just one? Why did Dee think of me when asked for a recommendation for an emotionally stable and healthy male? I have no idea. She knew hundreds of men in the swing dance community, many of whom I would have described as emotionally stable, healthy, and available.

I later asked her why she thought of me. She just shrugged her shoulders.

Louise blushed a bit and replied, "Well, maybe you might ask him first whether he might be interested. If he is, give him my phone number. "

Dee did just that. I had attended some parties and get-togethers she had sponsored, so I wasn't completely surprised when she called me one Tuesday in early April to explain that she had a coworker who was looking to meet me. Would I be interested?

Dee's inquiry did catch me off balance, though, as it reopened some old wounds unintentionally. After all, I had just given up on women! We talked for a bit, and I guess I just kinda gave in more than anything else. I certainly was not enthusiastic. Saying yes was more of a default reaction than anything else.

She gave me Louise's phone number, telling me that the best day to reach her was on Wednesdays. After her call, I left the slip of paper with Louise's number on the side table in my living room. But the phone number's existence stuck in my mind, and a day later on April 15, 1998, I decided, *Oh what the heck! The worst thing that happens is I get emotionally crushed once again.*

I picked up the phone and called her.

"Hello, my name is Walt Thiessen. A mutual friend, Dee, gave me your phone number. Is this a bad time to call?"

She replied, "No! Not at all. I was just doing some things around the house. Nothing important."

I decided before calling that I would talk to her for five or 10 minutes to be polite, probably lose interest, and then hang up. Two hours later, I modified my opinion slightly. Louise had a silly sense of humor that I found refreshing, and unlike so many other women I met, she had not yet given me any signals that she intended to play games with me.

Of course, it was just one call. I had too much experience with too many women to believe that the final verdict was in.

We hung up after agreeing to touch base again another time. To be honest, I wasn't so sure I was going to call again, but I did. The next week, again on Wednesday, I phoned her. That conversation also lasted more than two hours. So did the one the following Wednesday.

After three long phone conversations, I figured it was probably time to try to meet each other. I made it clear during the third conversation how tall I was, without actually specifying the height. I heard the hesitation in her voice, but she said she was 5'6" if she stood up straight.

I laughed at that, and we agreed to meet the following Saturday at a local restaurant halfway between our respective homes.

That Saturday, May 2, 1998, we met for lunch at the Maples Restaurant in Middlebury, Connecticut. The food was only so-so, but that was the least of our problems. Louise walked in the door wearing this battered old straw hat that she thought of as quirky, cute, and fun.

I thought it made her look like a hick.

To make matters worse, the entire time that we sat to eat and talk together, she refused to look me in the eye. Not once. For whatever reason, we just couldn't make eye contact.

She also knew exactly how tall I was now!

We parted company that day with me giving her a tepid promise to call her. She decided on the spot that she would never hear from me again, and if you had pressed me on the point, I probably would've agreed with her assessment.

Dee had previously scheduled a party for that night that I planned to attend. She, another woman, and myself all shared birthdays that week, so it was a combined birthday party for the three of us. When I showed up at her house, the first question Dee asked me was, "How did the date with Louise go?"

"Not very well," I replied with a roll of my eyes as I twisted my lips together like I had bitten into something bitter.

She asked why, and I told her the story. Dee did not blink an eye. She simply asked, "You're going to follow the three date rule, right?"

"The what?"

"The three date rule."

"Never heard of it."

"That's where you give it three dates before you make a final decision about whether or not the two of you might be right for each other."

I had never heard of anything so crazy in my life. We had no chemistry at all. Why would three dates matter?

I already knew that we had nothing in common. Well, that wasn't quite right. In our phone conversations we actually had quite a bit in common. But in person, we clearly were not getting along in, shall we say, a romantic way.

After the party as I drove home, I pondered Dee's suggestion. Once again, I kinda shrugged my shoulders and thought, *Oh well, what could it hurt?* My emotions are so frayed these days that one more disappointment won't hurt ... much.

For the next date, I invited Louise to go with me to the Norwalk Aquarium. We had a really nice time, and when I took her home, she asked me if I might be interested in rollerblading. It was one of the many subjects we had discussed that day. I told her I wasn't really good at it, but I was willing to give it a shot.

The rollerblading date went okay too, but when I took her home she "inadvertently" left her sweater in my car. She called me later and asked me if I'd found her sweater. I asked her to hang on and went out to check the car.

When I came back to confirm that I found it, she asked if I liked strawberry shortcake. I said that I did. She invited me over, and when I got there she introduced me to her new kitten, Eli.

Being the romantic man that I am, I spent most of the evening playing with the kitten.

Louise was not impressed, but she was also not deterred.

I had already told her about my interest in swing dancing. I wanted a partner who knew how to dance. So for the next date, I brought over to her apartment a cassette tape of swing dance music so I could teach her the basic steps.

To this day, we can't agree who pulled whom in, but that was the night we became a couple.

I had been in love before, but this was different. It wasn't that, "Oh god, I desperately need you," kind of love. This love felt more real, more solid, and surprisingly relaxed. It was the love of a best friend as much as the love of a lover.

A new feeling began to well up in me, one that I hadn't experienced in … well, in a very long time. How long, I couldn't have said. Perhaps I'd never felt anything like to before. I wasn't sure, but I also didn't care one way or the other whether I had.

In short, I was happy. I mean, I was really happy. I even smiled. A lot. It wasn't that sexual chemistry kind of happy. It was more like a deep-in-your-being kind of happy, the kind that feels real and permanent.

Some days later, she pulled out that "wish list" she had written all those years before. To my surprise, I matched every important requirement on her list.

The height issue didn't go away without a fight, however. A month after we got together, Louise called me one day to say that she needed a break for a few days because we'd been spending so much time together.

That nasty little voice in the back of my head piped up.

Here it comes, I thought with a cringe.

We stayed apart for one night …

I thought it was over.

Little did I know, Louise called her friend Lesley about her situation with me. Lesley asked her what was wrong.

"He's just so tall!" Louise said.

"Okay, what else?" Lesley asked.

"Well, that's it. How will we ever fit together?"

"Louise," Lesley lectured her, "If that's the worst thing you can say about him, what are you really afraid of?"

When she examined her feelings even deeper, Louise realized that she was just so emotionally overwhelmed by being with a guy (me) who was the first guy she had ever met who just loved and accepted her for who she really was.

She wasn't used to being treated this way by a lover and a mate, as a woman who deserved to be loved, respected, with emotionally healthy boundaries and being treated as an equal in every way.

She called me right after that conversation with Lesley to invite me over.

A little more than a year later, we married.

For all those years, I felt defeated. Little did I know that all I had to do was give up trying so hard, give up feeling unhappy and depressed about my lack of intimate relationships, and the universe would happily deliver my life mate within a matter of weeks.

Surprise!

Walt Thiessen is the founder of LOA Today, where he does daily podcasts on the Law of Attraction with co-hosts: David Scott Bartky, Cindie Chavez, Joel Elston, Wendy Dillard, and Tom Wells. He lives with his wife, Louise in Simsbury, Connecticut.

Website: www.loatoday.net

Friends Delivered to Me By The Law of Attraction

by Wendy Dillard

Having a close friend to share my thoughts and deepest desires has always been important to me. When I was married, my husband was my best friend and the one with whom I shared deep and meaningful conversation. However, when he and I weren't getting along, I wished I had nurtured my before-marriage girlfriend relationships. I found myself without a close female friend to discuss difficulties I was facing. Since I have a big need to express myself verbally, I know that almost every time *I talk out my thinking* to someone, I gain new insights. I love receiving new insights. I practically live for them.

After the divorce, I found myself in quite the conundrum. Even though my ex and I parted on good terms, reaching out to him for good conversation was no longer an option, as we had chosen to end our marriage so we could spread our wings and move on in different directions.

At this point in my life, I was using the Law of Attraction the best I knew how. As I pondered my situation of not having any close friends, I was clear that I wanted a girlfriend that lived close to me, so that I could call on a whim and ask her to share a meal at a local restaurant. This girlfriend needed to love deep and meaningful conversation like I did and be actively involved in her own personal development.

I wondered if this was too much to ask. But, having studied Law of Attraction, I recalled learning that *if I have the wherewithal to desire something, the Universe has the wherewithal to deliver it to me.*

So, I set my intention on my new female friend. Then I quickly revised my request to have several close friends, not just one. The others didn't have to live as close, just close enough that we'd be within driving distance for in-person time together.

In my area, we have hundreds of Meetups where you can connect with others locally on practically any given subject matter and I regularly received email notices when a new Meetup group had been launched.

One day I saw the name of a new group that captured my attention. It was called the "Wonder Tribe of North Texas."

I thought, "Hmmm, let's read the description to learn more."

I could tell the description was written by a very positive, upbeat, highly energetic woman. The thought of being with like-minded people like her really excited me, so I joined.

I got to the first Meetup a bit early where I was greeted by Rhonda, the leader of the group. She was as energetic and welcoming as her group description. While engaging her in conversation, I started to hope no one else would show up so I could spend more time getting to know her. Also, I was wondering if maybe she would become my new bestie. But then she mentioned where she lived, and I realized it was too far for an impromptu dinner.

Once other participants arrived, the Meetup began. The group conversation was definitely to my liking, so I knew I wanted to do this again because it felt so invigorating to be in the presence of like-minded people. Near the end of the gathering, Rhonda made a point to let me know that the lady sitting across from me (Keisha) lived in the same town as I did. So, Keisha and I agreed to car-pool to the next Meetup.

The next Meetup was a month out, and as promised Keisha and I drove together. Our conversation was quite stimulating both there and back. As the drive home was coming to an end, I asked if she'd be interested in sharing a meal sometime. She said she'd absolutely welcome that. I went home that night with a sense that I might have met the new friend I was hoping to find that lived near me!

Even though I was eager to schedule a dinner, I wanted to go slow because I'd been burned before – thinking I'd made a new friend only to find subsequent conversations were boring. But, driving together to the next *Meetup* was around the corner, so I knew we'd have another opportunity to see if our conversation was just as satisfying. *And it was!*

We spent hours in deep conversation during our first dining excursion, not leaving until the restaurant was closing. And we knew we'd not even begun to scratch the surface of the things we could talk about.

We began to meet for dinner more often until it became a weekly event that we both looked forward to with great anticipation. During the week, I'd keep track of the things I wanted to talk about with her, so that when Friday night came, I was prepared with all sorts of fun ideas to discuss. And little did I know, she was doing the same thing. Our conversations went all over the place from personal development to technology to childhood stories to our thoughts on global consciousness. We could literally talk about anything with one another.

As a life coach, having a friend where we could engage in coaching conversations was an aspect I really desired in a friendship. During one of our weekly dinners, I asked Keisha for some coaching to which she was agreeable. I found her insights refreshing, and I definitely appreciated the different point-of-view she came from.

One hiccup we faced as friends was that even though we both spoke English, *how* we expressed our experiences was very different. I come from a left brain, logical and linear perspective. Whereas, Keisha comes from a very right brain, etheric perspective. She sees the world through Energy (the unseen level of our existence). I'd never met anyone like her before that interpreted the world through Energy and the non-physical. We often had to interrupt our flow of conversation to define terms to try to get to the heart of what was being communicated which left me feeling very frustrated.

I recalled that when I was requesting a like-minded friend, I had specifically said to the Universe that this person didn't have to know the same personal development systems that I knew, so long as she was passionate about her own personal evolution. If she was schooled in different techniques, that could be even better because I could learn new ways to work on issues that could benefit both myself and my clients. (Be careful what you wish for!) Keisha was definitely as passionate about personal growth as I was, but her terminology was so different from mine.

But even with our communication challenges, our conversations were fun, exciting, and incredibly inspiring. One night, as we were saying our good-byes, Keisha said, "I can't wait to see how much our lives will have changed by next week."

And she was right, our lives really were making dramatic changes from week-to-week. Whatever topics we discussed fueled our desires to easily show up by the following Friday night (or at the very least, we'd see evidence of the desire making its way into reality).

Keisha and I were tenacious and eventually came to a place of more easily understanding each other. We're continually amazed at the amount of personal growth we've each experienced in the time we've been friends.

One of the Meetups Rhonda arranged was to attend an Abraham-Hicks workshop. Since I'm a huge Abraham-Hicks fan, I immediately signed up for this road trip that I knew would give us a four-hour drive to talk. During the drive, I shared a painful childhood story, to which Rhonda coached me into new empowering beliefs. And since then, Rhonda and I have shared girlfriend / coaching conversations on numerous occasions.

Rhonda's Meetup came to an end after only a handful of gatherings. But Rhonda believes (and so do I) that the primary purpose for creating this Meetup was because it was the Universe's way to connect us and for her to introduce me to Keisha.

A short time later, at an Abraham-Hicks land-cruise in Cancun, I met Clarissa. While sharing an elevator ride, we learned that we both lived in the same city, so we exchanged business cards promising to be in contact when we arrived home. Humorously, a year later when planning to go to a local Abraham-Hicks workshop, I texted her to see if she planned to attend and she responded that she would be there.

Clarissa and I hugged at the workshop, laughing at how we'd not been in touch since Cancun. I found out that Clarissa was a practitioner of services I could use. So, we purposely scheduled my appointments at the end of her work day, so we could grab dinner afterwards and enjoy some juicy Law of Attraction conversation. As our friendship was blossoming, I'd had the internal nudge to introduce Clarissa and Keisha.

So, my next impulse was to schedule a lunch for the four of us (me, Rhonda, Keisha and Clarissa). Our synergy was unlike anything I've ever experienced. The four of us now meet periodically where we're never at a loss for conversation or laughs! We are so on the same vibrational wavelength. It's truly inspirational! (And as I suspected Keisha and Clarissa struck up a wonderful friendship for themselves.)

I now have individual friendships with Keisha, Rhonda and Clarissa that are unique, each satisfying a different aspect of me. But, having all four of us like-minded women hanging out together is *game-changing!* We now call ourselves the "Fab Four," which perfectly suits us. We are four fabulous women choosing to live our lives at the highest level. When we're together, we support one another, share our latest epiphanies, and do a lot of laughing!

Even though I've been applying the principles of Law of Attraction for a number of years, it never ceases to amaze me when experiencing the full manifestation of something for which I've asked. I'm always surprised and delighted at *how* it shows up because it's always so much better than I could have planned.

Wendy Dillard is a Masterful Law of Attraction Teacher & Coach. Her expertise is in knowing how to apply the Law of Attraction to any situation. What other people call miracles and coincidences, Wendy considers normal and the way life is intended to be. Website: www.wendydillard.com

Personal Journeys

Overcoming Five Devastating Losses

by Debra Oakland

In the span of four years, I lost my 21-year-old son, my unborn baby girl in my eighth month of pregnancy, both brothers, and my father to prostate cancer.

Those few, tragic years could have led to a dramatically worse outcome had I not embraced my inner power, but I knew that the combined power of thought, feeling, and action was required to build a strong inner foundation of courage.

I look at life as my own personal, ever-changing movie reel. While some may question how I could be writing my own script when there was so much sadness in such a short period of time, I firmly believe we are where we are at any given moment in time based upon an infinite and sequential series of choices we make on our journey.

The seemingly random events that occur are our cues to speak, to act, or to respond. Which direction the scene takes is not based on the events occurring in our lives but rather upon how we script our response.

As the lead character in our own mental movie, we deliver our feelings, our emotions, and our words while we direct our inner movie, sometimes with very little editing but always in living color.

My ultimate goal was to become the conscious director of my personal life movie, rather than the reluctant supporting character.

Let me share my story as a script with two different endings.

SCRIPT #1 – FADE IN

My husband, Cody, answers a call from the hospital at five o'clock on a Sunday morning. It is news a mother never expects to hear. There has been a car accident. My son has died.

First: disbelief. This can't be happening! You never expect to lose a child before your own life is complete. *Please God, make this go away.*

Shock sets in; indescribable pain permeates my entire being. I had been through so much loss already. Now I have lost my only child and am heartbroken.

In a state of shock, feeling disconnected and out of body, I have to decide how to begin handling this news. Family is calling; people are trying to connect out of concern and love.

I want to sit and be still. No, that doesn't feel good. I need to get up and move around, go somewhere. No! That doesn't work either. What to do, where to turn, how to function?

Cody is my rock, but he is in shock as well. How do we get through this loss? How do I comfort us both? I can't. Not now!

Depression sets in, unable to function on any level; the days drag on to become weeks, months, and years. Life has lost its luster. There seems to be no hope of feeling normal again. Tears flow endlessly, guilt, self-pity, and hopelessness become close friends.

My marriage is lifeless, and I see no hope of it changing. My greatest fear is to be hurt again by loving so deeply. Cody can no longer live in this sad and broken marriage. As he takes his leave, he wishes it would have all turned out differently.

FADE TO BLACK

SCRIPT #2 – FADE IN

My husband, Cody, answers a call from the hospital at five o'clock on a Sunday morning. It is news a mother never expects to hear. There has been a car accident. My son has died.

First: disbelief. This can't be happening! You never expect to lose a child before your own life is complete. *Please God, make this go away.*

Shock sets in; indescribable pain permeates my entire being. I had been through so much loss already. Now I have just lost my only child and am heartbroken.

In a state of shock, feeling disconnected and out of body, I have to decide how to begin handling this news. Family is calling; people are trying to connect out of concern and love.

I want to sit and be still. No, that doesn't feel good. I need to get up and move around, go somewhere. No! That doesn't work either. What to do, where to turn, how to function?

Cody is my rock, but he is in shock as well. How do we get through this? I make a conscious choice to find a way out of this despair. I must believe Love is greater than even this situation. Cody and I decide to comfort each other as we talk about how to get through this loss.

I ask myself an important question: *What would my son, who loves me as I love him, want most for me?*

I say to my husband, "Knowing the love we all carry for each other is on a deep soul level, the only answer is that he would want us to live a happy life, celebrating his life as a gift, grateful for the time we had together."

I choose to define my life by handling this loss with courage, strength, and peace. My marriage to Cody grows stronger, and we become more resilient together.

I realize there are different ways of responding to hardships and that we can change our perspective from within. Both Cody and I rely on a strong foundation of inner power that houses our courage and strength, knowing this is the way to celebrate and honor our son's life, to carry him in our hearts as a precious gift. I embrace life with peace, gratitude, and compassion. I find the silver lining by going into the world courageously and helping others through the process of loss and grief.

This is my true story, and I am happy to report that Script #2 re-directed my life in miraculous ways.

After losing my son, something powerful awakened in me: courage, fearlessness, and determination. I had nothing to lose. I needed to share my voice, and through writing I found my silver lining.

During the years that followed, I pursued various interests. I love photography, so I took a class at a local college and learned to develop my own photos. I also took art classes. Fashion has always been something I gravitate to. I collaborated with a friend who owns a boutique and entered into the clothing business for several years. Best of all, I was not afraid to step outside my comfort zone any longer.

I committed myself to my passionate purpose by showing up to write each day. Every experience and challenge I went though led me back to my passion and was instrumental to my growth, molding me into the woman I am today. It is a true joy to be living my passion.

Courage became a welcome companion as I pulled up my big girl boots and continued on with my life, editing and rewriting my script as I went along. Every day as I sat down to write, I said to myself, "I am the author of my life movie, I am unlimited, I am a successful author with a powerful voice."

I later released my book, "Change Your Movie, Change Your Life: 7 Reel Concepts for Courageous Change," to the world.

Had I continued with self-limiting beliefs, I would have never written my book, which became a bestseller in the categories of happiness and personal transformation.

It's never too late to consciously choose to change the movie of your life. I have connected with people around the world through my Living in Courage platform. Before the loss I experienced, I was hesitant to use my voice, but no longer. I have been invited to share my story on over 70 radio shows, podcasts, and videos. I have collaborated on several books and support other inspirational writers.

Gratitude fills my heart. We each have our own unique voice. My goal is to shine a bright light into the world and to support others going through some of life's biggest challenges. What's yours?

Rather than dancing our life to the beat of other people, dance to the beat of your own heart. When the Universe asks you to dance, say YES!

Debra Oakland

Founder of Living in Courage - A Spiritual Oasis for Overcoming Life's Biggest Challenges
Author of Change Your Movie, Change Your Life: 7 Reel Concepts for Courageous Change

Web: DebraOakland.com

The Bath That Keeps On Gifting

by Keisha Clark

I have my own birthday tradition of taking the day for myself to do whatever I want, creating it spontaneously with no particular plan or schedule. And so I did with this particular forty-somethingth birthday, letting the day unfold as I enjoyed my hermitage.

I let myself sleep in. I spent extra snuggle time with my fur-babies. I received "happy birthday" calls and messages from friends. I treated myself to a nice lunch and a big screen movie. I was having a delightful day.

I began to notice my body was asking for some attention. I got the idea of a hot bath for my birthday. It *was* my *birthday* after all; the day of the forty-somethingth anniversary of me and my body being together (the longest relationship I've had in this lifetime). Wouldn't it be perfectly fitting to give my body what she desired?

In the year leading up to this birthday, I had come to see my body as an equal partner in this venture, though I had not always treated her that way. She has been with me through every adventure and had not kicked me out yet, and I was not always very good at acknowledging, much less thanking her.

On this particular birthday, I had a different idea of what my birthdays were really about – celebrating my relationship with my body. And so I chose to include my body in the celebration. She desired a bath, and I desired to co-create that with her, because truly, I love baths … I *LOVE* baths.

For me, there is something so sensual and soul-healing being immersed in a bath of steaming hot water. It is like a sacred ritual.

I begin disconnecting from the noise of the world as I set out tea candles in beautiful colored glass holders, lighting each candle and watching the flame catch and glow. I pick fresh towels from the cabinet and lay out the big cotton bath mat.

I begin filling the tub with hot water, dripping essential oils into the bath, taking in their scent on the rising steam as each drop disappears into the water. Shedding my burdens as my clothes fall to the floor, I dip my foot into the hot water and allow my body to acclimate to the heat, letting the rest of me relax into the bath, enveloped by it.

I suspend myself in the delicious steam, wet, and white noise of the water. I turn the faucet off and soak in the silence. I breathe in the aromatic steam and let it soothe me into the beyond-cognitive space of me. I exhale and let my body become liquid as the water alters the effect of gravity. I am peaceful and present in a perfect moment. I am in communion with the Universe, receiving from and offering my gratitude in a deep state of grace.

I float for a while, then slowly return to my earthly awareness. I give thanks to the water as it drains from the tub. I wrap myself in a thirsty towel and sit in the afterglow, reacquainting with my body as the slightly cool air of the room caresses her fresh skin. I give thanks to her as I extinguish the candles and tidy up the space, feeling refreshed, renewed, and ready to open the door to the world once again.

With this dream in mind, I found myself in a wee bit of a pickle. In order to experience a hot bath, it would require a place with a bath tub and hot running water, which I did not have at that time! That would require a hotel room. Was I willing to rent a room in order to have a nice hot bath?

Hmmm... At first, it was a "no," so I looked closer. Was I willing to stretch into a new choice simply because I could choose it? My "no" quickly turned into a slightly excited "yes".

"I am choosing this," I said to myself, and the excitement began to build. The moment I said "yes", I perceived something shift in my world. It felt like the air in the room got lighter and more joyful.

I asked the question, "Where do we go for this bath?" I quickly got a picture of a particular hotel that was only a couple of miles from where I lived.

"Really?" I asked. I was a little surprised because it was not the place I would have thought to check into. I got a definite *yes*-sense in response, and I chose to trust it and go with it.

"This should be interesting," I thought with a laugh as I began to collect my things to pack for *my bath getaway.*

It was a bit of fun actually, like a special something I was getting to do just for me (hehehe)! I collected my clothes and towels, bath pillow, candles, essential oils, my iPad, and a few other items. I set up my fur-babies for the evening, then put my bags in the car and headed to the hotel.

Nature had set the perfect backdrop for my birthday adventure. A light rain wet the ground, the air thick and cold outside – just the kind of weather that makes you want to get inside and get warm.

I pulled into the hotel parking lot, surprised to see it was pretty full. I went into the lobby to check in. There was one person ahead of me.

As I waited in line I kept asking my body if this is where we really wanted to go. I kept getting a clear sense of "yes", so I took a deep breath and reminded myself to trust my guidance.

I stepped up to the front desk and asked for a room. The lady behind the counter said it was my lucky night because they had only one room left. I grinned and said I felt very lucky. She asked for my license and credit card.

She looked at her computer screen for a moment and added, "And I'm really sorry, but this room has a Jacuzzi tub. Will that be a problem?"

It took a couple of seconds for what she said to register in my brain. Then I let out a burst of laughter.

"A Jacuzzi tub?" I asked in total surprise.

"Yes," she said, "I know some people don't like them, so I wanted to let you know, in case you wanted to change your mind about the room."

She had no way of knowing how hilariously awesome it was to me that the one room she had left had a Jacuzzi tub, and it just so happened I *LOVE* Jacuzzi tubs!

At this point, I erupted in full blown giggles at the joy of such delightfully surprising news. I could feel the excitement in my body, in the gleeful expectation of what a Jacuzzi tub meant for her! I felt like I had just won a fabulous prize!

"You have no idea how happy a Jacuzzi tub makes me," I said. "I actually came here to enjoy a hot bath for my birthday, and a Jacuzzi tub is perfect!"

She laughed and wished me a happy birthday. Then she printed up the room bill, said the weekend rate was in effect and the total would be $45. I giggled even louder as I handed her the charge card, amazed by what was taking place.

I had not put any specific expectation out for this experience other than having a hot bath, and the Universe delivered to me a room with a Jacuzzi tub at less than the weekday rate! How does it get even better than that?

I drove around the building to find my room. It was in a perfect spot near the back of the property where it was quiet. Behind the property was a large pasture and the soft night lighting of the moon and stars.

I got my bag and went to the door, still giggling to myself at the way this experience was unfolding. I opened the door, stepped into the room, and there it was: the Jacuzzi tub. I walked over to it and just marveled at it for a minute. It was huge! And it was mine for the night!

I turned the heat on to warm up the room and set up the space: clothes, towels, candles out, iPad set, and music on.

It had been quite a while since I had gotten to do this, and every part of it felt particularly yummy. I savored each step, each action, being even more present to the sacredness of this ritual on this night.

I filled the tub almost to the top and slowly slid into the water. It was as hot as I could stand it, and it came all the way up over my shoulders. I breathed in the scent of the oils in the water and on my skin and let the soft glow of the candle light in the rising steam carry all my cares away in this oh-so-peaceful, perfect moment.

As I melted into the sheer bliss of the experience it occurred to me: my body, the Universe *and* I had co-created this. It had not occurred to me in this way before, but at this moment I was so aware of her part in this creation, and I was in awe.

I would never have thought to ask for a Jacuzzi tub, yet the Universe knew how much I loved them. I never would have imagined this hotel even had Jacuzzi tubs, yet the Universe knew! And my body was totally willing to assist me in receiving the guidance to get there.

I would never have imagined I could have a room with a Jacuzzi tub at a price that worked for me. Yet when I became willing to let go of my resistance and my reasons for not choosing something I actually desired, I got out of the Universe's way, and it brought a perfect experience for me and my body to enjoy.

I sat in total gratitude and wonder of how the elements of that day had come together so perfectly, so brilliantly – and on my birthday. Happy Birthday, Body ... Happy Birthday to Us ... and Thank You, Universe!

That forty-somethingth birthday continues to give me inspiration and awareness. In the moments that I slip into feelings of doubt or uncertainty, I am reminded of my birthday bath and how completely the whole of the Universe is right here with me, knowing me intimately, ready to co-create with me at every moment, and oh so excitedly willing to deliver to me what I truly desire in greater ways than I can imagine!

Keisha Clark is a Spiritual Medium and Intuitive Living Coach. She teaches people how to develop and incorporate their intuition as a practical and powerful tool for creating, living and loving their lives.

Website: keishaclark.live

The Third Degree

by Linda Armstrong

I was a first degree black belt in karate. It was suggested to Gavin (my husband and Sensei) that I be put up for the upcoming promotion test by the USA World Chief Instructors. Gavin, who has his sixth degree belt, had not yet considered putting me up for promotion to second degree. In our style of karate, when you go for promotion (grading) in the black belt grades you test before the four World Chief Instructors of Kimura Shukokai Karate, held at the World Chief Instructors course attended by hundreds of people from all around the globe.

I had three months to prepare. Others going for black belt grading had already been told to prepare for the test many months prior. Gavin told me that if I worked hard enough, and if he thought I was ready, he would let me go for testing. Gavin does not give out gradings easily. He expects a lot from his students and does not want to put someone up for grading unless they meet his standards ... especially me, his wife. Well, I took this as a challenge. In my mind I thought ... *Oh yeah, I'll show you I'm ready!*

So I started training harder. I went to more classes. I practiced my katas (which are like a choreographed fight, only without any opponents). I worked on my impact and worked on fighting. *But, this is not where the real work was done.* You see, I practiced in my mind. I did my best training inside my head.

It's sort of like meditation, only I did this all the time, anywhere I was. I could be riding in a car, taking a shower, sitting at the Motor Vehicle station waiting to renew my license. It didn't matter where I was. I imagined in my mind. I did my katas in my mind and often actually worked up a sweat. I would spar (fight) in my mind, and my heart would beat rapidly. I felt the adrenaline. I felt all of the emotions attached to showing these four Chief Instructors that not only was I second degree, *I was actually **third degree**!*

Yes, I was going for second degree grading, but I told myself, *I am a third degree black belt.* I would have no trouble getting my second degree. They would observe me at the test and pass me with flying colors. I imagined what being a third degree might be like (even though I didn't really know).

"Anything that you have the ability to visualize you have the ability to have a physical manifestation of!" -- Abraham-Hicks

The test is given after two days of intense training, with one hour instruction by each of the four Chief Instructors both days. The facility accommodated 300 to 400 participants on very hard, carpeted floors. Usually when training we work on thick padded floors.

Prior to these two days we had had another two days of training, again four hours each day. Needless to say, by the time the testing took place my feet and legs (along with everyone else's) were feeling some pain.

The Chief Instructors ran us all through our punches, kicks, blocks, and combinations, both in the air and with the impact pads. Then we did a variety of katas. We did whatever we were asked to do during this test despite feeling extremely tired.

Then the test was over. There were close to 30 students testing. All of the participants in the test stood still as the Chief Instructors deliberated. In karate, when standing still we stand in Yoi position. This is ready position, basically standing still but ready to move if needed. You dare not fidget or lose focus. You stand ready.

Well, I have to tell you, standing still while they deliberated was the absolute hardest part of the whole week. My legs were killing me! I could see other students struggling like me with the simple act of standing still. Everyone's legs shook.

The Chief Instructors spoke to each other for what felt like hours. It was probably only 20 minutes, but it felt like an eternity. Finally, they asked each student to go up and stand before them as they awarded their new gradings. I'm happy to say that I passed the test and received my second degree black belt.

Shortly after the test was over, each of the four instructors came to me individually and told me that they had been deliberating for such a long time because they wanted to jump me to third degree! Whooooo hooooo! Thank you Law of Attraction!

They never jump black belt degrees and didn't want to start a precedent. This just was not done in the black belt grades. Instead, they asked me to test again the following year for third degree, which was an honor because normally going for third degree requires a minimum of another three years of training. It normally takes as long as it takes until you show your Sensei you are ready.

I did return the following year to test again and was awarded my third degree black belt in karate.

Linda Armstrong is a Master Certified Law of Attraction Energy Coach, and Energy Healer. She works with The GATE Healing Method and Theta Healing® Technique. She is also a Reiki Master Teacher, and Light Body Meditation Practitioner.

Web: www.lovemylife.coach

Hide and Seek

by Louise Thiessen

Around my 10th wedding anniversary, I was working as a lead teacher in an infant room in a day care center in Virginia. Halfway through one particular morning, I sat down to give a baby his bottle. I looked down at my left hand and noticed the center diamond from my engagement ring was missing. My ring is a center-round cut diamond with baguettes on either side running side to side, not up and down as in most settings. I was perplexed but not worried and certainly not panicked. I didn't remember looking at my ring that morning, so who knew when the stone fell out ... here at work, at home, in the shower?

I looked around my classroom and even donned gloves to go through all the discarded gloves that had been used so far that day changing diapers. No diamond. I called my husband and asked him to check the bathroom shower drain, while I would look elsewhere in the house when I came home soon for lunch.

I remained calm and knew that our insurance would cover the loss if need be. I just didn't feel anxious or panicky.

A search at lunchtime turned up nothing, so I went back to work leaving the rest of the engagement ring at home. A closer look showed that three of the six prongs that held that center stone were broken. I had no idea how they got that way.

I walked back into my classroom not phased by the loss. My co-worker who covered my lunch break greeted my with, "How much do you love me?" In her outstretched hand sitting in her palm was my diamond. She found it when she picked up one of the babies from his bouncy seat. There was the gem, which he had been sitting on. It must have come out of the setting just as I lowered the baby into the seat earlier that morning.

I had not felt confident that we would find it, but I also had not panicked. I did not block it's recovery with anxiety or negative feelings.

Louise Thiessen is a former psychotherapist and currently owns a local gardening services and maintenance business, Gardens By Louise. She is also an occasional co-host of LOA Today. She lives with her husband, Walt, and two black cats, Harmony and Joy, in Simsbury, CT

Out Of The Darkness

By Michael Craig

I only discovered the real Law of Attraction at a time when my life was at its lowest point, a time when I realized like Janis Joplin that, "Freedom's just another word for nothing left to lose..." Money was really scarce. I got divorced (again), was fed up with my career, and felt I had nothing of value to share with the world.

Oh, and I also did affirmations. Religiously. I woke up, looked at myself in the mirror and repeated the "I love you, you are good-looking, rich and loved" mantras.

For years.

Nothing but grief followed me. As much as I tried to shut out this negative force, my dark side kept pounding into me like a pile driver into the sand.

I felt hurt, poor, unloved, and generally miserable in spite of my efforts to talk myself out of this condition.

The lowest point came after my first divorce when my girlfriend killed herself.

I spent the next year feeling numb – not caring who I slept with, earning money any way I could, and generally becoming a genuine S.O.B.

It was then that the migraine headaches started.

Another marriage didn't help. I ended up divorcing her as well after cheating on her several times and feeling so worthless that I contemplated my own suicide.

The headaches only got worse.

The Silent Prayer

It was at this point that I consider my darkest night of the soul that I fell to my knees and admitted defeat. I knew no way out and finally asked God to help.

I didn't expect anything, but after my acknowledged defeat, life suddenly switched on. I found I didn't need affirmations ... just the ability to let go of the chaos!

Soon I met the woman of my dreams. Brigitte brought me back from the brink. She stayed with me while I released all the pent-up anger. She worked with me to discover and establish a powerful method of healing and self-discovery that I've used successfully on myself and others for many years.

It even cured my headaches.

Now, over 25 years later, Brigitte and I are still happily married and living in our paid-for home. We also have some vacation property, paid off our debts, and developed a way to earn a comfortable income from home. We are also pretty active and healthy.

I don't say this to brag. Far from it, I am most grateful for the gifts I've received in my life ... especially those painful episodes that awakened me to the limitations of my thoughts and affirmations.

You can do this yourself

Look around you. What do you see? Who are you with? Well guess what: these are things (and people) you have already attracted!

I found this out when I became honest enough with myself to know I didn't know squat! My "saying" some affirmation also carried with it the opposite of the affirmation ... each thought contained within itself its own mirror.

If I affirmed, "I easily attract $5000 or more each month in personal income," I may have felt good about "doing something" to attract more wealth, but to no avail. I soon discovered that the hidden decisions my subconscious mind drove home were just the opposite, i.e., "This is total B.S.; I always lose more money than I make!"

283

Using a technique based on affirmations and testing, I was able to discover in myself and others the pathway to communication with the hidden being in all of us. The ancient Hawaiians had a name for it; they called it the Ku or Unihipili (I started using Ku because "The One Who Makes Things Happen" was too damn long).

Years of testing proved my method worked. The people I worked with reported that they were more in touch with the hidden decisions that ran their lives, and were able to start attracting more good things into their lives; soul mates, more money, diseases and infirmities disappearing, and an overall sense of happiness with themselves and with life.

I found out I didn't have to live a life full of struggle. My struggles, in fact, were simply a reaction to the hidden decisions that constantly goaded me to create more drama.

I found out what my hidden self wanted, then negotiated with "him" to change the direction. Then I relaxed and let life come to me. It's much easier ... and it works!

Dr. Michael Craig is a licensed chiropractor in the Atlanta area. He has published several books and works with patients and groups using his technique, the Logical Soul®. For more information, check out his website at www.logicalsoul.com

Anybody But Me

by Ruby Gangadharan

For as long as I could remember, I wanted more than anything else in the world to be someone other than me. I lived, breathed and dreamed of a time when I could stop being the person I was and become someone else.

This was me at age 12, and this intention stayed with me until I finished college and started my first job. I am not entirely sure of the exact moment it took hold. However, I do remember being very aware of the conversations and experiences that helped me to reach it, a mixture of what I was told, what I perceived, and what explanations I was given.

There were remarks that were directed towards me from my immediate and extended family, from the teachers in school and our neighbors, while others were more indirect like things I watched on television, saw in movies, or heard between adults.

At the heart of this was my list of "flaws". There are too many to list, but here are the few I remember because these had the greatest impact on me.

I wasn't an early riser, so I was lazy.

I was loud and vocal, so I wasn't a decent girl.

I didn't like Math and numbers, so I wasn't intelligent.

I didn't help with chores in the kitchen, so I would experience a hard life ahead.

My skin was dark, I had a big belly, and I was short. So I was going to create difficulties for my parents when the time was right. (Years later I realized it meant marriage and finding a match.)

I didn't show a natural talent in the arts, so I was average and lacking.

I was sure about what I liked and wanted, so I was stubborn and inflexible.

I wore cheap hand-me-downs, so I was uncool and a lesser being.

I asked for things that others my age had, so I was ungrateful and greedy.

The other thing that shaped my intention was the confidence and happiness I perceived in other people, either in real life or on television. My cousins were so bold and articulate.

My aunts were flawless in everything they did. My school mates had all the answers.

I also clearly remember being constantly asked to replicate all these actions and behaviors.

"Why can't you do that?"

"That's what a good girl looks like."

"You should try this. It will make you more likable, successful, and popular."

The messages sank into my being until all I did was compare everything I did with what I saw in others. I still struggle to recall an early memory of being told what I was doing was good enough. It was always about the chase of getting something else. Every achievement was overshadowed by what needed fixing next.

At 12 years old, I didn't like my life, my body, my voice, my clothes, my people, my circumstances, and everything else in-between. I lived the cliché, "The grass is always greener on the other side."

I acted out this desire to be someone else and to fix my flaws. I hid my truth and played a role, acting and pretending to be someone else. I learned how to pretend and project strength and confidence. I learned what worked, what did not work, and what would make me seem … not me. It became my M.O.

The pretense forced me to flex my curiosity muscle to read more, to investigate, to ask questions, to try new things, to keep up the facade of "being anyone else but me".

I hoped and wished for someone to give me a helping hand, a cool someone who would validate who I was becoming. I believed that external validation is the only thing that counts.

I became alert and aware of people around me, noticing every individual that crossed my path. I developed my communication skills and got good at reading the room: faces, expressions, and everything between the lines. Soon, I could catch every emotion that people knowingly or unknowingly communicated through words, tone of voice, or physical actions. Eventually, I got so good at it that I kept finding myself in a unique position to support others even before they knew they needed it.

In my mid 20's, I was introduced to the literature of the Law of Attraction and Yoga Sutras. I was so taken with everything I read, I decided I must dive in deeply. I quit my job and decided to become a yoga teacher and a coach.

I learned new practices and techniques on my spiritual journey. I read everything I could get my hands on. I found discussion groups and started an introspection that revealed what had been happening to me all my life. It was as if in one swift stroke someone had articulated everything I had been feeling all these years.

It was liberating. I finally understood myself through this literature, and I now had the tools and a language to explain my experience.

And that's when it happened, quick as a blink. My wish, something that I was hoping for since I was 12, had come true.

I had become someone else!

I was now a person who loved her life, body, voice, clothes, and the people I knew, a person who was self-aware with the ability to self-correct.

I WAS living the good life.
I WAS interesting and articulate.
I HAD the best deal with opportunities and people I trusted
I WAS living in greener pastures.
I WAS the person that had it made.
I HAD become the opposite of the old me in every way.

In retrospect, I realize that the universe had heard the request of my 12-year-old self to be anybody else but me. The change was not so much about who I was but more about how I thought about who I was, about embracing all that I had and loving what I could do with it.

The Law of Attraction, the universal truth of creation, of action and subsequent consequence, is always working. This is absolute and without exception. It is always responding to our intentions and feelings.

We don't need to be anybody else but ourselves.

Ruby is a Transformational Life Coach and Yoga Practitioner who combines Law of Attraction with the Yoga Sutras.

Web: www.everydayloamagic.com

rubygangadharan@gmail.com

The Only Choice

by Louise Thiessen

After graduating from high school, I attended a local community college for two years. My older sister was finishing up her college education at Boston University. Having two kids in four year institutions at the same time just wasn't in my father's budget, although I still marvel at how he managed to pay for our educations without loans or scholarships.

I went to Washington, D.C. to visit two friends, one at Georgetown University, the other at American University. Georgetown is a very large school with a sprawling campus. I didn't know how many students were in attendance, but I knew by its shear size it wasn't for me. I liked small classes with professors who know you.

American University was squashed onto a small plot of land in the northwest corner of D.C. The campus is so small that when they designed the new library they had to put most of it underground. The small size of the campus and the fact that most of the classes were only 30 students and lectures were about 100 students appealed to me. I felt like I could maneuver around this campus and not get lost. I could make friends here and not feel anonymous.

After that visit, I decided this was where I wanted to transfer to. I wasn't willing to look at any other schools much to my parent's chagrin. I was confident I would get in. I didn't have the grades or SAT scores needed to get accepted. I just felt that this was the only school for me. I could see myself walking to classes, living in the dorms, and feeling I belonged here.

I completed the required paperwork and sent it off. The interminable waiting began. It helped that I had a second semester of my second year to finish, so that took my mind off the waiting. It came as no surprise when they accepted me.

Louise Thiessen is a former psychotherapist and currently owns a local gardening services and maintenance business, Gardens By Louise. She is also an occasional co-host of LOA Today. She lives with her husband, Walt, and two black cats, Harmony and Joy, in Simsbury, CT

My Boat Was Taking On Water

by Tom Wells

About seven years ago, the tidy, previously ever-upright sailboat of my life was overturned in one fell swoop. Within a 12-month period, my lovely wife and soulmate of 15 years divorced me; I lost my half-a-million-dollar home; I lost my very lucrative business and income source which I had enjoyed for 25 years; I lost half of my already inadequate life savings; and I got quite sick with a debilitating sinus condition that had built slowly for years and now manifested like the plague itself.

To top it all off, I found myself growing and changing so much that I was no longer able to believe in and rely upon the foundational support of the spiritual teacher I had so happily depended on to carry me through the previous 40 years.

I awoke each morning with my guts in a knot, a litany of unanswered questions flooding my mind.

Where was I going to live?

How would I ever be able to own a home again?

How would I create a new business and income? (I had been self-employed my whole life and wasn't likely to get a job. Nor did I want to get hired for a job.)

How would I ever recover enough money or enough health to get me through my later years (which I was already entering at age 61)?

How would I fare without the support of the spiritual teacher and his philosophy and meditation that I had relied on so long for my stability in life?

At first, I embraced it all with my characteristic "I've got great sea-legs" resilience, righted my little boat in the water, and began to act as if, "Of course, I'll nail all of this! Before long I'll have a brilliant new career firmly established, doing exactly what I love, a beautiful, super-compatible new partner, and plenty of money to buy a new home and replenish my devastated life savings! I know I can overcome this sinusitis and am sure I will unfold a magical, transformative, and supportive spiritual experience that will guide me to happiness and my wonderful new fulfilling destiny!"

It took about a year and a half for me to realize that I was decidedly *NOT* as resilient as I had assumed I was. Suddenly it seemed my life was adrift on a sea of dilemmas as I sailed into a three-year period of the most choppy, "dark night of the soul" waters that I had ever encountered. I realized that seasickness really could affect me, and drowning was a distinct possibility. I had only a vague idea of where these winds and waters might take me.

I felt a calling to do life coaching, so I invested many hours and dollars in learning two different forms of coaching ... but they just didn't inspire me enough. Even though I saw some clients, I wasn't yet in the groove of doing my life's work, doing what I loved, although I knew I was close.

I took every kind of workshop that came along that spoke to me, whether it was for my heart and my spiritual development or for the development of my business. But throughout it all, my worries about spending too much money with practically nothing coming in haunted me day and night. I watched my life savings dwindle away week by week, feeling a nearly ever-present dread of time and money running out. I remember the day I found myself walking into the natural food store to buy my weekly groceries thinking, "I'd better be really careful what I buy because I really can't afford what I want anymore!"

Every morning, the seasick pain in my stomach reminded me once again of how anxious I felt. My solution was nearly always the same. I knew I had to create a new business, and I knew I had to do it NOW!!

Work harder! I told myself, *Be more diligent! Hoist the mainsail! Learn more! Make more effort to apply what you're learning! Get it together!*

As you might imagine, my solution was the problem. The rigid expectations I put on myself only added to my stress.

Patiently, characteristically, I set in for the long voyage to find land. I put my back into the rowing and worked on my situation day and night from the little living room of my condo, one lonely anxiety-ridden month after another. I felt like I was literally in the doldrums, with false start after false start, feeling increasingly disempowered, no wind in my sails, and not exactly enjoying my life. The harder I rowed, the less progress I made.

With so much of myself hyper-vigilantly focused in this fearful, survival-based mode, I imagined I had little time for fun, family, and friends.

So of course it was true ... I had little time for fun, family, and friends.

I began to experience the breakdown of my friendships with many people I had known for years and years. And of course, this felt crappy too. Loneliness and isolation quickly set in.

Woe was me ... no land in sight!

I remember the day I sat in my recliner launching into yet another day of plodding along, when it hit me so clearly that with all the self-criticism I felt toward myself, my pessimistic thinking, my feelings of unworthiness and shame, poverty consciousness, perfectionism, and over-thinking everything ... the biggest obstacle to my forward progress was no one else but ME!

I had a close friend who spoke to me often about his thoughts of suicide, and I found myself thinking, *Things can't really be this hard, can they?? If it all seems this impossible to have the life I want, and I am so prone to make it so hard on myself, I can really understand how my friend has gotten to this place of kind of wanting to check out.*

(I knew I wouldn't really do it, but, by God, to actually think this way for the first time in my life was shocking to me!)

One summer's night, I finally had enough. I determinedly jumped up and pulled out a large piece of newsprint along with 10 colored markers and started feverishly writing and drawing pictures all over the page of the things I absolutely knew I loved about life ... passionately ... freely ... joyfully ...

I drew people dancing, playing music, singing, rivers flowing through mountains, deer, trees, the moon and sun, the things I knew beyond a shadow of a doubt that I believed in and was passionate about.

In that moment I made a new commitment to myself that from that evening forward, I would only settle for doing things, as my work in life, that authentically inspired me and brought alive my passions and bliss!

One day, a big, burly, sensitive friend named Ray invited me to a local fair of psychics and healers of all sorts. I didn't particularly want to go, but when the day came, I showed up midway through the event, even though Ray bowed out.

As I wandered through a room full of these gentle healers, for some reason, I was drawn strongly to connect with one woman in the far corner. Her whole aura, attitude, and mannerisms stood out in stark relief for me from the other practitioners in the room.

I handed her my 20 bucks, and she began to move around me as I stood there motionless. Clicks, sighs, and sounds of various indescribable sorts emanated from her, and I recognized the shamanic roots she drew upon as she circled me, touching me lightly on my head, heart and neck. Strangely, happily, I felt she put me in some kind of altered state. I felt light, floating, suspended as if in liquid, less in touch with my logical, reasoning self.

To my surprise, when she finished, she told me she had three messages for me:

1. I should look into the work of Abraham and the Law of Attraction, as received by Ester Hicks;

2. I should take local classes in developing my psychic abilities; and

3. I should get into a practice called Matrix Energetics.

Her recommendations felt like they came from some deeper knowing within myself, that this was very different from following my mind's lead in choosing yet another book or seminar or teacher to look for hints to my life's work. I didn't hesitate at all in following through on all three suggestions.

My work with the entities that call themselves "Abraham" most massively transformed my life and continue to transform my life every day.

Days later, I attended an event in my hometown of Boulder, Colorado with a roomful of about 20 people on a Saturday morning. As we ate our pot-luck brunch, we watched a live four-hour video feed from San Diego of Ester Hicks receiving these non-physical entities as they answered the questions of various audience members about various subjects.

I couldn't write fast enough to keep up with the constant stream of insights, answers, and wisdom flowing through this woman! All that mattered to me was the immense sense of *RELIEF* I received with all I heard. Land Ho! My wandering vessel finally reached terra firma.

Everything I had ever wondered about, struggled with, suffered with, worried over, had angst about, longed for wisdom and clarity about, needed to know what to do about, needed to know how to do it, ALL OF IT, was answered by these funny and wise entities speaking through the pleasant, normal voice of this distinguished, well-spoken woman.

Needless to say, I went back the next weekend for yet another four-hour screening. EVERYTHING in my life began to transform.

I dove into a six month long joyful process of compiling playlists of music gathered from indigenous and ethnic peoples throughout the world, music I had largely obtained from my shaman friend in New Mexico.

I created six consecutive freestyle conscious dance events over a four-month period, proving to myself the beauty and fulfillment of following my bliss.

Could I make a living putting on dances?

Would my idea of being a life coach satisfy the level of passion I had gotten in touch with?

I enrolled in a Law of Attraction life coaching academy to more formally augment my learning with tried and true coaching principles.

One warm summer's day while hanging out at the vertical-walled Boulder Canyon, I realized that I needed to start a practice of telling new, better-feeling stories about my life.

As the creek rushed by murmuring it's reassuring water words over the tiny rapids, I took out my journal and drew a line down the center of a page.

On the left side of the page, I wrote my oh-so-familiar thoughts about my life's difficulties: money woes, career dilemma, failing to find a life partner, struggling to make new friends, wondering where to live, and so on.

On the right side of the page I finally, finally, *finally* wrote what I wanted to see happen instead, with a knowing and a commitment to accepting that it was truly possible to have my life start to show up as the new better-feeling stories on the right side of the page!

Inspired by a nice couple I know, I also soon vowed to stop talking about things that I didn't want to happen in my life.

I'm back to sailing on the vast sea of my life, but no more in the fragile, un-seaworthy vessel of a troubled, struggling existence. Now, it's more like a streamlined, double-hulled ocean-going catamaran, tacking steadily to the winds of solutions and ease! I'm clearly the captain, and I'm clearly at the helm ... and that's a good thing!

It's clear sailing from here on out. When the storms come, as they surely will do, I'm ready for them. Drowning is no longer my focus. I'm in wide open waters, and I can raise my sails and head for any destination I choose. The sun shines, the winds blow strong and steady, and I love this infinite ocean!

Tom Wells is a Certified Life Coach, but wishes he were out on the open sea right now in a catamaran, tacking along to a stiff breeze! He offers a free first coaching session. He is also a co-host at LOA Today.

Website: YouAreJoy.com

Vienna Station

by Walt Thiessen

One of the last years we lived in Virginia, my brother, Mark contacted me to ask if he could bring his girlfriend's family to stay at our house for a few days. They were visiting from Trinidad, and they wanted to see Washington D.C.. Since we lived about 50 miles from D.C., we provided the perfect spot for a visit.

The visit we had with Uohna's family those few days was very pleasant and featured some cookouts combined with a lot of opportunities to learn about each other's cultures and families. But when the day came to head into D.C., we had a bit of a quandary.

For those not familiar with the D.C. area, Washington on a weekday is chock-full of automobiles. Finding parking places can be impossible. Even the parking garages fill up. That's what happens when you take a city of two million and add a few hundred thousand government workers to it all at the same time. It literally overflows.

Want to beat the rush? You have to leave at about 3 AM. That wasn't an option.

The ideal way to go into D.C. is via the Metro train system. That way, you don't have to deal with parking. The only difficulty with the Metro is that the parking lots outside of the city at the various Metro stations also fill up completely every day.

So I used the Internet to do some research to look for some ideas about how we could find a way to get into the city. To complicate matters, there were so many of us that we needed to take two vehicles. That meant we had twice as much of a problem – how to find two parking places in a place where even one available space is a miracle.

The only useful piece of information I could find was that there are about 10-15 parking places reserved right near the station itself for people who pay a very high monthly fee to have access to these highly prized spaces. You could accurately call them the "millionaire spaces". It is not completely unusual for one or two of those spaces to go unused on any given day. At 10 AM, if there are any of those spaces that have not yet been used, then anyone can use them!

Of course, this means that once again they're only available on a first-come, first-served situation. There is no way to reserve one of those spots in advance without forking over tens of thousands of dollars.

Fortunately, Louise, Mark, Uohna, and I were all aware of the Law of Attraction. So we did our best to visualize the Universe holding two of those spots for us, while we planned to be there right at 10 AM.

On the day of our trip, we got off to a good start, but we ran into some unexpectedly slow traffic on Interstate 66, which is the only main route from our area into the Washington D.C. area. As we waited for the jam to clear, we anxiously looked at the clock. We were going to be late! Someone else would get those spots.

After conferring between the two cars via cell phone, we decided to try some drastic action. My wife noticed that an exit ramp was just off to our right. If we could somehow get onto that ramp, maybe we could find back roads that would get us to our destination, the Metro station in Vienna, Virginia.

Since no one else could think of a better plan, I turned on my right turning signal, asking the jam of cars around us to let us over to the right lane. Miraculously, they all moved out of our way! It's hard to convey how unusual that is, because drivers on Interstate 66 usually are not that polite during a traffic jam. But that day, they must have been in a good mood.

We made it over to the exit ramp with both vehicles in just a minute or two, and as we drove on it we realized that it was one of those exit ramps that actually connects two or three different exits to the highway. It's a sort of byway that ultimately empties back onto the highway if you don't take one of the exits. Hoping against hope, I decided to stay on the byway, and lo and behold as we reached the merge we found that we were ahead of the source of the traffic jam where a fender-bender had occurred!

Suddenly, we found ourselves flying down the highway hoping we could still get to Vienna Station by 10 AM. When we reached the exit for Vienna Station, we took it as I tried to decide which side of the highway to go for. The station has two parking lots, one on the right-hand side of the highway, and one on the left-hand side of the highway. Since we exited on the right-hand side, I decide to try that parking lot first.

We drove to the special row of 10-15 reserved parking spots, but they were all taken. So there was only one thing left to do. We crossed the highway over the bridge to try the parking lot on the other side.

As we drove down the access road past all the rows and rows and rows of parked cars, we saw off to our right the special row of parking places. Only partly astonished, we saw there were exactly two spaces left empty next to each other. Louise asked me to stop so she could get out and walk over to guard the two spaces while we navigated our way through the gate further down the road.

After I dropped her off, I continue to the gate. Apparently, our hurdles were not completely done. There were two cars sitting at the entrance to the gate, but they were going nowhere. A sign set by the gate said, "Lot Full." The drivers of those cars were trying to figure out what to do.

Now what? I wasn't sure what I could do with those two cars in our way. So I kind of inched up to see why the two cars were just sitting there. To my astonishment, I saw that there was actually a gap of about 10 feet between the first car and the gate. I waited about 10 seconds more as I got my nerve up, saw that neither of the two cars ahead of us were going anywhere, and with my brother following me in the second car we zipped around them, drove through the gate, and claimed the last two parking spaces.

All of us expressed astonishment, joy, and amazement at how well the Universe had reserved those two parking spaces for us, the only two parking spaces left in a 35,000 space parking lot.

Thank you, Universe!

 Walt Thiessen is the founder of LOA Today, where he does daily podcasts on the Law of Attraction with co-hosts: David Scott Bartky, Cindie Chavez, Joel Elston, Wendy Dillard, and Tom Wells. He lives with his wife, Louise in Simsbury, Connecticut.

Website: www.loatoday.net

A Steinway Piano

by Anne-Marie Cannata McEwen

At the north end of Main Street in Middletown, Connecticut sits The Buttonwood Tree, our beloved community arts center. It was named for its birthplace, once known as the Avenue of the Buttonwoods.

In 1989 Wesleyan University alumna named Susan Eastman Allison opened a used bookstore, called the Ibis. It soon became a hub of activity where creativity and community flourished.

Besides being a bookstore, the Ibis became an informal gathering place for people to share their ideas and talents. It bustled with activity and brought positive energy to the neighborhood.

Two years later the Ibis morphed into a nonprofit arts organization, North End Arts Rising, while retaining its nickname, The Buttonwood Tree. It served the community by offering books, poetry readings, and programs for personal enrichment and the cultivation of artistic talent.

Jump to February 2007.

I found myself needing to "re-create" myself after my retirement from my career as a dental hygienist and more recently from my business as a food truck operator. I decided to volunteer in areas that interested me and see where it would lead me.

In addition to serving Miles for Smiles and the Coalition for Children, I responded to a newspaper ad looking for volunteers to help write grants for The Buttonwood Tree. I had a brief, very positive experience years earlier with The Buttonwood Tree, and knew they were about music and the arts. So I joined.

Three months later, one of the people on the grant writing team, Kunle Mwanga, invited me to join the Board of Directors for The Buttonwood Tree.

My first board position!

I accepted, not knowing what it entailed, but believing that they were doing good work in the community. For about nine months I volunteered for all three organizations and learned all about North End Arts Rising and The Buttonwood Tree.

Simultaneously, I focused on learning and growing to make myself the best person I could be, diving into reading all the *Conversations with God* books by Neale Donald Walsch, Louise

Hays' *You Can Heal Your Life*, and studying the teachings of Abraham books by Esther and Jerry Hicks.

Meanwhile, The Buttonwood Tree operated in low gear. Suffering from the economic downturn and a lack of leadership after Susan Allison stepped down due to illness, programming and funding reached their lowest ebb. I helped write some grants and did my best to inject hope, but half of the board members wanted to shut our doors. Our executive director stepped down to have a baby, and things looked dim.

I resigned from everything but the North End Arts Rising board, then took a trip to Hawaii to see my daughter. I stayed for six weeks. While there I was offered a job to run a sustainable seafood "fast food" truck. I'd have jumped at the chance if it weren't in Hawaii, but I knew that my daughter wouldn't be there very long, and all my family was in Connecticut. I declined.

Returning to The Buttonwood Tree, I learned that soon we'd have no executive director. There had been much discussion about closing for months. At our next board meeting, three directors voted to close down. Three others, including myself, voted to keep our doors open. The only problem was that since we had no funds, one of *us* needed to take over as executive director. As I voted to stay open, I felt the tug inside me – a nudge and a knowing that said THIS was my new job.

We all looked around the table in silence. It was a scary moment. I knew nothing about administration and nonprofits. I had no qualifications or experience. But knowing that my gut wouldn't lead me astray, I said I would take the job.

I told them I knew nothing and didn't know if I was capable. John Basinger, the president, looked at me reassuringly. He convinced me I could do it and offered to mentor me, helping as much as I needed.

My saving grace was that I had a passion for keeping The Buttonwood Tree open, with some decent writing skills, a love for music, and an even deeper love for humanity tossed in for good measure.

As executive director, it's my job to keep everything running smoothly, all systems "go" you might say. I was in charge of everything from programs to posters, including booking the acts, paying bills, and maintaining all the equipment.

Over the years we held many poetry events and classes of all sorts from painting to yoga. But the main focus of our arts programming was to provide concerts by local and touring musicians.

For a small arts organization, we had some good basic equipment in the music department, a great sound system with top microphones.

One item that was not quite up-to-par, however, was the piano. It was with great distress that I would bring in world-class pianists to perform at The Buttonwood Tree on a very inferior piano with various mechanical problems and issues with tuning stability. Their performances would suffer as a result.

Our piano tuner and repair man was one of the best in the area, Bruce MacLeod, who would make repairs until it couldn't be fixed anymore.

At one concert the piano rolled away from the pianist! We had to laugh about it at the time, and the pianist was more than cordial about it, but I was mortified. We needed another piano soon.

In our small space, the issue of the piano often brought up the question: should we get an upright instead of the baby grand that we had? Because we attracted pianists due to having the piano, and the piano happened to be my favorite instrument, I was emphatic about keeping the baby grand size. So Bruce bought a rebuilt piano from his friend and did his best with it. That held up fairly well, but it was still far from perfect.

We are fortunate to have many world-class musicians at The Buttonwood Tree. One music teacher, Carolyn Halsted, performed classical piano concerts at The Buttonwood Tree occasionally throughout the years. After we had the piano rebuilt, I invited her to play again. The concert was nice, and afterward I asked her to come back some time. I'll never forget her response. She said to me in the most gentle, kind and sympathetic tone, "I'm sorry, but I can't play that piano." Her softened facial expression revealed how painful playing it had been to her.

That pain embedded in me a very strong desire to get a fantastic piano so she would return and be happy to play at our place. I told her I'd do what I could to get another piano and asked what kind of piano I should seek to be suitable both to her and to the many other pianists we hosted. With humility and reserve, she sweetly said that she had a Steinway at home.

I could see in her eyes that she knew we couldn't afford one and that we'd probably never get a really good piano, but I felt

313

otherwise. I felt hope and a drive to remedy the situation. In that moment I vowed to myself to get a good piano, one she deserved to play on, worthy of the very best pianists in the world – a Steinway.

The next day I added "a Steinway" to our online wish list. I talked with our piano tuner and told him that I wanted a Steinway. He chuckled, and said it would never happen.

I replied, "I can hope can't I?"

He smiled and nodded, "Of course, you can. Good luck with that."

So I hoped. I imagined having happy pianists, and I talked about it with anyone who would listen.

Concerts came and went. Pianists asked to perform, and I'd turn many of them down, saying some day when we have a better piano we would be happy to host them. When I stood in front of the audience, welcoming them and introducing the musicians, I'd tell them that we are hoping one day to get a Steinway piano for these wonderful pianists.

I put the word out that we wanted a new piano, preferably a Steinway, and my passion for it never died. We actually got several calls from people offering pianos, but their pianos were no better than what we already had.

Concerts came and went.

Three years later, in early September I received an interesting phone call from a gentleman who lived about an hour away. Steve Gorden was moving and had a piano he couldn't fit into his new home. Though he had someone who offered to purchase it, he wanted to know who we were and what we would do with the piano.

After having fielded several such calls in the past, I learned that many people just wanted someone to take their piano away. Being cautious, I asked about his piano and its condition. It turned out his was a Steinway in perfect condition! I was thrilled at the possibility.

He wanted his piano to go to a good home where it would be played often and appreciated by many. We spoke for 45 minutes all about The Buttonwood Tree and how we serve the community, who would be using the piano, who our performers are, and all the other details. He said he would think about it and talk to some people about our organization and then call me.

I waited with bated breath but felt deep down: this was it. I could sense it happening … and it felt so exciting!

A few days later Steve called back and confirmed he would give us the piano. I was ecstatic and beside myself with joy. We were getting a Steinway in perfect condition! It took three years, but it was worth it.

And then it got even better.

The next issue was the timing. Steve didn't know when the move would happen. So we put things on hold. He said he'd call me and let me know when I'd have to pick it up. When that call came in I'd have to be ready – so I called the movers.

In this same time frame we planned to put down a new floor at The Buttonwood Tree. We had received a grant and planned the job to be done in late October. Our space has a lovely performance room that doubles as an art gallery about 20' x 20', and the other room is a small bookstore. To redo the floor we'd have to move everything from one room to the other, and of course the piano had to be disassembled.

I talked to a local moving company about a moving our old piano. We arranged for the piano to be disassembled and moved on Monday, then returned to its space after the floor was done.

On the Friday before the floor job was to be done, I got the call from Steve. He said the piano needed to be picked up on the following Tuesday, serendipitously the same week we planned to redo the floor! This meant we could pick up his piano, store it for a few days, and then move it into the performance space after the floor was done.

So we moved the old piano to the moving company for storage until we eventually traded it away. The moving company didn't even charge us for storing the Steinway!

Only the Universe could have planned it so well.

Anne-Marie McEwen has been studying the Law of Attraction since 2001 and is an incessant learner and teacher. She is the executive director of The Buttonwood Tree Performing Arts Center in Middletown, CT.

Website: buttonwood.org

I'll Have an Owl, Please

by Cindie Chavez

If you could ask for anything and have it show up in the next 48 hours what would you ask for?

I asked for an owl.

I know, that sounds a bit weird looking back on it, but I think owls are really cool, and I guess I was having a hard time believing I could manifest world peace or a new Mercedes in 48 hours.

It all started when a friend of mine popped into an online group we both frequent and asked if anyone had ever read the books E^2 and E^3 by Pam Grout. These two books are a collection of Law of Attraction experiments: easy to follow exercises to put the Law of Attraction to use and to the test!

I read E^2 a few years before, but had never even heard of E^3, so I ordered the new book, went to my bookshelf, and grabbed E^2 to give it a quick re-read. As I opened it I saw a bookmark on a particular experiment.

This experiment was very, very simple. It basically consisted of two parts:

1. Ask the Universe for something.

2. Receive it within 48 hours.

Hmmm, well that sounded easy enough. And that's one of my mottos: "Easy Peasy". So I decided to dive right in with my request to the Universe:

I'll have an owl, please.

Like all of the experiments in these books, this one had a lab sheet with a space to record date and time. I recorded January 14, 2015, 10:15am Central Standard Time.

This was certainly not the first time that I asked the Universe for something or the first time that I decided to "deliberately create" an outcome using the Law of Attraction.

However, it felt a little scary doing it "in public". Even though I'd been teaching the Law of Attraction for over a decade, I didn't usually declare in a public way what I was going to consciously create. After all, it was easier to share the whole story *after* I got the result. This was probably my biggest fear: what if nothing showed up?

I dealt with this fear right away by recognizing that if nothing showed up I'd just let everyone know that nothing showed up (or that I missed seeing it somehow!). After all, it's just an experiment, right?

So it was settled. I asked for an owl.

I wasn't sure how the owl would show up. I figured that someone would send me a greeting card with an owl on it – or maybe the postage stamp on the electric bill would have a picture of an owl – or some product I needed would arrive with an owl on the label – or that I'd get an email with an owl in the banner – or I'd see a child at the grocery story wearing an owl plushie – or something like that.

I didn't know how the owl would show up, but I felt absolutely certain that it would.

Each time I worried that maybe nothing would show up, I had an equally strong feeling that an owl was definitely going to show up.

However, I did not expect what happened just 26 hours later.

I sat in my office sitting at my desk, which faces a window. While working on a writing project and lost in thought, I heard a loud rustling sound and looked up to see a huge owl, with a wingspan of more than four feet, fluttering close enough to my window that his wings brushed against it. This beautiful owl seemed to fly up from the ground, skimming my window all the way up to the roof.

Now, that might not seem like a miracle to you if you live in the country. However, I live in the city on a busy thoroughfare. Occasionally I see a cardinal or a blue jay from my window, but the only owl I've ever seen in person was at a renaissance fair until this owl appeared at my window. It was real, and it was spectacular.

My heart beat fast, and I almost burst into tears when I realized that my owl had arrived in such a wondrous demonstration. Every "vision" that I had imagined for the possible manifestation of my owl was so much smaller than what actually happened.

Never in a million years had I expected a real, live, gorgeous, fluttering owl to appear at my window!

If you could send the Universe a request for something to appear in your life in the next 48 hours, what would it be?

Cindie Chavez, the "Love & Magic Coach," is the creator of MOONLIGHT: A Course in Manifesting Love, and is a best selling author, Certified Life and Relationship coach, and Energy Leadership Master Practitioner. She co-hosts on LOA Today.

Web: www.cindiechavez.com

Fins Up

by Leslie Shew

It was our last day at the beach, and my friends were still sound asleep. The weather was perfect. I wanted to get in a morning run while it was still quiet outside, but also wanted to meditate and journal a little. I made the decision to journal first and write down what was whirling around in my head to maybe bring some order to my thoughts.

I came here to get away, attempting to escape the pain from previous months. My life had recently been turned upside down in the most difficult year I could remember. It was not the first time I faced serious adversity, but this was different. Recent failures and set-backs unleashed my deepest fears, and I was now forced to deal with them once and for all ... only I felt alone this time.

The ocean has always been a source of comfort to me. It's so godlike in it's magnificent power and beauty: intimidating, mysterious, yet calming to my soul.

I embraced the opportunity to face my darkest fears and sadness through the power of meditation. I understood that what we think about creates our emotions and reality, but there was still a part of me that challenged Law of Attraction principles.

I guess you could call it disbelief. Attraction Law didn't align with my strict religious upbringing ... or did it? Perhaps the basic concepts and beliefs are just packaged differently. Either way, there was something I wanted to fully trust, yet I was still a bit skeptical.

I sat and journaled about what I wanted my life to look like when I got back to the real world. I wrote about what I wanted to manifest, what I wanted to feel, and who I wanted to be. I wondered: is it really as simple as shifting my belief? Decide what I want and focus on that until it manifests? Is it really possible?

It seemed simple when listening to the gurus who lived out their dreams and desires in their own personal lives of manifested creation. According to these masters of manifestation, thoughts would manifest whether I believed it to be true or not, but what if it didn't apply to me somehow? I mean, who am I to have the kind of power to create what I desire in my life, to evoke the emotions I want to feel instead of the ones that imprisoned me since childhood?

It seemed that lots of people were capable of making this powerful shift in mindset, so maybe it was real.

I had recently studied Dr. Joe Dispenza and his research into the power of the mind and manifesting your desired reality through meditation. For the first time in my life, I began meditating. It was not easy at the beginning, mind you. My life was a hot mess, and my mind was full of even more chaos and craziness. Attempting to quiet the voices inside my head was becoming a full time job.

However, I was determined. I wanted to see if meditation really worked and remembered hearing a powerful testimonial from a woman at one of the workshops I had attended who manifested seeing a red balloon while practicing a walking meditation on the beach. I rolled my eyes when I first heard it, but as the story unfolded, I found myself intrigued. What would be the point of manifesting a stupid balloon? That seemed like a lot of work for something insignificant. Why not try and manifest a hundred dollar bill or something more useful?

I obviously missed the point about how it wasn't what's manifested but rather the fact that it happened that matters. The woman believed she could do it, and she did. Many people around her watched it unfold. She couldn't deny the truth. I eventually thought, "Good for her for picking something so outlandish to manifest that her mind couldn't rationalize it away."

That's when everything changed for me.

I hopped out of bed, put on my running shoes, and decided to finish my quiet time alongside the ocean, my happy place.

I stepped outside where the smell of salt in the air, the warm breeze coming off the ocean, and the sounds of sea gulls fighting over their morning meal hit me in the face.

I put on my head phones, turned up the volume, and began to lose myself in my music and thoughts. The only thing that would have been more perfect would be to run with my eyes closed as I felt the warm sun beaming down on my face.

I smiled for the first time in a long while; you know, that deep smile that comes from within your soul, the one that makes you feel in the moment that things will be okay.

I have always loved running on the beach. I love to see who is out so early in the morning ... the other joggers and walkers ... the early risers dragging their beach chairs and coolers to the beach while the rest of their crew sleeps off the rum runners from the night before ... the fishermen determined to catch a yummy lunch or just enjoying the peace and quiet.

Just as I began to enjoy this welcome peace in my soul, my subconscious mind bullied it's way in to remind me of my past emotions, the ones that keep me paralyzed, the ones that are so familiar and in some strange way, comforting.

At first I thought I could just run harder and maybe that would shake them off. If I turned up my music, then maybe I couldn't hear them any more.

Dangit. Here came the tears, the feeling of loneliness, the despair, the regrets, the fears, the shame. It was like they all played in unison, joining forces to disrupt the few minutes of peace I had found in my morning of triumph.

How can the mind shift so quickly? And if it can happen so easily then how in the world would I ever experience true and lasting change?

Maybe all this stuff is just bullshit. Maybe this Law of Attraction and meditation talk was just for gurus and yogis ... or maybe all of those people were just being scammed and brainwashed.

Ironically, I have since come to realize that I was the one being brainwashed by my own subconscious mind, by my own demons, my repetitive thoughts and beliefs that had brought me to this place in my life to begin with.

I decided to do an experiment. What did I have to lose?

One of the happiest memories of my entire life was when my husband took me to swim with the dolphins for my birthday a few years prior.

As a teenager, I had dreamed of working with dolphins. You know, one of the marine biologist folks who get to train them, study them, teach them sign language, and whatever else they do. I didn't care, as long as I could just be in their presence. I had actually never seen one up close, other than the ones who swam in front of the boats when I would go on dolphin watches. But there was just something about them that captivated me.

Being in the water with them was such an incredible experience. The energy coming off the dolphins was intensely beautiful and invigorating. They made me laugh, smile, and cry all at the same time. It was literally the most amazing thing I had ever done and in that moment I felt more alive and happier than at any other moment in my entire life as I experienced the feeling of a powerful energy that is indescribable.

I began smiling just thinking about it. I remembered Dr. Joe say that to manifest something you must feel the emotions that you will feel when it becomes your reality.

So, I halfway closed my eyes and began to feel that energy and happiness I wanted, the feelings I had felt years before. I began imagining seeing a dolphin swim up to the shoreline and giving me a "fins up" that everything was going to be okay.

Immediately my subconscious mind began sending back "hell no" thoughts.

The first one was, *Leslie, you have been coming to this beach since you were a child and have never once seen a dolphin in these waters. So what makes you think you will see one today?*

But I knew they were there … it's the damn ocean! I knew they were in there, and if a women can manifest a silly red balloon for God's sake, then surely I can manifest something that actually lives.

I thought, *Okay, maybe, but you might have to sit and watch for a while. I mean, do you really think it's just going to happen right away just because you are willing it to happen with your newly discovered mind powers?*

Why not, I answered myself. *I will even ask God to help me. He loves me and wants me to see that I have the ability to do it, so maybe I will ask Him to throw in a little help from above.*

So, I did. I prayed to God and asked if He would just do this. Give me a sign that I'm on the right path and that things were going to be okay.

I approached the end of the boardwalk and stopped to lean over the wood railing to look out at the ocean. I saw a guy feeding the seagulls, a couple walking on the beach, and a man fishing on the edge of the water. It was beautiful and calm.

The ocean looked like a glass floor. It was almost still. The sunrise was stunning. I took a deep breath and waited.

In what seemed like only half a second, I saw him. A single dolphin leapt out of the water right in front of me!

I literally began laughing out loud and jumped up and down. I couldn't believe what I was seeing. And it wasn't a pair of dolphins, which is what you would normally see, it was just one single dolphin swimming alone, dancing his way towards me as though he could tell that I had seen him.

He immediately turned around and swam back into the ocean. I continued to smile, that big hard smile I had when I had gone swimming with the dolphins years before.

I thanked God and the dolphin out loud. I didn't care who saw me or what they were thinking. I had done it! We had done it!

I guess this Law of Attraction thing is for real.

I could barely see to get back to my condo from the tears pouring out of my eyes. It felt like I floated back to the room. I couldn't wait to write down what had happened in my journal. I wanted to be able to preserve this manifestation and memory feeling in my mindset arsenal for the next time my subconscious mind tried to tell me I was a fool.

Everything is going to be okay. I just have to keep believing in what I want to have in my life. When I can see it in my mind and feel it in my heart, I see the beauty of my desires manifest before my very eyes. The feeling is as beautiful as watching a dolphin jumping for joy at sunrise.

Leslie G Shew, PhD, CTN is a Certified Holistic Wellness Coach, a Member of The American Nutraceutical Association, DSHEA Certified, a Certified Nutritional Consultant, and a Certified Life Strategies Coach.

Web: DrLeslieWellness.com

Weather

Hurricane Floyd

by Walt Thiessen

Louise and I married September 26, 1999. I asked her to marry me the previous Valentine's Day. We rushed the wedding date because her father's health was poor, and we were not sure how long he would be around. (He died three months after the wedding.) So you can imagine how busy we were that year preparing for the wedding.

By the time September rolled around, we had just about everything worked out. We knew where we would marry and had a venue for the reception. Louise bought her dress. Invitations were sent and RSVPs received. With just two weeks to go, we both desperately needed a vacation.

My parents had retired to Smith Mountain Lake near Roanoke, Virginia in the mid-1980s. That was my go-to place when I needed to get away, and it was the first place we thought of for a quick vacation.

That same week the news was full of stories about Hurricane Floyd forming in the Caribbean. As we planned our Virginia escape, the weather people projected that Floyd's eye had an 80% or greater likelihood of plowing right through Smith Mountain Lake at the exact time we planned to be there.

We needed this vacation badly, and something inside me refused to give in to the weather. I knew nothing about the Law of Attraction at this point in my life. All I knew is that we needed this week of vacation to happen right now.

So from a very determined emotional place, I shouted to the Universe, "Get that hurricane out of here! We need sunny skies and warm temperatures for our week on the water."

As we prepared to drive to Virginia, Louise expressed her concern that Floyd was going to get in our way. I have no idea why, but for some reason I felt confident in assuring her that we would get our wonderful vacation in all its glory.

As soon as we reached Virginia, we heard news that Floyd had hung up in its path over the Atlantic. Hoping our luck would hold, we arrived in Huddleston, Virginia at my parents' house.

The weather was exactly as we had hoped it would be, and we wondered how long Floyd would stay away.

The folks on the Weather Channel were not optimistic. They were already in the process of warning people who lived in low-lying areas about potential flooding.

We rented some jet skis with the intention of getting in as much water sports activity as we could.

According to Wikipedia, "Floyd triggered the fourth largest evacuation in US history (behind Hurricane Irma, Hurricane Gustav, and Hurricane Rita) when 2.6 million coastal residents of five states were ordered from their homes as it approached."

By Thursday of that week, Floyd settled over the coast of North Carolina as it drenched shoreline communities in that vicinity.

Weather forecasters expressed their astonishment that it wasn't moving anywhere. All of their computer models had shown that the most likely path was right through inland Virginia, yet there it sat.

By Friday, we felt much more relaxed and refreshed from all of our fun on the water and visiting family. We felt like we had dodged a storm, and I suppose that had literally been true.

But what really surprised us was when we started on our trip back north to Connecticut for the wedding.

To our astonishment, Hurricane Floyd followed us up the coast. The storm very politely waited for us to get home before it reached Connecticut as a tropical storm, drenching New England.

Wasn't that a considerate thing for it to do?

Nine years later, I learned about the Law of Attraction, and when I told Louise about it, one of the first thing she said was, "Maybe that's how you kept the hurricane at bay when we got married."

I had not thought about it, but you know what? I think she was right.

Walt Thiessen is the founder of LOA Today, where he does daily podcasts on the Law of Attraction with co-hosts: David Scott Bartky, Cindie Chavez, Joel Elston, Wendy Dillard, and Tom Wells. He lives with his wife, Louise in Simsbury, Connecticut.

Website: www.loatoday.net

Altering the Weather

by Louise Thiessen

During our week of "staycation" one January we had plans to go to Old Town Alexandria, Virginia to visit a metaphysical bookshop, have lunch, and window shop.

For those of you who have never been there, Old Town Alexandra is paved with cobble stones, the streets are named after British royalty, and many of the streets contain small townhouses that have a definite lean to them where the ground has settled throughout the centuries.

The previous day's weather had not been conducive to outdoor activities, so on the Friday before we were to go, I projected that Saturday would be sunny, warm, and mid 50's (remember, this was January), and no clouds.

We awoke to cold, gray, overcast skies, and I began to wonder what happened to my lovely day.

We decided to go anyway, and as we drove my husband reminded me to envision what I did want, not to focus on what was currently happening.

As you drive the D.C. beltway to Alexandria, the view of the skyline is pretty well unobstructed by hills and tall buildings, so you can see quite a distance ahead. All I saw were gray, cloud-filled skies, but I kept picturing the sunny, warm day I had projected.

As we approached the exit for Old Town Alexandria, I watched as the clouds began to part and a sliver of sun began to shine down solely and only over our destination.

Could this really be happening? Only in the area where we were headed? Not to the north, not to the south, not to the east or west?

It remained sunny and warm long enough for us to walk around, shop, and even eat lunch outside in January. Even in temperate Virginia, this is uncommon.

We got to eat ice cream and sit down by the Potomac River for awhile. My husband and I love good, homemade ice cream, and I had no more than fleeting thoughts about finding some in Old Town Alexandria in January. We saw people walking by us and asked someone where they had gotten their delicious-looking cones. They pointed us in the right direction. The ice cream proved scrumptious, and I was thrilled that they had my favorite winter flavor, maple walnut.

What a lovely, restful, fun day we had as the clouds remained parted over our area!

Just as we finished our treats and talked about heading back to the car to drive home, the clouds began to gather. We had done all we set out to do, so we headed back to the car for the ride home.

As we drove out of town, the clouds closed in and covered the previous area of sunshine, and we marveled at the power we were coming to believe was ours to tap into anytime we wanted.

The Law of Attraction is real, available, and powerful. I now know that by staying in a positive, happy attitude, many wonderful experiences, people, objects, and things will come into my life.

Louise Thiessen is a former psychotherapist and currently owns a local gardening services and maintenance business, Gardens By Louise. She is also an occasional co-host of LOA Today. She lives with her husband, Walt, and two black cats, Harmony and Joy, in Simsbury, CT

The Microburst

by Walt Thiessen

I don't remember exactly which year it was, but it was one of the last couple years we will lived in Virginia. That would make it 2012 or 2013.

I was working in my office in one of the spare bedrooms of our house just outside of Warrenton, Virginia. Rumors of possible tornado activity had surfaced, and I periodically double-checked the online weather forecasts to make sure nothing was developing in our area.

By late afternoon, a number of small storms, often known as microbursts, began to form in our area. A microburst is a sudden, powerful, localized air current, especially a downdraft. It can be destructive like a tornado, but it doesn't cover as large of an area.

When I checked the radar map and ran the tracking animation to watch the progress of the storms, I realized that one of the worst ones was headed right toward our house.

Zooming in, I discovered that our house would be smack dab in the center of the projected path of that storm. The National Weather Service issued a tornado watch for our area.

According to the radar map, we had maybe 5 to 10 minutes before the storm would rush through our area.

Louise was working on something in the living room, and I called out to her that we needed to, "do our weather thing again."

We both began to visualize our favorite ideal weather patterns in our minds.

My favorite weather pattern is one where there are blue skies with a gorgeous sun, little puffy white clouds, and temperatures in the upper 60s to lower 70s.

I spent a few minutes on that image, making it as clear in my mind as I could, while believing mightily that it would come to pass. I also made sure that I got really excited about the prospect of the weather changing to my desired alternative .

This was just the second occasion that I could ever remember since we had learned about the Law of Attraction trying to influence a storm intentionally, and it was the first time that the storm was really dangerous, just minutes away.

Our Old Town Alexandria day trip Louise told you about didn't have a microburst – just a cloudy and rainy day. So I was really curious to find out what would happen this time.

After I finished my visualization and let it go to the Universe, I walked outside to see what was going on.

We lived in a house on a one-acre plot in a rural setting, surrounded by trees in all directions. Everywhere I looked, I could see trees bending fiercely in the wind as far off as I could see.

The only exceptions were the trees within our property line. Those branches barely moved, swaying gently if at all. I half smiled at that, thinking it was noteworthy.

I called Louise to come out and take a look herself.

As we watched the sky above us, it started to clear. I don't mean the whole sky. I mean only the part of the sky directly above our house changed. The rest of the sky remained gray and threatening.

It was like the heavens had carved out a hole in the storm right where we stood. This was getting really weird!

I must have stood out there for up to 10 minutes watching the storm as it bypassed us on all sides. When nothing else seemed to happen other than the blowing of the trees, I finally lost interest and walked back inside the house.

The next day, Louise and I got in the car to drive into town to run some errands. We decided to check out the neighborhood to see if there had been any damage from the storm.

Within about a half mile of our house in all directions, there was no damage at all. But beyond that radius, no matter which direction we drove, we saw trees, large branches, and even a telephone pole down.

The extent of the damage was astonishing!

We later learned that our part of the county had been hit hard by this microburst. Only the island of our little neighborhood was spared any damage at all.

If I needed any confirmation that we have the ability to influence the weather, I got it that day.

Walt Thiessen is the founder of LOA Today, where he does daily podcasts on the Law of Attraction with co-hosts: David Scott Bartky, Cindie Chavez, Joel Elston, Wendy Dillard, and Tom Wells. He lives with his wife, Louise in Simsbury, Connecticut.

Website: www.loatoday.net

Blue Skies, Please

by Walt Thiessen

I like to walk every day if I can during warm weather. There is a rails-to-trails path near our home in Simsbury, Connecticut that gives me as many miles of outdoor paths to walk as anyone could desire. It was one of my favorite reasons for us moving back to Connecticut from Virginia a couple of years before.

Most often, I walk a portion of the path that is two miles down and two miles back, giving me a total walk of four miles.

One day as I left the house, I looked up and saw gray skies in all directions. You could see that there was even a threat of rain. That particular day, I needed blue skies and sun. I mean I really needed it! I needed the piece of mind that good weather brings. I craved feeling delighted in a way that only a beautiful day can make me feel. Since I have a history of successfully influencing the weather, I decided to give it another try today.

So as I walked along, I half-closed my eyes and imagined that we had blue skies, a nice, bright sun, and warm temperatures, but not too hot. I kept thinking to myself, "All I have to do is keep focusing on what I want the weather to be like, and these gray skies will go away."

Like most folks, I am quite capable of harboring doubts when it comes to manifesting things via the Law of Attraction, but that day I stubbornly focused determinedly on the idea that on this occasion, I would be able to produce my ideal result.

I stayed happily focused for the first two miles of the walk, keeping my eyes closed half the time so that my attention would not be diverted or discouraged by what reality showed me.

I just kept imagining that beautiful, sunny blue sky scene in my head, getting myself more and more excited about it by the minute.

In my mind's eye, I kept filling in more details. I imagined the fragrance of beautiful summer flowers. I smelled the scents of the trees. I imagined the warm, comforting, gentle breeze that would accompany such a scene. I imagined animals happily frolicking on such a beautiful day. I could practically taste the sweet flavor of fresh, clean, sunlit air on my tongue. I heard nature sounds thrilling to the beautiful summer's day my mind was inventing. I could practically touch the nearby trees in my imagination, feeling their course, warm bark.

When I reached the turnaround place at the two-mile mark, I opened my eyes fully and looked up to the sky. Darn! Gray skies all around. A bit dejectedly, I felt completely deflated. All of that mental work for nothing? I felt so let down.

I turned 180° to head back home.

I glanced up in astonishment to see blue sky as far as the eye could see. I looked straight up. The dividing line between the gray sky and the blue sky was precisely, directly above my head. Apparently, the weather had been clearing behind me as I walked, and I did not even know it!

This weather-influencing stuff is really crazy!

Walt Thiessen is the founder of LOA Today, where he does daily podcasts on the Law of Attraction with co-hosts: David Scott Bartky, Cindie Chavez, Joel Elston, Wendy Dillard, and Tom Wells. He lives with his wife, Louise in Simsbury, Connecticut.

Website: www.loatoday.net

No More Snow

by Walt Thiessen

In March 2018 as I began editing the story submissions for this book, a series of snowstorms blanketed the Northeastern portion of the United States. By the end of the month, my wife's gardening services business was preparing to open for the season. This would be a problem with snow on the ground. Finances were tight, so we needed to get going as soon as possible.

With a fourth nor'easter scheduled to hit the area on March 21, 2018, I decided it was time to take action. As I detailed in other stories in this book, I have quite a bit of experience influencing the weather. It was time to put my influence to use once again.

The weekend before the storm, weather forecasts projected anywhere up to 14 inches of snow. The day before the storm, the forecast had resolved down to the range of 10 to 14 inches.

I decided we would have zero inches. How do you do that when the weather forecasters have better information than you do? I do what I always do in such situations: I focus on my ideal weather situation.

I began to imagine a beautiful sunny day with blue skies and little puffy white clouds. Temperatures would be around 70°F, with only a slight breeze to gently caress the skin. This is my favorite, go-to vision to imagine whenever I want to influence the weather. I do not claim the ability to control the weather, only to influence it. But I do know that if I want to influence the weather, I can do it provided that I become really focused and excited about my ideal weather vision.

A belief is a thought that you think over and over again, as Abraham-Hicks teaches. I take that definition to heart by continuing to focus on my beautiful imagined weather scene continuously for as long as I am able to maintain my focus. Hold my focus for a minute, and some level of manifestation will happen. Keep focusing for minutes at a time, and the manifestation will become closer and closer to my ideal.

While I have never succeeded at completely manifesting the ideal weather conditions on the day of a scheduled storm of some kind, I have often wondered if I could manage it by focusing on my idealized scene for, say, 24 hours straight. That would take a lot of concentration. It might be an interesting test to try someday.

For this moment, I merely settled for focusing on my idealized scene for perhaps 10 to 15 minutes. I kept focusing until I really believed deep down that I was going to see a major shift in the weather pattern. I went to sleep that night believing that at the very least we would end up having no snow.

The next morning, I awoke to find no new snow on the ground. The weather forecasters were not convinced. They assured us that the snow would start falling by 8 AM. I smiled quietly to myself and disagreed, sticking to my original intention. By 11 AM, there was still no new snow on the ground. Forecasters were now saying that the snowfall would start at around 1:30 PM.

Of course, 1:30 PM came and went with no new snow falling on the ground. My smile started to get really big by this point. At 3 PM, as I prepared to do my daily afternoon podcast with Wendy Dillard, I took one quick glance at the latest weather report and learned that a new and unexpected high pressure system had surprisingly formed above northern Connecticut, and this was inhibiting the projected snowfall.

I laughingly told Wendy about this at the beginning of our podcast, sticking to my original intention that we would have no snow, although I did modify it to say that we might possibly get a dusting of it in the morning.

That night, I went to bed with still no new snow on the ground. The next morning I woke up and found a dusting of snow on the windshields of the cars. That's it. The 10 to 14 inch projection had reduced to a dusting. I take full credit.

New Jersey and downstate New York got blanketed with snow. Most of Connecticut got little to none, despite the fact that we were the next stop on the storm's projected path.

This is not a power that I hold exclusively. Everyone can do this. You just have to learn to focus, believe, and let it go.

Then stand back and watch as the weather system produces a new result that makes you marvel at the power of the human mind.

Walt Thiessen is the founder of LOA Today, where he does daily podcasts on the Law of Attraction with co-hosts: David Scott Bartky, Cindie Chavez, Joel Elston, Wendy Dillard, and Tom Wells. He lives with his wife, Louise in Simsbury, Connecticut.

Website: www.loatoday.net

Contests

The Junior Achievement Writing Contests

by Barbara Pinti

At the age of 15, when I knew nothing about the Law of Attraction, I had an experience that made me wonder what exactly was going on.

As a sophomore in high school, among my other activities, I joined Junior Achievement. There were approximately 10 J.A. companies in my school, and each company had about 10-12 students in it.

My company made a simple three-candle candelabra. Our job was to organize the company with a president, vice president, secretary, and treasurer to manufacture and sell our product at a profit.

Toward the end of that school year, it was announced that there would be an essay contest about what Junior Achievement meant to us. They told us that there would be one girl winner and one boy winner of the contest and that all J.A. members could participate. They would fly winners to the Eastern Region Junior Achievement Conference in Atlantic City. Wow! I had never flown before, a really exciting prospect for a young girl who had not traveled.

My boyfriend was also a member of a Junior Achievement company. I began to picture each of us winning and going together to Atlantic City. Everyone was in a tizzy about this opportunity. Some weren't interested in writing an essay, but many of my friends were. There was a lot of competition, so I knew that I had to do my best.

I started writing some notes in my journal about different things I would say about my experience as a Junior Achiever and all the things it meant to me. I became more and more excited about the prospect of winning the contest with my boyfriend.

I began daydreaming. I started visualizing what the conference would be like and what the hotel would be like, not easy to do since I had never stayed in a hotel or seen a conference before! We would stay on the boardwalk in Atlantic City, and that seemed incredibly exciting to me. Going to the ocean was not something I had ever done before because I lived in a city in the center of a state with no seaside access.

At night before I went to sleep, I imagined walking along the boardwalk with my boyfriend and seeing the beautiful ocean close by. During classes I found myself thinking about the contest instead of paying attention to the teacher. I went to the library and took out a book about Atlantic City. It was a well-known city and had so many interesting places to visit. I literally became an expert on the city. Of course this was back in the late 1950s, so things have changed since then.

I felt strongly this dream was going to come true. I confided in my best friend that I truly believed I would win the contest and that my boyfriend would as well. She listened as she always did, but I'm not sure what she really thought about what probably seemed like a pipe dream.

I continued writing notes in my journal and shortly began to write a rough draft of the essay. My paper looked a mess with the many cross outs and changes I kept making to the wording.

After reworking it for another week, I felt it was ready to hand in to our adviser. Before handing it in, I put my hand on it and said a little prayer about this paper being the winning entry.

The next two weeks were the most difficult. The winners would not be announced until our Friday assembly. That gave me a lot of time to daydream and visualize my boyfriend and I both winning that contest, flying on an airplane, and landing in Atlantic City among all the other Junior Achievers. My visualizations were probably just as exciting as the real thing.

The morning of the assembly arrived. I wore my best skirt and sweater in anticipation of being called up to the front of the auditorium and being announced as the winner. I was very nervous thinking about this. It truly never occurred to me that it would not happen the way I imagined it.

As the principal spoke, my foot tapped in expectation. He gave a talk about Junior Achievement, about all its benefits, and how proud he was of all of our accomplishments in learning about business. Meanwhile everyone in the audience waited impatiently for the results of the contest.

The next thing I knew, I walked up to the front of the auditorium amidst much clapping. Even though I expected to win, it was still a shock when it happened. I was exhilarated! When I reached the front of the room I saw my boyfriend coming up the aisle to receive his congratulations on being picked as the other winner. Oh wow, was this really happening?

Yes, it was! From the moment I heard about the contest, I *knew* I would be chosen as the representative from my town. I soon realized that my strong desire to win and my daydreaming about it might have been what made it all come true.

I stored these thoughts in my mind and used them in later years when I wanted something badly. I thought of them as a kind of magic way to get what I wanted. It wasn't until I learned about The Law of Attraction that I fully understood it.

Barbara A. Pinti, MA, MA, ABD, LMFT, LPC

I am a psychotherapist in private practice in West Hartford, Connecticut. I have taught the Law of Attraction in many groups, workshops and in my private practice.
Email:
barbarapinti@comcast.net

356

The People's Choice Awards

by Patricia Framo

Not many of us can say we were on *The People's Choice Awards*. I didn't think I would ever be one of them either.

In January 2011, I was in the middle of a divorce after 25 years of marriage. At first glance one might think it was not the best time to be manifesting cool things into my life, but it actually turned out to be the perfect time.

The divorce was amicable, and I wished my ex-husband well, I felt so relieved to be free from an unhappy marriage. Not to say there weren't ups and downs, but overall, I was flying high, open to new experiences, and looking forward to an adventurous life that I could create on my own. I was in a new relationship with a really nice guy and I was … well … happy.

As a life transition coach for women going through divorce, empty-nesters, etc., I voraciously soaked up as much as I could, as fast as I could, about the Law of Attraction and how to use it in my life and work purposefully. I employed the concepts in my individual and group coaching and had recently manifested spontaneously meeting Esther and Jerry Hicks (Abraham-Hicks) in a restaurant in Del Mar, CA (that's a whole other story!).

So, for the most part, I was in the vortex (in a good place, connected with my "higher Patty") and feeling hopeful about my future. I put on my big-girl panties, joined my first Meetup group, and started connecting more with other like-minded people.

One day, I got an email from someone I had only met once, asking if anyone was interested in being on the red carpet at the upcoming People's Choice Awards. I replied with the requested information and included my friend Teresa as a guest, thinking, *What the heck, I may as well go for it!*

The following week, I got an email announcing that we were accepted, with instructions to follow. Well, that in itself got me pretty excited. I had no clue how all of this worked, but it sounded like a fun adventure to me!

We were told to wear a nice party outfit, dress as if we were going onto the show, and show up very early in the morning in Los Angeles the morning of the event. On the drive up from San Diego, Teresa and I stopped at a Mexican restaurant in L.A., and made the bathroom our dressing room. I can still remember what that dingy bathroom looked like and what a contrast it was from the glitz of the show. We got into our fancy outfits, helped each other with makeup, and because it was chilly and we wanted to be comfy, threw on sweatshirts and flip flops.

When we got back into the car, we talked about the day ahead and got really excited.

I distinctly remember asserting, "Teresa, we are going to get onto the best part of the red carpet. We'll be chosen to go into the show. We will sit down in the front of the theatre, surrounded by stars!"

We were almost giddy in our excitement, and I felt a buzz run through my body.

When we drove into the multi-level parking structure, it was very confusing and chaotic with cars and people milling around and no clear direction. We never found our group, so we ended up just parking and getting in line with the first group we saw.

Such a wide array of people! A long process followed, and it soon became clear that this was more of a casting call than anything else. The powers-that-be queued us all up in various lines, stood back, evaluated and re-evaluated their choices, made changes, moved people from one line to another, etc.

While in the parking garage, they placed us in a line with people dressed in jeans, flip flops, some looking as if they had just rolled out of bed.

Teresa and I looked at each other and said, "No way are we staying in this line; we need to get into the cool line so we can get into the show!"

We tore off our sweatshirts, ditched our flip flops, donned our heels, and within minutes, we were re-assigned to a line of women and men dressed to the nines. We stayed positive and relaxed throughout, feeling the anticipation of what was to come.

Eventually Teresa and I ended up in the chosen line that they told us would be on the best part of the red carpet, the area sponsored by CVS Pharmacy.

After a long, chilly walk to the theatre along the sidewalks of South Figueroa Street, our group arrived at the Staples Center. And true to their word, they sat us in the best area of the outdoor red carpet, right across from where all the stars stopped to be photographed.

While we sat crammed side by side in bleachers, those in charge were constantly moving people around to other less desirable areas of the red carpet, adding new people, etc. ... kind of like pawns in a chess game. This selection process went on for many hours throughout the day.

There was a group of well-dressed executive-looking men and women who stood at the bottom of the bleachers on the red carpet, looking at each person, whispering to each other and then moving us around some more. God forbid anyone got up to use the restroom, or they'd be out, never to return! No jackets, no water, no food, no bathroom runs!

Eventually a couple of celebrities from E! Entertainment arrived, fashion gurus Bobbie Thomas and Robert Verdi. They explained to our group that three of us would win the opportunity to go into the show with a friend, as well as valuable gift cards and a bag of pricey cosmetics from CVS, and they would film the winners. They practiced over and over with pretend winners, moving from place to place throughout the bleachers. All the while, the executives below observed, whispered, pointed and nodded their heads, as if selecting secret agents for the CIA.

At one point, Bobbie sat next to me on the bleachers, and we chatted a bit. She seemed really sweet. I kept smiling throughout the afternoon, as Teresa and I were moved about within our red carpet section, no longer seated next to one another. No worries! We were having fun, and it was so cool watching celebrities walking down the red carpet, smiling for the paparazzi.

Then it was time to announce the winners. I was feeling so calm and happy, and it almost seemed natural when they pointed to me as one of the winners. Crazy but true!!

Bobbie and Robert sped up the bleachers to me, gave me instructions on what to do, what would happen, etc. They filmed the clip over and over, as noisy helicopters hovered overhead, in an attempt to get uninterrupted video. By the fourth time, my face was aching from smiling so hard, but we finally got what they wanted.

Bobby and Robert announced who I was, what I had won, and that I would be going into the show. I had no idea where that tape would be shown, but figured it would be on their website or something down the line.

Bobby told me that she suggested choosing me after sitting next to me earlier and chatting with me. I thanked her profusely, and off we went, into the show!

Teresa and I were hustled down the bleachers, with many well wishes from our red carpet companions. The woman with the headset leading us into the theatre told us the show was about to start, so we needed to hurry. We begged to stop at the restroom and I never peed so fast in my life. She briefed us on what would happen next: we would enter the theatre, be seated in a group of pretend friends, and they would film us all cheering as if we all had won $250 gift cards to CVS Pharmacy. I actually have no idea if anyone else won this, but Teresa and I did, along with an amazing bag of cosmetics, so we were happy!

She rushed us through the doors and what a sight ... this huge, packed theatre filled with elegant-looking people and floor-to-ceiling TV screens as the backdrop of the stage. Sparkles everywhere and search lights scanned the theatre making designs across the ceiling and walls.

She walked us down, down, down the aisle until we were seated in the third row, maybe 20 feet from the stage. Totally surreal! Queen Latifah was hosting, and there she was, right in front of us, along with the winners, including Jennifer Aniston and Neil Patrick Harris.

It was a little overwhelming, and I was trying to just soak it all in, when a few people said to me, "Look! There you are on TV!" And there I was, up on those big TV screens, as they played the clip of me winning. A camera swung around and was in my face, and we waved our gift cards and cheered like crazy. Later on, I got a string of text messages from friends all over the country asking if I was really on *The People's Choice Awards*. What an amazing manifestation!

Some may say it's a lucky coincidence, but I have no doubt what allowed that manifestation into my experience is that I was aligned with my inner being, in a positive emotional state, without resistance, and believed it could happen. I asked source to make it happen, and I allowed it in.

Since then, I have learned so much more about how to purposefully create my own life experience. I went from believing this process may be true, to knowing it is absolutely true. I've seen it over and over again in my own life and in others', including my friends, family and clients.

Daily meditation, listening to Abraham-Hicks audios, being present and appreciative of whatever I can, and focusing on positive aspects are the most effective ways I know to allow what I want into my life.

Is that the coolest thing, or what?

Patty Framo is a licensed clinical social worker and trained life coach who has over 10 years of experience counseling and coaching people regarding life's challenges, transitions, & losses.

Email: Pattyframo@gmail.com

Phone: +1-858-945-8822

Did I See You In A Commercial?

By Rhonda Burns

Even though the previous 18 months were chock full of bold new adventures, radical life choices, out-of-my-comfort-zone experiences, beautiful new friendships, and so much more, I recognized myself in a familiar space one afternoon in 2012 as I reflected on what I really wanted my life to be like. I was feeling pretty down and wondering if I'd made a mistake moving back to the area I'd left just three years before, as I was feeling quite "stuck" and stagnant in my life. In the three years I'd been away, I'd stretched myself, healed, loved, forgiven, supported, celebrated, took big risks, moved states three times, and grown more in that time span that I even knew was possible.

I had this gnawing sense within me that maybe my dreams and my desires were just too big. Maybe what I wanted was just too much ego talking, or for the "wrong" reasons. It was like trying to push away one of those large inflatable plastic clowns that are weighted at the bottom. Every time I would push the thought or the dream away, it would just come bouncing right back up at me! BOINGGGG!

I finally decided to actually use some of the tools I knew to use. I pulled out my journal and started to write down the things I wanted as I talked to the Universe.

"I don't know how this is going to look, or how it's going to show up, and it doesn't have to mean anything at all, but I REALLLLLLY want to show up in the world in a much greater way. I'd like to be visible and make an enjoyable contribution to the world. I know I have so much joy, laughter, humor and kindness to offer the world; so Universe, please, what will it take for me to be more visible and to be seen?"

I wrote down some lines of gratitude and appreciation, then was able to close the journal and get myself off the couch and out into my day with a smile back on my face.

Some of the things I jotted down included, "I love knowing that the Universe is a friendly place – it gives me great comfort. I appreciate knowing that all my needs are always met, even when I sometimes allow myself to stress when it's not required. I love having the freedom to have deeply, soul-fulfilling desires that I know I can manifest. I'm grateful to know my own power and possibility now."

A few months later, I received an email passed along by a friend from a financial services company looking to interview people about their experiences with financial services advisers.

In exchange for 30 minutes of our time, there was $300 cash for those they picked.

I saw that email and thought to myself, "Hey, I have flexibility in my schedule, and sure, I'd love $300 for 30 minutes of my time. What would it take? How much fun can I have with this whole thing, no matter what happens or how it goes?"

As I strolled through the produce aisle at the grocery store between the grapes and the lettuce, I called the number in the email. The woman who answered and I exchanged pleasantries, and she asked me if she could ask me a few preliminary questions while we were on the phone. I agreed, and as I was picking out plums and checking the ripeness of the avocados, I answered her questions with ease.

Within just a few minutes of the Q&A, she asked me if I was available two days from then to come into an area hotel and answer questions on camera for her client. She said I'd be in a four-person panel, and they would do it on camera, so that the client could see each individual's responses to the subject of money and finances. She also said that the client might need more information after that first round, so I needed to be able to come in for a second session at a later date if they determined more was necessary. I told her that wouldn't be an issue and thought to myself, "I think I just made $300 and maybe even $600 for an hour's worth of my time!" CHA-CHING!

The day of the event, I woke up and started running through some fun questions I loved to ask myself to keep me out of my head and away from, "figuring things out".

I wonder how much fun I could have with this? I wonder how many new people I can connect with and make smile? I wonder how much more of me I can show up as today with no expectation of how that has to be. I wonder what magic is awaiting me today.

It's like priming the pump with goodness and curiosity – a fantastic elixir.

I arrived at the hotel on time, checked in with the registration staff, and was asked to wait my turn. When I was called, they placed me in a panel with three men. Immediately, I thought to myself, *Oooh, I'm really going to be a ham with this. I feel like being totally nonchalant and like I don't have a care in the world.*

That was in stark contrast to the guys I was seated next to. They were quite stiff, matter-of-fact, and seemed to keep trying to show how impressive they were with their knowledge and their understanding of financial services. It really did feel a little like a competition of "mine is bigger and better than yours."

I laughed on the inside, as I could feel just how ridiculous this felt to me. I just wanted to have fun, so I did!

I answered questions to the best of my ability, but I didn't try to impress or prove anything. I was the only one laughing during my portion of the Q&A, and I was having a grand time with the folks running the video camera and the computer.

Hey, I thought to myself, *I'm thrilled that I'm getting to be me, to be happy, and I'm making $300 – in CASH – yeah, keep it coming, Universe!*

As we wrapped up our time together, I collected my envelope of cash and said goodbye to the staff. They said that if I was going to be called back, it would be after the holidays, so to just keep an eye on my email. I told them that would be great, and off I went with even more bounce in my step!

Just a couple of weeks later, upon return from a holiday trip with family, I got another email from the coordinator I'd spoken with originally. She said that the client did in fact want to meet with me again, only this time, I'd need to come to downtown Dallas to a high rise office to meet with an actual financial adviser. The plan was for the adviser to talk with me for 30 minutes and I'd walk away with $300 cash again. I responded and told her I'd love to. We set the date and the time.

Just a few days after our email exchange, the day arrived for me to head to the downtown office to meet with the financial adviser. I met the registration staff member down in the lobby that I'd seen at my last meeting, and she escorted me up to the 38th floor of this beautiful office building that bustled with busy corporate executives and office workers from the various companies in the building. I walked into a chic lobby with a company nameplate across the wall, shook hands with a well-groomed, neatly coiffed man typical of that of what you'd imagine when you think of a financial planner: navy blue suit, crisp white shirt, beautiful silk tie, and a short but stylish haircut.

We shook hands and smiled at one another as he escorted me to a long, mahogany meeting table in a well-lit conference room. We sat near one another, and after the initial greetings and ice-breaking, he began to ask me general questions about financial planning and my experience with various companies and nuances of the experience.

I was relaxed and at ease and was really being quite cheeky and irreverent having so much fun with it, considering the topic was a bit "dry". I had him laughing with me at some points and after about 20 minutes of this exchange, he asked me if I would be willing to invest my money with him.

A bit shocked, I immediately responded with expletives that weren't quite as mild and polite as the "HECK NO!" here on the page. I told him that he seemed very knowledgeable and professional, but I didn't have enough information to make a decision like that.

He then proceeded to say, as he clicked a button on a remote aimed at a big screen television at the end of the table hanging on the wall, waiting for the image to illuminate the screen, "Well, that's good, because I'm not actually a financial planner. I'm actually, a DJ."

I then saw an image of him in long, blond dreadlocks, in a cut-off t-shirt, tattoos, rings, and a nose piercing leaned over a turn-table record player, smiling. On the right side of the split TV screen was his current form and fashion as he appeared to me during our meeting.

I immediately burst out, "No waaaay!"; laughing; dropping F-bomb after F-bomb, asking him what in the world was going on and was this some type of joke? I was so amused and so confused, but it was really the most hysterical experience, and I loved being part of it.

370

He then proceeded to wave to the wall sconces directly across the table from where we were sitting and told me that they were actually filming a commercial and they wanted real-world reactions to the content. I think you could have fueled a city with the wattage coming out of my smile in that moment!

Just about the time I was composing myself from laughing so hard, the side door opened up and a producer walked in to meet me. She was thrilled with my reaction, and as she escorted me through the door into unfinished office space behind the conference room that was filled with production equipment and people, I received a round of massive applause and high fives for my reaction. I was elated!

The producer then filled me in on what was actually going on and that yes, I had just been secretly filmed for a potential part in an upcoming national commercial that their client was going to run for financial planning services. She said that the client would be picking who they wanted to use in the commercial, but would I be willing to fill out a SAG (Screen Actors Guild) card, as she felt sure that I was a strong contender.

I laughed and filled out the card in a heartbeat. In that moment, I looked up at the ceiling, tossed my head back and just roared with laughter as I whispered to the Universe:

Oh my goodness, I could have NEVER seen this coming, nor have planned for it. Thank you, Universe; this is the BEST surprise I've yet to receive. No matter what happens from here, I know I showed up, and you delivered by matching what I was choosing and being. Message received – got it! Now keep it coming!

I collected my cash from the producer, and as I drifted out of that downtown tower, I could have flown home on a cloud. I was so pumped with energy, enthusiasm and sheer gratitude. I had so much fun relaying the story to friends and family, and no matter whether I was cast in the commercial or not, I was so satisfied and felt such joy and elation at that experience that I was completely content that I got to experience it and be part of it. People could not believe the sheer "luck" I had, or that I might be part of something longer term.

Several months passed. I sat on my couch at home watching a favorite program one night when I felt my cell phone vibrate on the cushion beside me.

As I picked it up to see who texted, I laughed out loud as I read the following from a local friend of mine, *Did I just see you in a commercial?!*

I chuckled and smiled as I texted back to him, *Well, it depends. What are you watching, and what was the commercial about?*

To which he replied, *It was on a cooking show network, and it was for financial planning.*

In that moment, I literally shrieked out loud to myself as I clapped my hands together loudly, followed by a fist-pump or 10! I managed to calm down enough to respond to my friend that yes, that was in fact me, and then I flipped to the channel to wait and see if I could find the commercial.

Sure enough, within minutes, there I was on the screen. It was surreal and fun at the same time. I was still in shock that it manifested the way it did.

I muttered under my breath, *Well, Universe, it never shows up the way I think it will, does it? Thanks for rocking my world!*

Within a week, I began receiving checks from the talent company, and they continued for over three years. How's that for "ask and receive"? Simply by choosing to ask, committing to taking inspired action, showing up, being me – no matter the circumstance or audience – I was richly rewarded beyond my wildest dreams.

I still get tickled when I think back to all the emails, calls and texts I received from all over the country from friends and former colleagues, as well as strangers I would meet who asked me, "Did I see you in a commercial?!"

Even during one of the baseball World Series games, the commercial ran. How's that for "being seen" and being visible? Well, played, Universe ... well played!

Rhonda Burns is an Intuitive Freedom Coach & Pleasure Advocate who helps soul-hungry men & women powerfully and pleasurably create conscious harmony with their lives and bodies. Websites: tenaciousminx.com rhonda-burns.com

Cars

Accident, I think not!

By Wendy Dillard

We were driving home while engaged in casual conversation when all of a sudden … Bang – Boom – Crunch! Our lovely morning drive came to an abrupt end as we'd just been rear-ended. I hit my head on the side of the car really hard, causing me to go into a state of shock. What happened next was pretty fuzzy in my memory, but I do recall there was an ambulance and several squad cars at the scene of the accident within no time at all.

I only got a glimpse of the young guy that hit us. Based on the skid marks on the pavement, our best guess was that he was texting while driving and didn't notice when we came to a stop while waiting to make a left turn on a narrow two-lane road.

I didn't know about the Law of Attraction at that time, but I had a strong belief that we contribute to what shows up in our life. At the time, we couldn't think of anything that we'd been thinking that might have led to this car accident. But we recognized that we might receive greater understanding down the road, and we felt quite fortunate that our injuries were minor and that we had insurance to cover our many trips to the chiropractor.

Our insurance company considered our car *totaled,* which was a huge bummer because I'd just received this car as a gift from my mother-in-law about six months before.

We'd been through quite a fascinating history where cars were concerned. Less than two years before, I drove my limping Ford Taurus to the dealership (after hours) where I parked it, assuming it's condition was well beyond our financial ability to repair it. I left the key with a note explaining its troubles while sobbing as I mourned the loss of my much-loved car.

The next morning, the mechanic confirmed our suspicions ... the engine was a goner, and the repair would cost about $6,000. We'd have to walk away from my Taurus.

For a while we shared his car, but that was not a long-term solution.

We decided to ask my husband's parents if we could borrow one of their cars for a short time. They had two cars, but my father-in-law rarely drove anymore in favor of my mother-in-law chauffeuring him around. They said "yes," and I temporarily had wheels again.

A short time later, they decided to "gift" the car to us. We were both overwhelmingly grateful and relieved, because we still didn't have the financial means to replace my car.

For the first time I got a taste of not having car payments, as both the car given to us and my husband's car were paid off. I felt this wonderful sensation fill me with a knowingness I was tracking toward the financial freedom I desired.

Sometime later, my mother-in-law had her eye on another new car for herself, which we thought was crazy because she'd purchased a brand new Taurus (off the showroom floor) just a short time before. So, we assumed she'd pass her Taurus to her husband. Then, in a shocking conversation with her, she announced that they didn't see the need for two cars anymore. And what she wanted to propose was for her to "gift" her Taurus to us, and in return we'd "gift" the car I'd been driving to her brother.

Hello!!! Of course we accepted the deal, who wouldn't?

Within the next couple of days, cars were exchanged, and I was driving her gorgeous Taurus!

What no one knew was that the day she showed us her new Taurus two years before, I claimed that car for myself by silently saying in my mind, "That's my car!" I didn't tell anyone about this, not even my husband.

You see, I loved Tauruses. I'd already had three Tauruses, each of which I thoroughly enjoyed, but there was something special about the one that she had. It had lots of extras that my Tauruses didn't.

And the thing that really got my motor running was the sleek tail fin on the trunk which I thought looked really classy. Her Taurus gave me a feeling of *extravagance* that excited me.

So, when I say I wanted her car, *I really did*. But, I never thought it would happen. And yet, here I was in her Ford Taurus where my heart leaped for joy as I was completely blown away at this magical moment.

I love free stuff, don't you?

Now, with my fourth Taurus rear-ended and declared *totaled*, we received a check from the insurance company for $5,600. This was much less than we'd expected considering the car wasn't that old.

In the spirit of moving forward, my husband asked, "What kind of car do you want now?"

I gave it a moment as I pondered the answer.

"A Jaguar," I said.

My husband replied, "Really, you want a Jaguar? I've never heard you *ever* talk about Jaguars. Where did that idea come from?"

"I don't know," I said, "but that's what I want, a Jaguar."

He said, "You know you're not going to find a Jaguar for $5,600."

I blurted out, "Watch me!"

I'd never looked for a Jaguar before, so I had no idea what they cost. I had no idea what they even looked like. Even I was shocked to hear myself say I wanted one, but I knew I did. It just felt right to me.

So, I began searching for Jaguars.

I got quite the education. Jaguars really are expensive. Even pre-owned ones are expensive ... definitely more than $5,600.

I wasn't willing to settle for anything less than a car that made me smile every time I drove it. Also, I became aware of the growing importance that I desired to buy this car with *ALL cash,* because I never wanted car payments ever again ... and I meant it!

After finding some possibilities online, we headed out to see them. While on the car lots, we also looked at other cars just in case I might find myself interested in something other than a Jaguar. My husband and I walked in different directions to cover more territory, then called to each other when we found something good. We looked at a lot of cars over the course of one weekend, but nothing really hit the spot for me.

While heading back home, I recall my husband telling me that every time he called me over to look at a Lexus, BMW or Mercedes, he noticed that my attention was fixated on a Jaguar, and he had a hard time pulling me away to look at the cars he'd found. This interested me because I was unaware of this and wondered what it was about Jaguars that captured my attention so fully. Honestly, I didn't even know what *any* luxury car looked like by body style. I was generally drawn to a car for its color or shape.

The car lot experiences helped me to understand that *what I really wanted in my next car was the feeling of luxury.* Jaguars represented a huge step up from the previous cars I'd had because I thought of Jaguars as wonderfully exotic.

In the past, I'd had what I'd perceived as *average cars,* and I had a powerful readiness to drive something that gave me a feeling of *first-class lifestyle and wealth.* This wasn't because I wanted to impress anyone; it was completely for my own personal satisfaction. I wanted to experience feelings that "wealthy people" experienced … and I thought that having a luxury car would do that for me.

My husband recognized that I was doggedly determined to get a Jaguar and to pay for it with *ALL cash,* but he didn't see how it would be possible to find one for only $5,600 as the prices of the Jaguars we saw were significantly higher than the money we had.

Again and again, I said to him, "Just watch me!"

I knew where I was willing to be flexible and where I wasn't. And I really didn't want to budge on the idea of having a car payment. I knew *something* must be was out there that I could buy with *ALL cash.* I imagined a story that there would be a beautifully kept Jaguar that had been owned by an older couple who barely drove it. They kept it in a garage and traded it in when it was just out of warranty so it still had low mileage. The more I told myself this story, the more I believed a car like this existed, and it was just waiting for me to find it.

While searching online, I found a Jaguar with only 63,000 miles. It was six years old and cost $9,950. I wondered if the list price was accurate because it was so much lower than others I'd seen for this model year. The color was called *quartz* (which was a beautiful shade of gray). I thought being called *quartz* sounded snazzy! I know the price was higher than the insurance money I had, but I was drawn to this car.

So, we went to see it. It was more beautiful than I'd ever imaged. There wasn't one blemish on it. It looked brand-new (just like I'd been imaging in my mind). It drove like a dream and had awesome power under the hood. Test driving this Jaguar stirred up a delightful feeling of wealth within me, and I loved it.

I'd fallen in love with this Jaguar and wanted it really bad, but what about the price?

We sat in the lobby trying to figure out where the rest of the money might come from. My back was to the door while other customers walked in, when abruptly my husband said, "That man is asking about YOUR car, so if you want it, you'd better tell them now."

So, with barely a hesitation, I jumped up and headed over to the salesman behind the counter. I told him I definitely wanted to buy that quartz-colored Jaguar, but that I didn't have all the money right now. He said they could hold it for me for 10 days with a $2,000 non-refundable deposit. I said I could give him the $2,000 now, but I needed 14 days to get the rest. He said they could only hold it for 10 days. I asked again with a pleading tone of voice, but he didn't budge.

I asked if I could talk to his manager, and he kindly directed me to the manager's office. I told the manager how much I wanted that Jaguar, but I needed 14 days before I had the full amount. He repeated the same story about the 10-day holding limit. Then with a determination that filled my whole being (as well as the tone in my voice), I explained how I only had $5,600 from the insurance company. And in order to gather the rest of the money, I would use all the money in my saving account plus I'd use next my paycheck, which wouldn't come for 14 days.

I went on to say that by giving him a check for $2,000, I was guaranteeing him that I would return in exactly 14 days with the balance. After all, I couldn't afford to lose that $2,000 in my financial state. Thus, a $2000 deposit was my way of saying *this deal was as good as done*!

My impassioned plea did the trick as I watched his expression soften toward me. He extended the holding period to 14 days!

I was ecstatic.

I did have to do some creative juggling with the bills that I had intended to pay with my next paycheck, but it was worth it to buy my Jaguar with *ALL cash* so I could keep with my plan to not have car payments.

Two weeks later, I returned with the rest of the money to pick up *my* Jaguar. It was an electrifying moment! Not only was I going to own and drive a Jaguar, but I also got to experience paying for a car with *ALL cash* ... something I presumed only wealthy people did!

Each day, I'd look out of my second story window admiring my Jaguar as it was majestically parked on my driveway. Neighbors walked over to chat with me about my new car. It was their unanimous opinion that I'd benefited from a big promotion allowing me to buy it. They thought it was brand new and had no idea it was six years old.

Each neighbor spoke with a tone of voice filled with awe, but also slightly sarcastic ... as if to say they were jealous of me. This was evidence to me that my Jaguar had a perceived value that was far beyond the dollars I actually paid.

As a matter of fact, the neighbor who seemed the most jealous had just spent $65,000 on his new SUV that had all the bells and whistles. I chose not to tell him how much I actually paid for my sophisticated-looking Jaguar, letting him believe whatever he wanted.

Recognizing the power of perceived value, I decided to increase the fun by getting personalized plates. My license plate is IAMHPY. While fueling up my Jaguar, strangers often get my attention by giving me two thumbs up while wearing big smiles as they point toward my license plate. I love it ... not only does my Jag give me incredible pleasure, but it does it for others too!

Here's a fun addendum to my story... I had been encouraging my husband for the past couple of years to buy a new car, but he didn't feel we should spend the money while his car still ran. Then one very cold, wintry day, my husband got in his car to leave for work at 4:30 AM. His car didn't have a working blower, so that meant there was nothing to de-fog his very frosted windows, let alone provide heat to him. He headed off to work by sticking his head out the window to see where he was going.

Thank goodness he only worked three miles from the house, and at that hour no one else was on the road. However, this situation was a huge turning point for him.

When he arrived home from work, he told me about the conditions he endured that morning. He told me that while letting his car engine warm up, he looked over at my Jaguar knowing it had a working heater, a working de-fogger, as well as seat warmers. And there he was in his pitifully falling apart car.

That was the very moment that caused him to realize that if his wife could have a Jaguar, then he deserved to have a wonderful car too. I was thrilled my Jag provided the inspiration to up-level his thinking.

Around this time, the medical portion of our insurance claim was settled, and we received a check for $10,000. With that, we were ready to shop for my husband's next car. I did for him what I did for myself. He wanted a Jaguar too, but he wanted the sporty version, whereas I had the sedan. He told me the exact model he wanted and said it had to be the British Green one. And once again, he didn't believe it would be possible to find this specific Jaguar with only $10,000. To which I said once again, "Watch me!"

The same story unfolded ... I found the exact model he wanted in British Green. The cost was $12,500 for which we managed to find the extra cash needed within our personal resources. Once again, no car payments!!

Can you image the shock on our neighbors' faces when they saw a second Jaguar on our driveway? Yes, we now had His & Hers Jaguars. We became the talk of the town, and no one was the wiser that between our two Jags, we paid less than you would have paid for *one average car!*

Owning and driving my Jaguar did exactly what I hoped it would do. Every time I sit in my car or even look at it parked on the driveway, I swell with *feelings of wealth and abundance.* Owning this Jaguar has propelled my abundance quotient in a big way. Now I live in the *knowing* that I can truly have anything my heart desires.

Wendy Dillard is a Masterful Law of Attraction Teacher & Coach. Her expertise is in knowing how to apply the Law of Attraction to any situation. What other people call miracles and coincidences, Wendy considers normal and the way life is intended to be.

Web: www.wendydillard.com

Homes, Cats, and Cars

by Louise and Walt Thiessen

WALT

Louise and I celebrated our 13th wedding anniversary in September 2012 by doing the first-ever podcast of LOA Today. We had a grand total of zero listeners.

Less than a month later, my brother, Mark, and future sister-in-law, Uohna, did the second podcast with us. Both podcasts had technical difficulties, and our listenership hadn't increased at all.

Again, zero listeners.

By this point, I was the only one of the four who really wanted to do the podcasts on a consistent basis. Why? Because the podcasts were part of my own efforts to improve my mindset, they felt good to do, and I enjoyed the whole process, despite not having any listeners.

Well, I did have a few listeners after awhile. Not enough to shake a stick at, but hey! It's better than zero listeners, right?

About five years before this, in November 2008, I was despairing the world's financial state of affairs (as well as our own) following the onset of the financial crisis. I knew that my own business was completely at risk. Since 2003 I had been self-employed full-time building websites for small businesses and non-profit organizations, and most of my customers were very small non-profits. I knew enough about economics to know that my non-profit customers were very likely to shrink in number dramatically as the consequences of the financial crisis emerged over the next couple years. I had no clear idea what to do about it.

Louise had her gardening business, but since I'd had the foresight to know that the financial crisis was not only coming (I'd predicted it about a year before it happened), I knew that it would likely have devastating consequences for her business too. So she decided to sell it. After all, when money gets tight, gardening services become an unjustifiable luxury that people stop paying for.

So she found another gardener to sell her business to, getting a small sum of cash in return. While it wouldn't last, it would at least give us a bit of help.

More importantly, however, she sat me down one day and said to me something like, "Are you aware of just how negative you've become?"

No, I wasn't aware of it. In fact, I protested that I thought I was a pretty positive person, all things considered. But as we talked, it became more and more clear that I had far more negative thoughts going through my head in those days than I'd previously admitted. In fact, the closer I looked at my behavior, the less I liked what I saw.

So by November 2008, I was not only in despair, but I was thrashing around for any possible solution I could find.

I'd previously heard about this movie/phenomen known as *The Secret,* and while I was a disbeliever in anything metaphysical, I was willing to give it a try. Heck, I was willing to give almost anything a try.

So I ordered a copy of the movie and watched it. When I did, two things happened. On the one hand, something deep inside resonated with the contents of the movie. On the other hand, my subconscious mind screamed at me, "Are you crazy? That's a bunch of hooey!"

The battle raged in my mind for a few years afterward as I awkwardly tried, sometimes succeeded, and often failed to be a deliberate creator in my own life. Somewhat to my surprise, I refused to let go of this Law of Attraction notion despite the disappointments and failures. My attitude had improved marginally, but not enough that most people would have noticed the change. Consequently I still had more bad things happening to me with my business and with life in general than good ones.

By April 2012, became a bit of an obsession with me. One day when Mark and Uohna came to visit, I decided to risk bringing up this controversial topic among the four of us. After much discussion, I proposed the idea of doing something together, something like a podcast, on the subject of the Law of Attraction. There were sniffs of interest from everyone, but it didn't go any further at this point.

It wasn't until the following September that I took the bull by the horns and decided to go for it. After the first two podcasts, I started reaching out to anyone I could find on Twitter interested in the Law of Attraction, and I ended up setting up interviews to do on my podcast, some of which Louise was able to participate in. They were good interviews, and they continued to whet my appetite for more.

But soon my wave of interviewees diminished to a trickle, and I was finding it hard to keep up. By the following summer, I took an extended break from the podcasts, even though LOA was still a major interest of mine.

Then a series of events began to occur before I got it going again, events that would change our lives substantially forever.

LOUISE

It was the summer of 2013 in Northern Virginia, and I was well aware of the Law of Attraction and how thinking about something could draw it to you.

I was going to need a new vehicle in the not-too-distant future. I had been driving a 2001 Ford Ranger pickup for a number of years because I needed the cargo room to haul supplies and materials to the job site for my garden design and maintenance company.

When the economy took a nose dive, I sold the company. I kept the pickup, but the truck's lack of comfort for the driver and the lack of cab space for groceries and other personal purchases had me considering driving something else.

I still wanted cargo room for all my finds at garage and tag sales. I would buy low and take the items to local consignment shops to sell for a small profit. By no means did this hobby provide significant income. It was just fun.

An SUV seemed like a good fit, but what make and model? Since I didn't need to be concerned with **how** I was going to make this happen (since trying to figure out "how" it's going to happen is a no-no where deliberate creation is concerned), I decided to aim high. Lexus being a Toyota product, and me being a previous Camry owner three times over, meant I wanted to explore a Lexus to make sure it really fit my needs.

The fact that we didn't have the money for it didn't enter into the picture.

So off to the Lexus dealer my husband and I went to act as if we could purchase something in the near future. In Law of Attraction lore, this is sometimes referred to as "deliberate creation." Another word for it is "play." We needed to visualize and believe that we could buy such a vehicle even if we didn't have the funds at the moment.

We alerted the salesman of our intentions, and he seemed okay with us asking questions and trying the car on for size. I liked the amenities and comfort, but the headroom wasn't right for my tall husband. It was a better vehicle than a sedan, but maybe not for hauling pieces of furniture, since the back seat didn't fold down.

So we went back to our day-to-day lives, and since money was tight, I didn't seriously consider buying a new vehicle until one fateful day ...

WALT

That summer was eventful for a couple of reasons. Not only were we imagining and dreaming about new cars (my car was on its last legs, too), but we also acquired new, furry additions to our family.

One day in July, the people who lived across the street from us got evicted, although we didn't know it at the time. About a month later, Louise found a nearly all-black cat lurking in the front yard. She tried to lure the cat inside, but the cat ran away.

The next day, the same cat appeared. She lured it to the house because it looked hungry. The only thing even close to cat food that we had was some leftover swordfish from the previous evening. Oh well ... the poor cat would have to settle for a swordfish dinner!

We had both grown up with cats, and we had often talked about how it would be great to have two cats in our lives: his & hers cats, so to speak. Louise saw this cat's appearance as an answer to our prayers.

She lured the cat inside and tried keeping it inside, but despite enjoying some attention from us, the cat clearly wanted out. So she let it out.

The next day, there was no sign of the cat. We wondered what happened to her, particularly because she seemed malnourished. A day later, when the cat still didn't appear, we went looking for her. We'd seen her lurking across the street, so we walked over there.

As I looked around, I heard a very high-pitched mew under the car in their driveway, and out popped a small black cat that looked remarkably like our swordfish-loving visitor, except there was clearly something wrong with her front paw. *My God, I thought ... it looks broken!* It bent at an unnatural angle, and the cat hobbled on it awkwardly, not to mention that she looked even more malnourished than before. *Was that even possible?*

Louise called out, "Is that her?"

I stared at the cat for a moment, perplexed and perturbed.

"I don't know," I replied. "She looks like she's been hurt."

I picked the cat up, and she struggled a bit to get away, but very feebly. If you said this cat weighed four pounds, I'd have laughed at you. She was so thin and malnourished, I would have said two pounds, even though she was clearly fully grown.

I couldn't see specifically what was wrong with her paw, but my emotions had gotten the better of me, and I was determined to get this cat some food and, if necessary, some medical attention.

So I walked back to our house carrying this small, furry bundle. Around the same time as we got her some food, another black cat ... clearly the first one who visited us the day before ... made her appearance. So there were two of them!

I was still feeling upset about this second cat's apparent injury, and I told Louise I wanted to go over and confront the owner about it. She convinced me to wait until after lunch, which we did.

We took the second cat inside to feed both her and the first cat. This second cat, whom we later named Harmony, had a very peculiar habit. Apparently, she'd gotten the short end of the food stick for so long that she'd developed the habit of growling as she chewed her food, with a suspicious look at anyone ... human or animal ... lurking nearby. I'd never heard a sound like that: rwar, rwar, rwar as she ate her precious meal, growling a new growl with every chew.

We learned that the people across the street had just moved in, and they told us that they'd found the cats there when they'd arrived. That's also how we learned that the previous occupants had been evicted. We then learned that there were actually four cats, not two, and to complicate matters the new family had four dogs of their own. Four dogs plus four abandoned cats did not add up to a happy family in their book.

Just as we talked, a third, very large light gray cat came strolling around the corner of the house like he owned the place. The woman we spoke with said there was also a fourth one around somewhere. She was hoping to find a way to keep the cats, but apparently her husband was against it.

To complicate matters even more, we were renting our home, and our lease said clearly, "No pets."

It didn't look good for the cats.

I looked at Louise and knew instantly that she wanted to keep all of them. I liked the idea of cats too, but three of them? Maybe four? And what would our landlord say when he found out?

She convinced me to play it by ear. Three cats came to our home that night. We ended up naming them Joy, Harmony, and Yoda, which also represented the order in which we found them (or they found us, depending upon your viewpoint).

It turned out that Yoda, the gray cat with the Yoda-like eyes and ears, regularly displayed an uncomfortable interest in Joy, the first black cat. He'd chase her all over the house, and Joy didn't like it! We inferred that this meant they needed a trip to the vet to get fixed, and despite money being tight, we found that the local animal shelter did this kind of work relatively inexpensively. So we arranged appointments for all three.

We acquired some pet carriers, and on the appointed day we took them to the shelter and dropped them off. An hour later back at home, we received a phone call. We could come pick them up.

"Really? That was quick," was my reaction.

"Oh, we didn't have to do anything with them," the female voice at the other end of the line told me. "They've already been neutered."

She explained that they previously had been fixed as part of an international program designed to address the worldwide overpopulation of cats by capturing, neutering, and releasing stray and feral cats. Some cats also get adopted this way, and that's what had happened with these cats.

Why the evicted family who acquired them didn't take them back to the shelter but left them instead to fend for themselves … well, we never did get the answer to that question.

The way they knew the cats had already been neutered through that program was that the cats' ears had been "tipped," the international sign for cats that had been captured, neutered, and released.

I'd just thought they had some kind of weird genetic mutation that made their ears like that.

"Oh, and Joy is actually a boy."

Well, that was certainly a surprise!

We ended up having to keep them in separated areas of the house now that we knew that Yoda's interest in Joy was in driving away a rival rather than in something more intimate. We definitely did not want cat fights inside the house! So Yoda got the half-finished basement, and the two black cats lived upstairs with us.

This was also the beginning of what we called, "The Kitty Cat Shuffle," because we had to find ways to give Yoda attention upstairs in order to keep everything fair for all. So we played this little game where the two black cats would get let outside for a bit, Yoda would come upstairs to spend time with us, then we'd get him back downstairs, and the two black cats would come back inside while Yoda went outside ... and so on.

Soon afterward, Louise sat me down to tell me that she wasn't happy in Virginia. Could we move back to Connecticut where we'd previously lived?

Our home in Virginia sat in the middle of nowhere, about 50 miles from Washington, D.C. just beyond the Manassas battlefields. It took an hour just to go ... well, almost anywhere. Grocery shopping was usually an all-day Saturday event.

By contrast, Connecticut is a much smaller state where everything is much closer together. Simsbury, the town we'd last lived in together, was full of all kinds of interesting amenities, including a rails-to-trails bike and foot path, various annual events like craft fairs and flea markets, the permanent site for the Hartford Symphony Orchestra's summer concert series, an annual fly-in at the local airport, and other local activities, not to mention the Big E, a huge New England version of a county fair that took place about a half hour from our home, plus the fact that we lived within driving distance of Boston, New York, the shoreline, Cape Cod, and a host of other interesting places to go and things to do.

Louise wanted to move back to Simsbury. Because she had moved to Virginia 11 years earlier with me without hesitation because I needed to help my parents with their move from Smith Mountain Lake into a senior center in Lynchburg, there was no way I was going to decline her request.

The only problem, as usual, was money. 2008's financial crash hadn't been kind to us. We didn't have much money.

Moving would wipe out what little retirement savings we had left. Not for the first time in my life, I was terrified about how to make the money work at retirement age ... let alone how to make ends meet in the coming year.

But like Louise, I had been studying the Law of Attraction, trying and often failing to work it to our benefit. We needed to move back to Connecticut. She needed a job (I was still self-employed, but my annual income was dwindling). We needed new cars. We now had cats in the family, and we had no idea how to make any of it work.

Toward the end of October, the weather man said we should expect a particularly cold spell of weather with temperatures in the low twenties. Brrr!

It was after 4 PM, and I was working in the second bedroom that served as my office.

"WALT! There's another one!" I heard Louise call from the back door.

Coming out, sure enough I saw a fourth cat. This one was a mixture of browns and grays. We'd caught an occasional glimpse of her in the yard during the past few months, but now she was at our back door crying for help. Leaving her outside was out of the question given the impending freeze that night, but where could we put her?

Time once again for The Kitty Cat Shuffle! We ended up giving her half the basement, with the other half going to Yoda and a closed door between them. Louise resolved not to name her in case we couldn't keep her, so we just called her Lady.

One day, as Louise was tending separately to Yoda and Lady, she accidentally left the door open between the finished and unfinished sections of the basement. To her alarm, she saw Yoda casually walk directly to where Lady sat ... and Lady didn't move!

Yoda gave Lady a little sniff, then moved on to graze in Lady's food dish.

Hmm! Apparently these two not only knew each other, but they got along well, too!

Shortly after that, we found the two of them perched on a table near the basement slider door, admiring the view outside. Yoda was sprawled out like a *pasha*, and Lady lay with her head using his butt as a pillow.

Yes, they did indeed know each other! The Kitty Cat Shuffle now simplified somewhat. However, the problems between the Blacks and the Grays, as we called the two pairs of cats, hadn't disappeared.

One day, Louise called me from the basement to come quickly. I ran to the basement stairs and ran halfway down to the landing before turning to start down the other flight of stairs.

There, at the foot of the stairs, I saw Louise standing with a worried look on her face. The two male cats, Yoda and Joy, were clearing spoiling for a fight right there in front of her. They crouched facing each other, their noses about a six inches apart, with their ears back and their eyes in a squint, both ready to pounce with claws flying. I knew that in a moment I was about to see an all-out cat fight.

Well, that wasn't an acceptable situation. One or both of them could get seriously hurt (not to mention the two of us if either of us tried to intervene). This would mean some expensive medical bills, whether from a vet or from a medical doctor.

So I did the only thing I could think to do in the moment. I started running downstairs as loudly and quickly as I could. With my first step toward them, the two cats raced off in opposite directions.

Crisis averted.

There were other, similar confrontations to handle between the two male cats, one of which involved using a tennis racket as a temporary shield to block one of them (without any harm to either of them), but fortunately none of those situations ever came to bloodshed.

Meanwhile, the problem of how to pull off a move back to Connecticut combined with the twin problem of needing new cars had become much more acute. As always, money was the biggest issue, and we didn't know what to do about it.

So we did the only thing we could think of to do. We put it out to the Universe that we needed help now! Then we drove to Connecticut to house hunt and look for a job for Louise in the first week of November.

Staying with an old friend in Connecticut cut down on our expenses, but we still had to shave pennies. We had heard that an apartment was available in the complex where we used to live in Simsbury 11 years before, but when we got there the person who was supposed to meet us never showed up. The apartment got rented … to someone else. Our other attempts to find work and housing also fell through. This was heartbreaking because Simsbury is not a cheap place to live. Those apartments were the lowest priced rents in the area, but they were also nearly the most we could afford.

Discouraged and with bruised egos, after finding nothing else available in our budget, we tucked our tails between our legs, climbed back into my aging Camry, and headed back to Virginia, having no idea what to do next.

Knowing that if a move came up we'd have to find homes for the cats, I began a campaign to find someone to adopt one or two of them. I posted pictures everywhere I could find a place to post them, offering them to a good home, no charge.

We hoped that Christmas might bring us good news, but Christmas came and went without further developments with all these problems. The only good news that month is that I got the urge to start doing podcasts again, arranging an interview with one of my previous interviewees. That interview slowly got the podcast train inching along again out of the station.

By January, we decided that we really had nothing to lose. After all, the money was almost gone, so what the heck! We kept our chins up, hoping and daring to believe that somehow a miracle would happen to save us.

We drove back up to Connecticut again, this time for a pre-arranged job interview for Louise, and we finally got some good news. Louise got the job! Now we just needed a home, preferably one where we could keep cats.

Arriving again in Simsbury, we again checked out the apartment complex where we used to live, but there were no units available. I asked the woman in the office if she knew about any that might be coming available soon, but she couldn't help us.

Well, we'd come all this way, so I was determined to try something ... anything ... to find a place to live that we could afford. After all, we couldn't afford to keep making fruitless trips. The fact that Louise had gotten employment cheered us up and buoyed our spirits. Somehow, a home we could afford would appear ... we hoped.

I didn't even dare to think what to do about cars or cats.

I managed to find a local Realtor who specialized in helping renters. We met him, and he turned out to be this older gentleman who had basically been selling real estate since the town was founded, or so it seemed. Actually, the town is nearly 350 years old, but I wasn't going to quibble about it.

This Realtor said he'd sold the guy who built our old apartment the land to build them on some 50 years previously. He tried to find something we could afford (which was almost nothing) in their lists of available homes, but with no luck. Then he made an interesting comment. He said that our ex-landlord also had other properties around town and identified one on the other side of town, called Canal Place. Had we tried there?

Louise and I looked at each other. Canal Place? Never heard of it!

The next morning, we called the landlord's office again, and talked to the same woman I'd spoken with yesterday. Did they have anything available at Canal Place? "Yes," she said. "There are two."

I thought, *Why didn't she tell me that yesterday when I called about the other apartments? Oh well, never mind.*

We arranged to see one of the apartments with the head maintenance guy later that day. As we drove down the main road toward our turn, we passed a car repair garage owned by the same mechanic we used who owned the garage on the other side of town where we used to live, and I got a strange, prickly feeling running down my neck.

When we made the turn and drove into the complex, what we saw created a bit of a shock for us. The architecture was identical to the architecture of our old apartment complex from 11 years prior. I guess it wasn't a total surprise, since it was the same landlord, but we thought the similarity bode well for us. Louise commented that unless is was a really terrible apartment, she'd be okay with living here.

Upon walking into the apartment, it was like walking through Alice's looking glass. The apartment was a perfect mirror image of our old apartment 11 years before. Every room was in the same place as before, but reversed as if you were looking at the whole place through a mirror.

Most miraculous of all, the rent was identical to what we had paid 11 years before (and $250 less per month than what we paid in Virginia).

We took it.

That left three problems.

First, we had to move, and we had to do it fast. Louise's new employer wanted her to start at once, and we managed to get them to agree to start two weeks later ... but no more. This meant we had two weeks to complete a move from Virginia to Connecticut starting from scratch.

Second, we had two very, very old cars. Louise needed to replace her 12-year-old Ford pickup truck, and I absolutely HAD to replace my 15-year-old Camry with its 237,000 miles on it, because it might not survive the 500+ mile trip north again. Where would the money come from? I had no idea. Plus, Louise wasn't up to driving a car north by herself.

Third, we now had four cats. Fortunately, the lease of our new apartment allowed us to have cats! Unfortunately, we were only allowed to have two.

That meant we had to do the unthinkable. We had to pick two cats to keep while trying to find homes for the other two, all while packing at break neck pace for a move in two weeks while Louise continued to work her old job (which we couldn't afford to let her give up until the last minute.)

We had just two weeks to get it all done. *Two weeks!*

We needed new cars, and we couldn't afford them.

We couldn't drive up in the pickup because you can't put two cats in pet carriers in the back of a pickup truck in freezing January temperatures, not if you want them to survive the trip.

My old Camry probably wasn't up to another trip.

Plus we had a whole bunch of stuff that wouldn't go in the moving van, so we needed to bring it with us on moving day.

And this move would wipe out the last of our retirement savings.

ARRRRRGGGGH!

LOUISE

So, my husband and I were moving back to New England after being in Virginia for 11 years. He sold his car the day before we moved on the advice of his mechanic, who felt his 1998 Toyota Camry with 237,000 miles would not make the trip north.

When we contacted the moving company, they assured us that they could transport my truck on a hitch behind the moving van. Fantastic! We had two cats and a myriad of stuff we needed to bring with us, but not in the moving van. Add the two of us to the mix of things we just couldn't fit in the moving van in the dead of January.

We arranged to rent an SUV, and Walt would drive. I was good for only about three hours of actual driving time before my back would start to ache. This fact is very important to what happened next.

WALT

Here's how the sale of my old Camry went. I placed an ad on Craigs List to see if I could get a buyer for it. I figured if I could get $500 for it, I'd be happy. I advertised it for $800.

Then I called around for moving companies and found one that would work with our ever-shrinking budget. It would take every last penny we had, but they'd move us lock, stock, and barrel.

Best of all, I had an inspiration. Could they tow our pickup truck behind the moving van? That way, we could rent an SUV for the trip to carry the cats and sundries.

Yes, they could!

Woo hoo! It was starting to come together.

The afternoon before the move, I got a caller interested in buying the Camry while I was out running an errand in it. Could we meet in an hour? *Sure!*

The buyer drove up dragging a car trailer behind him. I gave him the keys to the car so he could check it out, then ducked inside to use the bathroom. When I came out, he inquired, "Did you know that it was out of oil?"

WHAT???

I'd just driven it without any issues for about 40 miles just an hour before. How could it not have any oil in it? But sure enough, when I checked the dip stick, it was bone dry. It's a wonder the oil deficit combined with engine heat didn't crack the engine block entirely.

"I can't give you $800 in light of this, but would you let it go for $500?" my buyer asked me.

I couldn't believe my luck. $500 was exactly what I was hoping to get for it, and now I was getting it for a car that clearly had a major oil leak.

"Yeah, okay," I said as nonchalantly as I could. He gave me five one-hundred dollar bills, I signed over the title, we pushed the car onto his trailer, and he drove off dragging it behind him.

We had packed and prepared as best we could, but by moving day the next morning we were barely three-fourths packed. The movers showed up early and started loading stuff and boxes faster than I could dump stuff into them and throw a piece of tape over the top. Louise was working like a mad woman trying to pack up the kitchen.

Midway through the madness, the boss asked me for a pow-wow. I said sure.

"I'm afraid there's been a misunderstanding. I know the lady in our office said we can tow your pickup truck, but the law doesn't allow us to do that," he informed me. "I could get an expensive ticket for doing it."

Oh no! What could we do now? I can do a lot when I have to, but I can't drive both a rented SUV and a pickup truck at the same time, and Louise can't drive more than three hours without her back screaming at her.

Still, I had managed to sell a 15-year-old car with 237,000 miles on it and a major oil leak the night before for $500, so anything was possible.

One of his crew members approached us. "If you want to sell the pickup, I'd like to buy it," he said.

Louise and I tried very hard to not let our jaws hit the ground.

Our plan had been to tow the pickup to Connecticut, use it as a vehicle until we could figure out a more permanent solution to our car problems, then sell it, maybe even get some value in trade for it. I hoped to get maybe $1,000 for it.

But now that we couldn't tow it ...

"Sure," I said. "What do you have in mind?"

"I'll give you $1,500 for it," he said.

Louise and I couldn't believe our luck. The employee didn't have the cash with him, so he asked the moving company boss for a loan against his salary. The boss looked at the truck and said, "Well, I don't think it's worth that much. It's probably worth about $1,200." So the boss cut $1,200 off the moving bill in exchange for the pickup.

Not bad for a $1,000 pickup truck.

Maybe this move was going to work out after all.

Sadly, the one thing that wasn't working was figuring out the solution to the problem of the cats. After much angst and agony, we agreed to keep Joy and Harmony while finding homes for the other two. Unfortunately, despite the fact that I had engaged in a feverish campaign to find someone to adopt them over a two month period, we found no takers. Winter is not exactly the ideal time to try to find someone to adopt a cat.

So with a heavy heart Louise volunteered to take them to the animal shelter in the hopes that someone would adopt them. This was a bit frightening because the shelter was not a no-kill shelter. If after a period of time they couldn't find a home for the cats, the cats would have to be euthanized.

This did nothing to improve our joint state-of-mind.

The only good thing was that we still had to deal with the move, so that's what kept us going ... that plus the firm belief (well, about as firm as gelatin anyway) that the Law of Attraction would deliver the goods for us when we needed them.

By late afternoon, the mover's boss came to me again to say that the van was packed solid and there were still a few items that they couldn't fit into the van. They couldn't squeeze a teaspoon in anywhere ... it was that jam packed from floor to ceiling. The back of the truck looked like someone had taken our stuff and run it through a compactor, it was so densely packed.

I improvised a late dump run to literally dump the few less-desired pieces that were left over before the dump closed. We made it with five minutes to spare, and the moving van headed north to Connecticut.

Once the moving van took off, we returned to the house to do some last minute cleaning while it got dark outside (and inside too ... we didn't have any lamps in the empty house any more except for the overhead fluorescent kitchen light and lights in the two bathrooms). Then we packed the cats and the stuff we were hauling ourselves into the rental SUV and hit the road for an eight hour drive ... starting at 8 PM.

It was a long drive, but it went well. The cats did surprisingly well, except for the last hour when Harmony kept crying that she needed out. We figured that she needed to pee, but everything was packed away, including the litter box. Well, we somehow made it to our new home at 4 AM, set up the litter box for the cats, threw an air mattress on the floor, and went to sleep.

45 minutes later, the moving van boss called my cell phone to tell me that they'd arrived. Could we let them in so they could unload our stuff?

The rest of that day is a blur, but we got moved in, boxes everywhere. That night, as we ate our well-deserved evening meal away from the mess, Louise and I discussed the fact that we didn't own a car. The only car we had was a rental, and we couldn't afford to keep paying $39 plus tax per day for it.

So the next morning I went online and did some searching, trying to find cars we could afford. It was a tall order, because we had no money for a down payment and couldn't afford much in the way of car payments. We didn't like it, but maybe we might have to settle for one old used car that we'd share. How we'd make that work day-to-day we had no idea.

Add in the fact that I stand 6'8" tall and that there are very few vehicles that can accommodate my height, and you can understand that the list of possible vehicle options gets very small quickly.

My online search proved fruitless.

A Toyota had saved our lives in an accident many years before, so we felt loyal to the brand. We ended up at a Toyota dealership near the Massachusetts border, and they convinced us to consider leasing instead of buying a used car in order to get a slightly lower monthly payment. At this point, I was willing to try anything, but I still didn't see how we could afford two cars ... and we really needed two cars! They tentatively got us to put $100 toward a lease, with the understanding that we could cancel if we found something better.

The next morning, we were getting desperate. We headed to another dealership near our new home to make one last attempt. There was a snowstorm coming, but we figured, *what the heck,* as we asked the snowstorm to hold off for a bit.

We walked into the dealership and met Jose, who would be our salesman. It was also a Toyota dealership. We told them our sad financial story and asked them if they could do anything to help us.

One of their V.Ps's, another man also named Jose, got involved and said he was going to make sure we had two cars no matter what it took.

They ended up putting me in the same car that the other dealership had (a Camry), and I liked it, but I told them sadly that I didn't see how we could swing it. Even at the lease price, we couldn't afford a second car ... and we really needed that second car.

They kept crunching numbers, lowering the price. I thanked them for their efforts, but we just couldn't afford it.

Finally, Jose the V.P. said, "Okay, here's what we're going to to. We're going to give you a lease on the Camry at our cost." That amounted to about a 40% savings on the lease price. I loved the idea, but what about a car for Louise? We'd been looking at a late model Corolla for her. The payment on it worked, but she hated the one we'd been looking at, and there were no other used cars on the lot.

By this time, it was about 3 PM. We'd been there over six hours, and Louise had a headache. So did I, if I was honest about it. We agreed she would take the rental car to go home to the boxes and a well-deserved nap, while I'd sign up to lease the Camry. The next morning, we'd return the rental and then try to figure out something about a car for her.

She left, and about two minutes later, Jose the V.P. asked, "Where's Louise?"

I told him.

He replied, "Call her back."

"Why?"

"Because we're going to lease her a brand new Corolla, also at dealer cost, for the same, low monthly payments we were going to sell her for the used car."

In shock, I called Louise to come back and went to pick her up. The bottom line is that we drove home in the snowstorm that finally showed up later that day with two brand new cars, the first time in either of our lives that we had owned a new car.

And we did it with no money in our pockets and at incredibly, impossibly discounted prices.

So life was good, right? I mean, with some huge help from the Universe, we'd pulled off the impossible. We had moved to Connecticut, got two brand new cars, Louise had a new job, we brought two cats with us, and all was well.

Well, almost.

First, within a week, Louise hated her job so much that she quit. It was in day care, and she was able to land another job with another day care right away. Improvement was good.

But within about a month, Louise started to experience pain in her legs and feet. It got so bad that she could barely walk, let alone do her job. Clearly, something had to change fast.

On top of that, there were still two cats in the animal shelter in Virginia, and it was **not** a no-kill shelter. The shelter has a website that enabled me to track their progress, and I was happy to report to Louise by March that Lady had been adopted out of the shelter. But Yoda was still there, and while there were cats that had been there far longer, Louise felt really upset about it.

So she started reaching out to people she knew in Virginia, people she'd worked with, etc. Would any of them have any interest in adopting a beautiful light gray cat named Yoda? One of them pointed her to a former co-worker who rescued animals. Might Mony be interested? It turned out that ... Yes! Mony loved Yoda and adopted him on the spot.

Drinks of relief all around.

Today, Joy is our ambassador to our apartment neighborhood, introducing himself to every passing neighbor willing to stop and pet him.

Harmony, the one with the bum paw whom I estimated weighed about two pounds, improved considerably over time to the point that we realized that her paw problem is probably due to a birth defect. She still hobbles, but she gets around just fine, and she's definitely not hungry any more. She probably weighs

10-12 lbs now and could even stand to be on a bit of a diet. She may be a little chunky, but we love her anyway.

And Yoda and Lady are living happily ever after with their new families.

Now we only had to deal with the fact that Louise was in pain every day and hated her job. Plus, while we had somehow miraculously manifested a new home and two brand new cars with almost no money, plus had two new members to the family ... well, let's just say that the money problems were still around. What to do?

A visit to a podiatrist led to adding off-the-shelf insoles to her shoes at a far lower cost than we expected, which helped clear up the pain. However, she didn't want to stay in day care any more. Maybe she should start up the gardening business again? So she did, but this time she'd do it by hiring help to do the work.

The first year was a good one, although it didn't generate a lot of income. It did, however, see Mark and Uohna become my co-hosts of the LOA Today podcast starting in August, a team that held together for another year with Uohna and I doing most of the podcasts together while Mark sat in occasionally.

The second year, Louise doubled her business size. Uohna and Mark quit doing the podcasts, so I contacted Joel Elston, who had been one of my first year interviewees, to ask him if he'd like the spot. He accepted quickly. That was great news!

The third year, Gardens By Louise doubled its business again, although my own business continued to decline.

Last year, her gardening business became our main source of income while my own business practically fell apart, just in time to turn in her Corolla at the end of the lease period and buy a used Toyota Sienna that she could use as a cargo van, one that had all the bells and whistles and was in fantastic condition for a used vehicle. I turned in my lease as well for another brand new Camry.

In April, Joel found himself in a new work situation and with a new foster son in his life, and he didn't have enough hours in the day. So he regretfully withdrew as my co-host on the weekly podcast of LOA Today.

A month later, I found David Scott Bartky, and he became my new co-host.

Louise's business got so busy that it threatened her health last summer, both mentally and physically. So I stepped in to help in a big way.

Meanwhile, something amazing started to happen with the LOA Today podcast. While I now had listeners, I was lucky if I had 25-50 total "plays" in a month.

But when David and I began to do a series of episodes on the topic of the book, *Ask And It Is Given,* by Jerry and Esther Hicks (with Abraham), our listenership started to rise.

During that same time, I made a big push to urge listeners to subscribe to the podcast so that they could get a permanent feed of shows to their smart phones ... and it worked!

By September, the growth path in LOA Today's listenership numbers was skyrocketing at an amazing rate.

By November, they'd reached some serious levels. We were getting more "plays" in a month than we'd gotten in all of the previous years combined!

Louise and I talked about it, and she could see how much doing the podcasts meant to me. I'd been working hard all of this time to improve my attitude, and the weekly podcast had really helped me in that regard.

I wanted to do the podcast daily instead of weekly, since I now could hardly wait for Sundays (the day David and I did our recordings) to arrive each week. Since we were in the gardening off-season, she said to go ahead and see where the podcast would take me.

So I reached out to seven more LOA coaches I found online, and three of them: Wendy Dillard, Cindie Chavez, and Tom Wells, came on board exactly one day after I put out my feelers. WOW! Now that's what I call responsiveness. Thanks, Universe!

Wendy and Cindie soon told me about experiences they'd had contributing to multi-author books that had sold well, which gave me the inspiration to create the book you now hold in your hands.

This year, we're fully expecting to break records again with Louise's business, finally shooting us solidly into the black. The gardening season is already under way, she has seven employees, and April 2018 turned out to be a record April for the business.

I now spend time six days per week doing the LOA Today podcasts while helping Louise manage the growth of her exploding gardening business.

Add in my role in putting together and editing this book, and you can see that life has gotten better and better.

Today, I smile every day. My own mental attitude has improved immensely. Everyone close to me has noticed it in a big way, and each step of the way where my attitude improved, what followed was yet another advance in a series of steps like what you just read.

We're now hunting for a house of our own to buy, instead of our small apartment, and of course we're using the Law of Attraction to make it happen. We're currently looking at houses that are way, way, way out of our price range, picking and choosing what we like and what we don't like, piecing together our ideal house while dreaming really, really big. We even found one, right next door to some kids Louise took care of when we first arrived. It meets all of our needs. We just need to figure out the money.

Want to bet that we won't find a way to get it? Here's a hint: it's a sucker's bet!

Walt and Louise Thiessen are the founders of the LOA Today podcast.

They live with their two black cats, Harmony and Joy, in Simsbury, Connecticut USA.

Subscribe to LOA Today

Visit us on the web at www.loatoday.net

One of the main reasons we created this book was to promote our podcasts. We call each podcast, "Your Daily Dose of Happy" because we want to help deliberate creators like you to use LOA to get themselves into a happy place every day. Listening to LOA Today is a great way to accomplish that goal.

The happier you get on a regular basis, the more of the good stuff will come into your life via the Law of Attraction.

If you haven't listened to any of our episodes yet, please do so. You can also listen to live broadcasts using the player on our home page. All of the instructions for playing live show, subscribing and sharing, and calling in to talk with our co-hosts during the live broadcasts can be found on our home page at loatoday.net.

You can subscribe on your smart phone. If you have an iPhone, just visit the iTunes store and search on "LOA Today". Your iPhone comes with a built-in podcast app that will capture and play every new episode we publish.

On an Android phone, search the Play Store for "LOA Today". You'll need to install a podcast app first. We recommend the free app called, "Podcast Manager".

And once you've subscribed, please remember to share! We live on a planet where there is so much negative stuff bombarding our senses each day. News, politics, entertainment, pop culture, and even social circles pound us all the time with every negative story, scenario, or experience imaginable.

So a podcast that emphasizes the positive and happy things in life is a wonderful counterbalance to all of that. Sharing it with others who don't know about LOA Today is one of the friendliest things you can do.

As you practice becoming more and more adept at applying the Law of Attraction in your daily experience, we wish you all of the love, success, happiness, joy, fabulous wealth, health, relationships, and general abundance anyone could ever want for the rest of your life!

Got a Law of Attraction Story?

Submit it to us for our next book!

Do you have your own, real-life Law of Attraction story you would like to share with the world? This is only the first book of many yet to come. We will be collecting stories from real people like you for future projects.

If you would like to have your story considered, please email it to: stories@loatoday.net

Please include your full contact information plus a statement that you give us the right to edit and publish your story without compensation to you.

We cannot publish all of the stories we receive, but if we like your story well enough we may include it in our next book!

Made in the USA
San Bernardino, CA
27 May 2018